U0918374

英汉财经新闻翻译研究

赵红霞　著

中国财经出版传媒集团
中国财政经济出版社

图书在版编目（CIP）数据

英汉财经新闻翻译研究／赵红霞著．--北京：中国财政经济出版社，2021.12

ISBN 978－7－5223－0969－9

Ⅰ.①英…　Ⅱ.①赵…　Ⅲ.①经济－新闻报道－英语－翻译　Ⅳ.①G212

中国版本图书馆 CIP 数据核字（2021）第 246152 号

责任编辑：彭　波　　　　责任印制：史大鹏
封面设计：卜建辰　　　　责任校对：张　凡

中国财政经济出版社 出版

URL：http：//www.cfeph.cn

E－mail：cfeph@cfeph.cn

社址：北京市海淀区阜成路甲 28 号　邮政编码：100142

营销中心电话：010－88191522

天猫网店：中国财政经济出版社旗舰店

网址：https：//zgczjjcbs.tmall.com

北京财经印刷厂印刷　各地新华书店经销

成品尺寸：170mm×240mm　16 开　13 印张　200 000 字

2021 年 12 月第 1 版　2021 年 12 月北京第 1 次印刷

定价：68.00 元

ISBN 978－7－5223－0969－9

（图书出现印装问题，本社负责调换，电话：010－88190548）

本社质量投诉电话：010－88190744

打击盗版举报热线：010－88191661　QQ：2242791300

前　言

经济、技术发展日新月异的今天，人们每天都被铺天盖地的新闻浸润，其中财经新闻关系着国家的经贸发展、地方的经济走向以及个人的财经信息感知。财经新闻主要向三类受众传递信息。首先，财经新闻为财经专业领域受众传递国内外各类财经信息，解释及时发生的经济现象，对“经济人”决策、判断提供依据；其次，财经新闻为非财经专业领域普通受众传播经济知识，培养民众财经方面的知识；最后，财经新闻向政府部门、相关行业、企业反映市场运行情况，为政府、相关部门制定、改善或创新相关财经政策提供参考。

财经新闻报道的现实性、时效性、专业性特点决定了该文体的特殊性。财经新闻具有社会导向功能，剖析经济运行现象，反映社会经济市场问题，为监测社会经济运行起着导向作用。财经新闻还具有互动联系功能，将政府、企业、个人三者有机结合，架起沟通的桥梁，保证财经活动的顺利运行。

在经济全球化和中国在国际经贸舞台上的活动日益频繁的今天，英汉财经新闻的翻译对中国的经济政策制定与传播、企业跨境投资和民众理财判断具有至关重要的作用。本书将系统介绍财经新闻的概念、特征、翻译原则与方法，助力英汉财经新闻信息的精准传播和交流。

本书共分五章，以财经新闻的概念、特征、翻译原则与方法为主，辅以若干财经新闻案例，并对案例进行了点评。第一章重点概述了新闻的英汉定义、特征与载体。第二章聚焦财经新闻的概念、功能、媒介，英语财经新闻的一般类别，每个财经新闻的类别后面以具体新闻案例说明。第三章高度概括了英语财经新闻的五大主要特征：词汇特征、句法特征、篇章特征、标题特征和导语特征。第四章介绍了英汉财经新闻翻译的七个主要原则：信、达、快、活、切、显、简，在每个原则后面予以案例说明具体原则在英汉翻译过程中的运用。第五章介绍了英汉财经新闻的常用翻译方法：直译法、意译法、节译法、摘译法和编译法。

应当指出，该书的理论框架还不够完善，许多问题还有待进一步的探讨，由于本人的学术水平有限，书中难免会存在漏洞和诸多不妥之处，欢迎广大读者批评指正。

本书在撰写过程中，学生张浩、常江等在图片收集、文本校对方面给予了很大的帮助，在此表示真挚的感谢！

赵红霞
西安财经大学
2021 年 7 月于陕西 · 西安

目　录

| 第一章 |

新闻概述

一、新闻的界定

新闻就在我们身边，与我们的生活息息相关。我们可以通过不同的媒体获取各类新闻，从而获取政治、娱乐、教育、体育、财经、科技多方面的动态信息。什么是新闻？古今中外，人们对新闻的概念有不同的界定。

（一）汉语语境中的新闻界定

早在唐代，"新闻"一词就已出现在大众视野。《南楚新闻》是成书于唐代的一本笔记，专门记载中国南方一带的奇闻逸事。《南楚新闻》这个书名中出现的"新闻"主要指社会奇闻轶事，有别于我们今天所说的"新闻"，但从传媒记事的要点来看，该书在新闻史料中也占有一席之地。20世纪八九十年代，许多学者在著作中都指出，《南楚新闻》一书首次展示了"新闻"的概念和一些内涵（阎景翰，1990：1205；刘建明、张明根，1994：763；戴元光，2001：57）。目前，据学术界的新考证，《南楚新闻》出现前，"新闻"一词就早已明确出现。尽管如此，《南楚新闻》题名方式与现代新闻几乎一致，所以其在新闻史上的意义和价值是不可忽略的。

人们普遍认为具有现代意义的"新闻"一词出现在南宋赵升著的《朝野类要》。该书记载："其有所谓内探、省探、衙探者，皆衷私小报，率有泄露之禁，故隐而好之曰新闻。"宋朝时期，小报是非法出版的非官方报纸，有些人专门在中央一级机关，以及寺、监、司等政府衙门打听消息，了解事情，称为内探、省探、衙探，这些人在交流传递信息的过程中怕走漏风声，于是创造出“新闻”一词，显然，这里的“新闻”多为情报。到了元明清时期，话本及小说流行于市井中，深受民众欢迎，“新闻”一词在话本和小说中屡见不鲜了。

在现代，有关新闻的定义已有很多。下面先列出一些典型的汉语定义。

《辞海》（第七版）对新闻的解释是：（1）新近发生或变动的事实信息。一般为受众所关注，并需经传播者选择，借助语言、文字、图像等符号载体及时传播。产生于人们沟通和了解情况的社会需要。由于生产力的发展与人际交往的频繁，出现从事采集与传播新闻的社会职业，并逐步成为各种政治力量、社会团体的宣传手段和舆论工具；在经济领域中，也成为一种商品。（2）指新闻文体。广义包括消息、通讯、特写等体裁。狭义专指消息。

《现代汉语词典》（第七版）给“新闻”的释义为：（1）报社、通讯社、广播电台、电视台等报道的消息。（2）泛指社会上最近发生的新事情。

我国新闻学术界的知名人士曾对新闻下过定义。

我国杰出的新闻记者，被称为新中国新闻事业开拓者的范长江（2001）对新闻下的定义是，“新闻就是广大群众欲知应知而未知的重要事实”。

我国著名的新闻学家、复旦大学王中（1956）教授引入传播学概念，把新闻定义为“新近变动的事实的传布”。

我国新闻教育家、新闻学者、中国人民大学教授甘惜分（1985）教授把新闻定义为“报道或评述最新的重要事实以影响舆论的特殊手段”。

中国新闻理论开拓者邵飘萍（1924）认为，“新闻是最近时间内所发生的事情，是认识一切关系社会人生的兴味实益的事物现象”。

被誉为“新闻教育界第一位大师”和“新闻学界最初开山祖”的徐宝璜（2018）在《新闻学》中提出：“新闻者，乃多数阅者所注意之最近事实也”。

（二）英语语境中的新闻界定

Just as Ekeanyanwu N T, Ofulue C I, Bel - Molokwu N J, et al. (2012：20) describe：News is one of the most difficult issues to define in mass communication. There are many definitions：

William S. Maulsbyl defined news thus：

• *News is an accurate, unbiased account of the significant facts of a timely happening that is of interest to the readers of the newspaper that prints the account.*

William G. Bleyer defines it like this:

• *News is anything timely that interests a number of people; and the best news is that which has the greatest interest for the greatest number.*

Mitchel Chainley defined news as:

• *The timely report of facts or opinions that hold interest of importance, or both for a considerable number of people.*

Prof. Charles Coates defined it thus:

• *News is what interests the reader, the viewer, the reporter, the editor, the producer, their spouses and their neighbours. News is what affects their diets and their lives.*

Sam Zelman of CNN says:

• *News is what is important because of its impact on society; it is what people need to know and what they want to know.*

And he defines news *as an accurate, unbiased account of a current, timely event, which is reported in the mass media and is significant to a large number of people in a locality.*

Agbese (2008) also sees news as finding out and publishing the things people do not want others to know and second, anything that will make people talk.

According to COBUILD Advanced English Dictionary on line, news can be defined as: (1) **News** is information about a recently changed situation or a recent event. (2) **News** is information that is published in newspapers and broadcast on radio and television about recent events in the country or world or in a particular area of activity. (3) The **news** is a television or radio broadcast which consists of information about recent events in the country or the world. (4) **News** is sometimes used in the names of newspapers. (5) If you say that someone or something is **news**, you mean that they are considered to be interesting and important at the moment, and that people want to hear about them on the radio and television and in newspapers. (6) See bad **news**/good **news**. If you say that something is bad news, you mean that it will cause you trouble or problems. If you say that something is good news, you mean that it will be useful or helpful to you. (From https://www.collinsdictionary.com/dictionary/english/news)

News falls into two basic categories: soft' news and "hard" news. 'Hard' news is characterized by Tuchman and others as having a high level of newsworthiness, i. e. news value (usually regarding politics, economics and social matters) demanding immediate publication. On the other hand, "soft" news does not necessitate timely publication and has a low level of substantive informational value (if at all), i. e. gossip, human interest stories, offbeat events. This fundamental typology has held steady for more than three and a half decades without any serious attempt to reassess its continued relevance or the adverse research consequences of such a dichotomous, and perhaps overly simplistic, categorization (Lehman - Wilzig & Seletzky, 2010)

A definition of news is rather elusive. The stock answer is easy: news is when man bites dog; news is something you haven't heard before; news is what editors and reporters say it is.

News is information that is published in newspapers and broadcast on radio and television about recent events in the country or world or in a particular area of activity. One thing is clear: news is different things to different people. Certainly, geography plays a role. News of unemployment in the steel industry will be on the front page in Pittsburgh but might not receive a mention in a local newspaper in a small town in Texas.

互联网上还有一些另类的新闻定义。

新闻是指报纸、电台、电视台、互联网等媒体经常使用的记录与传播信息的一种文体。

(https://baike.so.com/doc/782738 - 828179.html)

英文中 News 的来历有两种看法：一是取 new（新的）复数，表达新东西、新讯息之意，二是取北（North）、东（East）、西（West）、南（South）的首字母，意为四方所起之事即是新闻。（万维百科https：//www. wanweibaike. com/wiki－%E6%96%B0%E9%97%BB）

二、新闻的特征

从上述不同的定义可以看出，人们在给新闻下定义时，由于目标不同，视角不同，关注点不同，所以对新闻定义的表述不尽相同。

根据这些不同的表述，我们可以分析得出新闻应有以下主要特征。

（1）新闻具有真实性。新闻是对存在着的客观事实的描述，而不是对没有事实基础、凭空捏造的想象的描述。

（2）新闻具有新颖性。新闻是对新鲜事实的描述。

（3）新闻具有典型性。新闻是对典型事实或人们普遍感兴趣的事实的描述，而不是任何事实都能成为新闻的描述对象。

（4）新闻具有传播性。新闻是向人们传递某种信息的，并且可以通过不同的媒介传播。

（5）新闻具有展示性。新闻可以向人们展示时代文化，记录时代文化。

（6）新闻具有时效性。新闻迅速、及时地传播新人、新事、新情况、新问题，否则，它将失去价值。

（7）新闻具有简洁性。新闻简明扼要，篇幅短小。“三言两语，记清事实，寥寥数笔，显出精神，概括而不流于抽象，简短而不陷于疏漏”，用笔要简洁利落，内容集中精炼。

（8）新闻具有公开性。新闻能够利用大众传播手段向整个社会传播信息，为大众所知。

（9）新闻具有预见性。新闻向人们提前告知事物发展的新趋势，提出新建议、新举措。

（10）新闻具有实用性。新闻向人们提供生产生活所需的实用方法、实用信息等。

三、新闻的载体

新闻与其载体密不可分。任何新的、东南西北发生的事情只有通过适当的载体传播，才能被广为人知。

在当代，新闻的载体纷繁复杂，代表性的载体有报纸、杂志、电台、电视台、手机和互联网。这些载体各具特征，传播新闻的方式、侧重点、影响力各不相同。所以，新闻是指报纸、杂志、电台、电视台、手机和互联网经常使用的记录社会、传播信息、反映时代的一种文体。

四、小结

综上，新闻有较悠久的历史。不同时代、不同地域的人对新闻的界定多元丰富、趣味盎然。新闻是在报纸、杂志、电台、电视台、互联网、手机中经常见到的，用简洁语言，程式化的语篇，记录社会重要事件、传播最新信息、反映时代文化的一种文本。新闻的载体多种多样，功能不同，影响不同，且随着科技的发展不断更新，更便捷有效地为人们服务。

参考文献

[1] Agbese, D. The Reporters' Companion [M]. Lagos: Newswatch Books Limited, 2008.

[2] Ekeanyanwu N T, Ofulue C I, Bel - Molokwu N J, et al. News writing and reporting [J]. 1976.

[3] Lehman - Wilzig S N, Seletzky M. Hard news, soft news, "general" news: The necessity and utility of an intermediate classification [J]. Journalism, 2010, 11 (1): 37 - 56.

[4] 戴元光 .20 世纪中国新闻学与传播学——传播学卷 [M]. 上海：复旦大学出版社，2001.

[5] 范长江 . 记者工作随想 [A]. 范长江新闻文集 [M]. 北京：新华出版社，2001.

[6] 甘惜分 . 新闻理论基础 [M]. 北京：中国人民大学出版社，1985.

[7] 刘建明，张明根 . 应用写作大百科 [M]. 北京：中央民族学院出版社，1994.

[8] 上海辞书出版社．辞海 [Z]．上海：上海辞书出版社 [M]，2020.

[9] 邵飘萍．新闻学总论 [M]．京报馆，1924.

[10] 王中．论新闻．王中文集 [M]．上海：复旦大学出版社，2004.

[11] 武春河．深度影响 [N]．北京：经济日报出版社，2006.

[12] 徐宝璜．新闻学 [M]．北京：中国传媒大学出版社，2018.

[13] 阎景翰．写作艺术大辞典 [M]．西安：陕西人民出版社，1990.

[14] 中国社会科学院语言研究所词典编辑室．现代汉语词典（第7版）[Z]．北京：商务印书馆，2016.

| 第二章 |

财经新闻概览

第一节　财经新闻的界定、功能、媒介

一、界定

“财经新闻”是“新闻”的下位词，隶属上位词“新闻”的一个细分类目，财经新闻侧重采集报道财经领域的新闻。对于财经新闻的定义，目前学术界普遍认为财经新闻有广义和狭义之分，下面先看一些前人有关财经新闻的定义。

清华大学周乃蓤教授（2013）认为狭义的财经新闻的界定是“针对资本市场的报道，涵盖宏观经济、微观经济、货币、银行、金融产品等”。

上海交通大学的李本乾、李彩英（2006：3）从广义的角度来界定财经新闻，他们认为“财经新闻就是有关经济活动、经济现象、经济决策最新事实和情况的报道。它具体指涉的对象十分广泛，在现代经济生活中的象征性资产，如货币、股票、期货等，有关这些领域的动态、政策、现象自然是财经新闻的报道范围；传统上关于社会物质再生产所牵涉的生产、分配、交换、消费四大环节的活动也是其报道对象，甚至经营管理领域，因为最终影响到企业的市场表现，乃至整个市场格局，也落在财经新闻的视野里”。

邓涛（2004）认为“狭义的财经新闻一般是指与金融和证券市场、资本市场等相关的新闻报道。广义的财经新闻则是涵盖经济新闻和金融新闻的‘大财经’”。

中央财经大学的孙凤毅（2010：24）在《财经新闻报道与研究》一书中提到，现如今广为接受的财经新闻内涵包括两个方面，即：（1）在银行、保险、证券等市场发生的新闻是财经新闻；（2）从金融、资本市场的角度报道经济活动与现象的是财经新闻，前者是狭义的财经新闻，后者是广义的财经新闻。

武春河先生（2006）指出，可以从“宏观、中观、微观”的新思路来审视经济活动、经济现象，进而界定财经新闻。宏观财经新闻是指整个国民经济全局报道，中观财经新闻是指区域经济或产业报道，微观财经新闻是指公司新闻。武春河先生对财经新闻的界定提供了新思路。

财经新闻常与经济新闻相混，许多学者在著作中将“经济新闻”与“财经新闻”进行了细致区分。孙凤毅从形式和内容两个角度对财经新闻进行界定，并指出“财经新闻”概念的提出事实上是对传统经济新闻的一种否定，财经新闻的提出与市场经济体制相辅相成，随市场经济体制的确立与发展应运而生。

结合上述论述，可以看出，财经新闻是新闻文本的一个重要分支。因为财经新闻是重要新闻分支类别，传统主流媒体常特别强调财经新闻的公信力、专业性、权威性。简而言之，财经新闻有别于经济新闻。财经新闻是指经济、金融领域新近发生的事实的报道。财经新闻可以是证券市场、银行等小范围的新闻报道，也可以是金融、资本等大市场角度的新闻报道。

报纸被认为是最早出现的传播新闻的媒介报纸在国内外都有着悠久的发展历史。在我国，新闻出版业认为“邸报”是我国最早的报纸，“邸报”属于新闻文抄，是朝廷用于传知朝政的文书和政治情报的一种公告性新闻。基于它具有报刊特点，所以，我们可将其视为具有报刊特点的文书抄本。明末，活字印刷术广泛运用后，“邸报”的规模也越来越大。西方报纸的发展也走过了漫长的历史，目前，我们认为，西方最早的报纸约公元前60年，恺撒以白板公示国家事件为标志。

二、功能

财经新闻具有传递信息的功能。财经新闻主要向三类受众传递信息。

首先，财经新闻为财经专业领域受众传递国内外各类财经信息，解释经济现象，为该受众群体参与经济活动提供帮助，通过财经新闻得到信息，对“经济人”决策、判断提供依据；其次，面对非财经专业领域普通受众，财经新闻起着传播经济知识的作用，培养普通民众的市场经济意识，普及民众财经方面的知识；最后，财经新闻向政府部门、相关行业、相关企业提供财经方面的信息，能够向政府、有关部门及相关企业反映市场运行情况，有利于政府、相关部门针对市场经济情况制定、改善或创新相关政策，有利于相关企业根据经济变化调整企业经营运转情况或进行企业重组。

财经新闻具有社会导向功能。财经新闻能够反映社会、市场问题，剖析经济现象，为相关专业人士、相关部门规划发展蓝图提供新思路，促进社会经济平稳发展；此外，财经信息为监测社会经济运行起着导向作用，有利于营造良好的市场经济氛围。

财经新闻具有互动联系功能。财经新闻是政府、企业和个人沟通的桥梁，能够将政府、企业、个人三者有机结合。社会主义市场经济是政府宏观调控与市场机制有机结合，财经新闻是一座沟通桥梁，政府部门通过财经新闻传递的信息，合理制定相关政策。企业根据财经新闻反映的财经信息，结合政策动向，制定企业发展规划。经济职业人士阅读财经新闻，丰富自己的知识体系，开展新的研究，为政府制定相关政策建言献策，为企业良性发展出谋划策。普通民众通过阅读财经新闻，了解国内外财经事件，主动学习财经知识，丰富文化生活，积累财富。

三、媒介

随着科技发展和社会进步，传播新闻的媒介也愈发多样，传播方式不断变化，人们接受信息也越来越快捷，效果也越来越好。传播新闻的媒介指新闻传播过程中传播者和受众的中介，是用来表达某种含义静态和动态信息的一种物质载体。财经新闻的主要传播媒介有报纸、广播、互联网、电视、财经期刊杂志、财经新闻影片等。如今，大众性财经新闻的传播媒介主要是报纸、广播、互联网、杂志等。

报纸是最早出现的传播新闻的媒介。现在依然是最重要传播新闻的媒介。

毫无疑问，在传递财经新闻信息时，报纸是财经新闻最基础的传播媒介，起着重要作用。现如今，传播财经新闻的报纸，有专门的财经新闻报纸，如外国的《华尔街日报》（*The Wall Street Journal*）《金融时报》（*Financial Times*），中国的《经济观察报》《中国财经报》《经济日报》《中国证券报》等，也有综合性报纸开设专门的财经板块，如《人民日报》的财经板块。

广播是一种声音式的传播新闻的媒介。广播将声音通过无线电波传送给听众，使听众获得信息。20 世纪 20 年代，美国匹兹堡 KDKA 电台申领执照，是世界上第一座拥有执照的电台，这为广播的诞生拉开序幕。现在，广播传送新闻的技术已相当成熟。由于越来越多的人关注财经新闻，我国的财经新闻广播电台也雨后春笋般在全国各地相继涌现。在我国，不仅有覆盖全国的“中央人民广播电台经济之声”，还有一些区域性的财经新闻广播，如“上海第一财经广播”“江苏财经广播”等，这些广播电台，使听众不受空间和条件的限制接受财经新闻。

互联网在现实生活中应用十分广泛，互联网已渗透人们的生活，潜移默化地改变人们生活方式，甚至影响着整个社会进程。互联网应用走向多元化，为财经新闻传播的发生、发展提供了优良的沃土，互联网这一媒介为人们及时有效地接受财经新闻提供方便，还为人们提供了自发自收财经新闻的自由，人们还可以在互联网上就感兴趣的财经新闻相互交流。人们可以直接搜索相关财经词条来查阅信息，也可以通过登录专门的财经新闻网站来获取财经新闻。互联网上，点击量居前列的财经新闻网站有财新网（www. caixin. com）、新浪财经（finance. sina. com. cn）凤凰网财经（finance. ifeng. com）、雅虎财经（finance. yahoo. com）、福布斯（www. forbes. com）等。

第二节　英语财经新闻的类别

一、宏观类别

宏观层面，可以根据不同的标准对英语财经新闻进行分类。

根据传播媒介的不同，英语财经新闻可分为报纸财经新闻、杂志财经新闻、互联网财经新闻、广播财经新闻、电视财经新闻等。

也可按主题对财经新闻进行分类。如今，科学技术迅猛发展，学科交叉、学科融合逐渐形成一批交叉学科，这种综合性发展趋势使财经新闻涉及的各领域越来越细化，越来越有突破性。相应地，英语财经新闻也可划分成更具体、更细小的类别，如医药类财经新闻、钢铁产业财经新闻、汽车类财经新闻、农业财经新闻、能源开发财经新闻、区域合作财经新闻等。

从英语财经新闻的应用来看，财经新闻分为财经动态新闻、财经综合新闻、财经经验新闻、财经述评新闻等。

根据新闻体裁的不同，英语财经新闻可以用所有新闻的体裁来表现。但是，由于英语财经新闻的特殊性，按体裁划分，常见的英语财经新闻体裁有：财经消息、财经通讯、财经评论、财经特写、财经人物专访等。

二、具体类别

（一）财经消息

财经消息是一种常见的新闻体裁，它用概括的叙述方式，简明扼要的文字，迅速及时地报道国内外新近发生的、有价值的、公众最关心的财经事件。

财经消息往往用简明的语言交代财经事件发生的经过，引用当事人、目击者的话来说明财经事件的要点，并引用财经专家的话或权威性的观点来介绍相关的背景。下面列举几则财经消息如下：

Bitcoin surges past \$60000 for first time

Cryptocurrency Bitcoin has risen for the first time above \$60000 (£43100), continuing its record - breaking run.

Bitcoin - which has more than tripled in value since the end of last year - has been powered on by well - known companies adopting it as a method of payment.

But some analysts said this latest surge came in part due to the huge US stimulus package approved this week.

Bitcoin's total market value last month exceeded \$1tn.

However, Bitcoin has a track record of wild price swings and has fallen sharply a number of times since it was created in 2009.

The recent spikes have been fuelled by big companies.

In February, Elon Musk revealed that his electric carmaker Tesla had bought $1.5bn worth of Bitcoin and would be accepting it as payment for its cars in future.

Mastercard also plans to accept certain cryptocurrencies as a form of payment while BlackRock, the world's largest asset manager, is exploring ways it can use the digital currency.

The Covid-19 pandemic has also played its part in Bitcoin's price rise, as more people go online for shopping, moving further away from physical coins and notes.

Critics argue Bitcoin is less of a currency and more of a speculative trading tool that is open to market manipulation.

There is also concern over its environmental impact, with huge amounts of energy needed to conduct transactions.

(https://www.bbc.co.uk/news/business-56390409)

——BBC, 14 March, 2021

【译文】

比特币首次突破60000美元

加密货币比特币首次上涨突破60000美元（43100英镑），持续创造新纪录。

自去年年底以来，比特币的价值增长超过两倍，已有知名公司采用比特币作为支付方式。

但一些分析师表示，比特币这一最新涨幅是由本周美国批准的刺激计划导致。

上月，比特币的总市值超过1万亿美元。

但是，比特币在过去曾经历过价格剧烈波动的记录，自2009年创建以来已经大幅下跌了很多次。

大公司助长了最近的飙升。

今年2月，埃隆·马斯克（Elon Musk）透露，电动汽车制造商特斯拉（Tesla）购买了价值15亿美元的比特币，并将在未来接受比特币作为购买汽车付款支付方式。

万事达卡同样计划接受某些加密货币作为付款方式，而全球最大的资产管理公司贝莱德（BlackRock）正在探索其使用数字货币的方式。

随着越来越多的人上网购物，实物硬币和纸币减少使用，Covid-19新冠肺炎疫情在比特币价格上涨中也发挥了作用。

批评家认为，比特币不是货币，而是投机性交易工具，可以对市场进行操纵。

由于比特币交易需要使用大量的能源，人们也担心其对环境的影响。

► **点评：**

本篇新闻篇章简短，仅由12句英文组成。新闻消息由标题、导语、主体、结尾构成，新闻架构属于金字塔结构。读者可以通过阅读文章标题和文章导语掌握本篇新闻主要内容，即“比特币首次突破6万美元”，新闻导语对标题进一步解释“比特币这种加密货币在持续打破最高纪录”。

下面我们来再看一则关于“标准普尔指数”与股指走势的财经消息：

Stock futures inch higher after S&P 500 retreats from record

Futures contracts tied to the major U. S. stock indexes ticked higher in the overnight session Wednesday evening after the S&P 500 retreated from record levels during the regular session.

Contracts tied to the Dow added 53 points, while those pegged to the S&P 500 rose about 0. 15%. Nasdaq 100 futures advanced a similar 0. 15%.

The moves in the overnight session came after the S&P 500 slipped from record levels during Wednesday's regular session as pressure on tech offset optimism sparked by the first round of major corporate earnings that largely exceeded expectations.

The broad equity benchmark dipped 0. 4% after hitting a fresh record early on Wednesday. The Dow Jones Industrial Average gained just 53 points.

The Nasdaq Composite lost about 1% during regular trading as Tesla fell nearly 4% , Netflix and Facebook dropped more than 2% each, and Amazon, Microsoft and Apple all dipped at least 1%.

With the first – quarter earnings season now underway, investors will on Thursday pore over financial results from snack company PepsiCo, asset manager BlackRock and both Citigroup and Bank of America.

The season began in earnest with bank results on Wednesday, when Goldman Sachs climbed more than 2% after blowing past analysts' expectations with record first – quarter net profits and revenues on strong performance from the firm's equities trading and investment banking units.

JPMorgan Chase also topped forecasts on the top and bottom lines, helped by a $5. 2 billion benefit from releasing money it had previously set aside for loan losses. Bank stocks have climbed across the board this year, with the S&P 500 financials sector up nearly 20% compared to the S&P 500's 9. 8%.

Investors will on Thursday review the Labor Department's latest report on the number of Americans filing first – time claims for unemployment insurance. Economists polled by Dow Jones expect the government to report that another 710000 filed claims for the first time during the week ended April 10.

March retail sales data, also due Thursday morning, are expected show a robust uptick in consumer spending, with some economists seeing a gain of 10% or more thanks to the arrival of the $1400 stimulus checks. The consensus forecast is more modest growth of 6. 1%.

On Tuesday, the Food and Drug Administration called for a pause in administering J&J's Covid – 19 vaccine after six people in the U. S. developed a rare disorder involving blood clots. The announcement triggered a sell – off in reopening plays earlier in the week, but is not expected to have a material impact on the pace of the U. S. vaccine rollout.

(https: //www. cnbc. com/2021/04/14/stock – futures – inch – higher – after – sp – 500 – retreats – from – record. html)

——CNBC, APR 14, 2021

【译文】

标准普尔 500 指数从最高纪录回落　股指期货小幅走高

周三晚，标普500指数从正常交易时段的创纪录水平回落后，美国主要股指期货合约走高。

在与道琼斯指数挂钩的合约上涨了53点，与标准普尔500指数（S&P 500）挂钩的合约上涨了约0.15%后，纳斯达克100指数期货上涨0.15%。

隔夜交易的走势是在标普500指数周三例会期间从创纪录水平下滑之后出现的，因科技股承压抵消了因第一轮主要企业财报大幅超出预期而引发的乐观情绪。

周三早盘创下新高后，大盘股指下跌0.4%。道琼斯工业平均指数仅上涨53点。

纳斯达克综合指数在常规交易中下跌约1%，其中特斯拉下跌近4%，Netflix和Facebook的跌幅均超过2%，亚马逊、微软和苹果的跌幅均超过1%。

随着第一季度财报季的临近，投资者周四将关注零食公司百事可乐（PepsiCo）、资产管理公司贝莱德（BlackRock）以及花旗集团（Citigroup）和美国银行（Bank of America）的财报。

周三，高盛（Goldman Sachs）股价飙升逾2%，此前该公司股票交易和投资银行部门表现强劲，第一季度净利润和收入创下历史新高，超出分析师预期。

摩根大通（JPMorgan Chase）的收入和利润也超过预期，得益于释放此前为贷款损失预留的资金，该公司从中获利52亿美元。银行类股今年全线上涨，标准普尔500指数金融类股上涨近20%，而同期标准普尔500指数上涨9.8%。

投资者将在周四审查美国劳工部关于首次申请失业保险的美国人数量的最新报告。道琼斯（Dow Jones）调查的经济学家预计，在截至4月10日的一周内，政府将首次报告71万份索赔申请。

3月的零售销售数据也将于周四上午公布，预计消费者支出将强劲上升，一些经济学家认为，由于1400美元经济刺激措施的实施，消费者支出将增长10%或更多。普遍的预测是更温和的6.1%的增长。

周二，美国食品和药物管理局（FDA）要求暂停接种强生的新冠肺炎疫苗，此前美国有6人患上了一种罕见的血栓疾病。这一消息在本周稍早引发市场大跌，但预计不会对美国疫苗推出的速度产生实质性影响。

▶ 点评：

本篇新闻标题为“标普500指数与股票期货发生变化”，新闻正文第一句具体列举道琼斯工业平均指数、标准普尔500指数、纳斯达克100期货发生的具体变化。后面随即说明了标普的变化引发的纳斯达克综合指数、高盛股价、摩根大通以及零售销售数据的变化。信息反映及时，内容概括性强。

（二）财经通讯

财经通讯运用叙述、描写、抒情、议论等多种手法，具体、生动、形象地反映某一财经事件或与某一财经事件相关的典型人物。

财经通讯中，叙述、描写部分较详细，对一些普通民众无法理解或难以理解的术语都会借助各类修辞手段进行细致的说明，抒情部分的比例相对较少，议论部分则较客观。

一些财经通讯就是典型的专题财经新闻报道。专题报道的内容广泛，可以是当前发生的重大事件，如中国载人航天飞船成功发射，也可以是与财经有关的日常生活小事，如某电子产品对人们生活的影响。专题财经新闻报道包含信息量较大，这些信息一般是记者围绕某一经济主题，深入采访不同的人和机构，然后写成的。专题财经新闻报道中的信息是丰富多元的，包括具体的财经新闻事件、背景、被采访者的原话以及记者的一些简单评论。列举几则财经通讯如下：

Yahoo sold again in new bid to revive its fortunes

Two pioneering web services of the internet age, Yahoo and AOL, have been sold again after the latest owner failed to revive their fortunes.

US telecoms giant Verizon is selling its media assets, which include the two companies, to a US private equity firm in a deal worth $5bn (£3.6bn).

Verizon bought Yahoo in 2017 and AOL in 2015 for a combined $9bn.

Yahoo and AOL were once trailblazers, but were subsequently overshadowed by firms like Google and Facebook.

Under the sale of the media assets to Apollo Global Management, Verizon will retain a 10% stake in the division.

Verizon bought the two brands in the hope of a quick entry into the digital advertising market, believing they still had enough resonance with consumers.

Yahoo and AOL were pioneers in offering a wide range of free and informative web services to consumers, long before Googlecame into existence.

By providing free web mail and chat messenger services, the two firms had a cornerstone for online advertising on the market, as most internet users in the early 2000s were accessing their websites and software on a daily basis.

Yahoo also provided everything from the news, weather reports, sports results and movie release dates; to message boards, its own version of eBay – Yahoo! Auctions – and real – time markets data.

But over the last decade, Yahoo and AOL have faced an uphill struggle against more powerful rivals like Google, Bing, Facebook, Twitter, ESPN, Fandango and Weather. com, due to a saturated internet market.

Verizon also made a mistake in failing to acquire Yahoo's equity stake in Chinese e – commerce behemoth Alibaba, as well as Yahoo Japan, where Yahoo! Auctions is still thriving.

"Tremendous potential"

Apollo says there is still a considerable opportunity to build the two brands into a digital media and online advertising powerhouse.

"We are thrilled to help unlock the tremendous potential of Yahoo and its unparalleled collection of brands," said Reed Rayman, private equity partner at Apollo.

"We have enormous respect and admiration for the great work and progress that the entire organisation has made over the last several years."

David Sambur, co – chief of Apollo, added: "We are big believers in the growth prospects of Yahoo and the macro tailwinds driving growth in digital media, advertising technology and consumer internet platforms."

Verizon bought Yahoo to combine its search, email and messenger assets, as well as its advertising technology tools, with the AOL platform.

But the sale was overshadowed almost immediately after it was disclosed Yahoo had been subject to two massive cyber - attacks. Verizon eventually negotiateda $350m price cut for the acquisition.

However, today Yahoo's homepage still commands a huge audience, as "netizens" check their Yahoo! Mail accounts.

The brand is considered to be one of the top news aggregators on the internet, and is the eleventh most visited website in the world, with 3.8 billion visits over the last six months, according to web analytics platform SimilarWeb.

The sale by Verizon comes after it disposed of blogging platform Tumblr in 2019 and news website HuffPost last year.

(https://www.bbc.com/news/business - 56972205)

——BBC News, May 4, 2021

【译文】

为重振旗鼓，雅虎再次出手

新东家未能力挽狂澜，互联网时代的两家开拓性互联网公司雅虎（Yahoo）和美国在线（AOL）再次出售

美国电信巨头威瑞森（Verizon）正以50亿美元（36亿英镑）的价格将包括雅虎和美国在线在内的媒体资产出售给一家美国私人股本公司。

威瑞森2017年收购雅虎，2015年收购美国在线，共斥资90亿美元。

雅虎和美国在线曾经也是互联网行业的开拓者，但后来被谷歌和Facebook等公司盖过了风头。

将媒体资产出售给阿波罗全球管理公司（Apollo Global Management）后，威瑞森将保留该部门10%的股份。

威瑞森收购这两个品牌是希望能迅速进入数字广告市场，威瑞森认为这两个品牌仍能引起消费者足够的共鸣。

早在谷歌问世之前，雅虎和美国在线就已经成为向消费者提供丰富的免费网络信息服务的先驱。

通过提供免费的网络邮件和聊天服务，这两家公司为市场上的在线广告奠定了基础。21 世纪初，大多数互联网用户每天都在访问这两家公司的网站和软件。

雅虎还提供了新闻，天气预报，体育赛事结果及电影上映日期的一切信息；此外，雅虎还有自己的留言板 —— eBay - 雅虎拍卖 - 和实时市场数据。

但在过去十年中，由于互联网市场饱和，雅虎和美国在线面临着与谷歌、必应、Facebook、推特、娱乐体育节目电视网（ESPN）、Fandango 和 Weather. com 等更强大的对手的残酷竞争。

威瑞森未能收购中国电商巨头阿里巴巴对雅虎的股权，也未能成功收购 Yahoo Japan。但雅虎拍卖发展势头依旧不减。

潜力无限

阿波罗说，这两个品牌仍有很大的机会发展成为数字媒体和在线广告巨头。

阿波罗私人股本合伙人里德·雷曼（Reed Rayman）表示："能帮助雅虎及其众多品牌释放巨大潜力，我们感到很高兴。"

"我们对整个雅虎公司在过去几年中取得的巨大工作和进步非常尊重和钦佩。"

阿波罗联席首席执行官戴维·桑布尔（David Sambur）补充称："我们非常相信雅虎的发展前景，以及推动数字媒体、广告技术和消费者互联网平台增长的宏观因素。"

威瑞森收购雅虎是为了将其搜索、电子邮件和通讯资产，以及广告技术工具与美国在线平台结合起来。

但在雅虎遭受两次大规模网络攻击的消息被披露后，这笔交易几乎立即蒙上了阴影。威瑞森最终以 3.5 亿美元的价格达成了此次收购。

然而，今天雅虎的主页仍然拥有大量的用户，因为"网民"们需要查看他们的雅虎邮箱。

网络分析平台 SimilarWeb 的数据显示，雅虎是最一流互联网新闻网站，其访问量全球排名第 11，在过去六个月中访问量高达 38 亿。

威瑞森在2019年出售了博客平台Tumblr，2020年出售了新闻网站赫芬顿邮报。

▶ **点评：**

本篇新闻通讯主要讲述互联网服务平台雅虎再一次出售重振旗鼓。本篇新闻提供雅虎相关背景资料，例如“Verizon bought Yahoo in 2017 and AOL in 2015 for a combined ＄9bn.”以及“Yahoo and AOL were once trailblazers，but were subsequently overshadowed by firms like Google and Facebook.”等。新闻通讯通过分析“**Tremendous potential**”，即“雅虎拥有无限潜力”，详细解释“雅虎再一次售出”这一事件的原因。

（三）财经特写

财经特写选题范围广泛，内容丰富有趣，体裁也多种多样。广义地说，财经特写可分为两大类：财经人物特写和财经事件特写。两类特写旨在抓住某一财经人物或事件的某一富有特征性的部分，做集中的、精细的、突出的描绘和刻画，以便取得强烈的艺术感染力。财经特写举例如下：

Meet China's lipstick King，an outspoken 28 – year – old e – commerce streamer who fans adore and brands fear

At first glance，Austin Li Jiaqi looks like the boy – next – door：he's always clean – shaven and typically dressed in earth – toned，well – pressed button – down shirts. But when his stream on Chinese e – commerce platform Taobao goes live，a different side of him comes out to play.

“We're starting now!” he claps and proclaims loudly，as millions of followers and ardent fans pour in to see him try lipsticks and other beauty products live.

“Are you ready to buy，buy，and buy?”

China's ＄38.6 billion beauty industry is the second largest in the world behind the US（which rakes in an estimated ＄56 billion annually）and is on trend to be the biggest market by 2023，according to the Cheung Kong Graduate School of Business.

In the last several years, Li's built a following of more than 7 million on the Chinese social media platform Weibo and more than 35 million on TikTok. His recommendations can be the difference between a product selling out or sitting on the shelves collecting dust.

The live – streaming sales powerhouse has come a long way from his humble beginnings as a L'Oreal shop assistant in Nanchang, a small city in southern China. He now holds joint live – streams with Chinese singers and actors and has become a society fixture at political conferences, beauty conventions, and gala events for luxury brands and magazines.

Helped along by a full staff of assistants and live – streaming technicians, he rattles off his signature catchphrase, "OMG! Sisters, buy this!" and hawks products on his marathon live – streams from a snazzy studio in Shanghai.

What sets Li apart from other streamers appears to be his cutting—and often snarky—reviews of every product he dislikes, be it Calvin Klein or Chanel. His friendly, peppy tone of voice, combined with how he seems unafraid of offending luxury brands and major retailers with his scathing takes, puts him in stark contrast to other Chinese beauty streamers, who avoid treading on thin ice where key industry players are concerned.

Weibo users are especially intrigued by Li's often vivid descriptions of his products. Coral blush isn't "peach": it's the ripe fruit of summer, tender to the touch, a shade that'll make boys stop in their tracks. That necklace isn't just "shiny" — it reminds him of the stars, the shimmering of a million galaxies.

And then there's the lipstick.

From 2017 to 2018, Li cemented his position as the country's "口红一哥" (or "lipstick king"): first, when he tried on 380 lipsticks in a seven – hour marathon stream, and then when he sold 15000 lipsticks in 5 minutes, beating Alibaba founder Jack Ma in a one – on – one selling competition.

The South China Morning Post also reported that in 2019, Li set a Guinness record for "the most lipstick applications to models in 30 seconds," putting lipstick on four different models in just 30 seconds.

Most recently, Li was named one of the "Time100 Next 2021", a list of emerging leaders around the world who are "shaping the future."

Little is known about Li's private life.

Despite social media chatter about a rumored romance with his long - time assistant, Li maintains that he has "no time to date."

"I do 389 broadcasts in 365 days. I don't have time to eat or sleep, so do you think I have a personal life?" Li told news portal Sohu in 2020.

Li notoriously keeps to himself, but in 2020, the Chinese press reported that he purchased a swanky three - story penthouse in private apartment complex Yunjin Oriental, which is located in the middle of a glitzy riverside district just off the Shanghai Bund.

Chinese media estimates that Li earns anywhere between $10 to $20 million from live - streaming every month, and Time has projected that Li will be worth $15 billion by 2023 off of his earnings from China's live - streaming e - commerce industry alone.

Those lips don't lie: Li's path to becoming China's emperor of e - commerce.

Li's business model is simple: brands allot a certain amount of stock for Li to sell on his stream, and he takes a cut for his services. But the sheer volume of the items that Lee sells, coupled with the line - up of brands that want to foster a working relationship with him, has made him a force to be reckoned with in China's e - commerce market.

Products are sold in real - time during marathon live - streams that can last from anywhere between six and eight hours. These days, Li sells everything from skincare products to household appliances and snacks. Customers are motivated to lock in impulse buys as Li counts down from 10, making gleeful announcements on his stream when thousands of products sell out in a matter of seconds.

But just as it might be the pinnacle of success for a brand to get a shout -

out from Li, some might prefer he leave them alone.

Whether brands like it or not, Li's endorsement can have a huge impact on sales.

In 2020, it was reported by Chinese media Jing Daily that a five – minute segment on Li's stream caused the sales of a widely – anticipated 24 – shade line of lipsticks from Hermès to tank in China.

When reviewing the Rouge Hermès line on his Taobao stream, he told his 12 million viewers that the shades looked "cheap."

"There's no soul in these colors," Li said, sighing. "It's unflattering, just like the shades your old mother would use."

A clip of his Hermés live – stream went viral on Weibo, as the hashtag #李佳琦的表情 (translated: The Look On Li Jiaqi's Face) trended, praising him for his honest—albeit cutting—reviews.

His bluntness makes him a standout in a crowded e – commerce market and wins him a devoted cache of supporters.

"Never change, Jiaqi," a fan wrote on social media after the Hermés stream. "This is why we know we can rely on you!"

(https: //www.businessinsider.com/austin – li – jiaqi – chinas – lipstick – king – online – shopping – taobao – 2021 – 3)

——Insider, Mar 31, 2021

【译文】

中国的口红一哥，一个直言不讳的28岁电子商务主播，深受粉丝们的崇拜和品牌的畏惧

乍看之下，李佳琦（Austin Li Jiaqi）看上去像是隔壁邻家男孩：他总是剃光了胡子，通常穿着大地色纽扣衬衫。但是，当他在中国电子商务平台淘宝上直播时，李佳琦则展现出自己的另一面。

"我们现在开始!"李佳琦鼓掌大声疾呼，瞬间数百万的追随者和粉丝涌入直播间，等待口红试色，观看其他美妆产品直播。

"准备好下单了吗，下单了吗？下单了吗？"

长江商学院的数据显示，中国美妆产业规模达386亿美元，次于美国世界第二大产业（估计每年创造价值560亿美元收入），并有望在2023年之前成为最大的市场。

在过去的几年中，李佳琦在中国社交媒体平台微博上的追随者超过700万，在TikTok上的追随者超过3500万。李佳琦的建议可以决定商品是即将售罄还是放置于架子上蒙尘。

直播，李佳琦体现出销售一哥的形象，这与当时在中国南部小城市南昌市担任欧莱雅店员时谦卑的形象相距很远。现在，他与中国歌手演员一同直播，并已成为政治会议，选美大会以及奢侈品牌和杂志的联欢晚会的社会人物。

在助手和现场直播技术人员的全力帮助下，李佳琦在上海一家时髦的录音室录制马拉松直播中，他大声疾呼出自己标志性口号——“OMG！姐妹们，买了！”。

李佳琦与其他主播与众不同的地方在于对于不喜欢的每件商品（无论是Calvin Klein还是Chanel），他常常采用较为机智的评论。友善，敏锐的语气，再加上严谨举止，他似乎不怕冒犯奢侈品牌和主要零售商，这使李佳琦与其他中国主播形成了鲜明对比，后者避免在关键行业参与者关注下踩雷。

李佳琦经常采取生动的方式描述产品，微博用户对此特别感兴趣。珊瑚腮红不是“桃子”，而是夏天成熟的果实，触感柔和，阴影产品会使男孩驻足留步。这条项链不仅是“闪亮的”，它还会让人想起星星，一百万个星系闪闪发光。

再者是口红。

从2017年到2018年，李佳琦巩固了自己中国“口红一哥”（或“口红之王”）的地位：首先，他在长达7小时的马拉松直播中尝试了380支口红，然后在5分钟内卖出15000支口红，在一对一的销售竞赛中击败了阿里巴巴创始人马云。

《南华早报》曾报道，在2019年，李佳琦创下“30秒钟内给最多人涂口红”的吉尼斯纪录，仅用30秒钟就将口红涂到了四个不同嘴唇上。

最近，李佳琦提名在“Time 100 Next 2021”榜单之中，该名榜单列出了正在“塑造未来”的全球新兴领导者。

但人们对于李佳琦的私生活知之甚少。

尽管社交媒体传言称，李佳琦与他的长期助手发生恋情，但李佳琦坚称，自己“没有时间约会”。

“我在 365 天里开展 389 次直播。我没有时间吃饭或睡觉，所以你认为我有个人生活吗?”李佳琦在 2020 年新闻网站搜狐采访中提道。

但广为人知的是，他坚持做自己，但是到了 2020 年，中国媒体报道，李佳琦在私人公寓大楼云锦东方购买了一套豪华的三层顶层公寓，该公寓位于上海外滩附近繁华的滨江区。

据中国媒体估计，李佳琦每月从直播中赚取的收入位于在 10 万到 2000 万美元之间。《时代》杂志预测，到 2023 年，仅从中国的流媒体电子商务行业的收入来看，李佳琦的市值就将达到 150 亿美元。

无须多言，李佳琦成为中国电子商务之王

李佳琦的商业模式很简单：品牌方为李佳琦分配了一定数量的存货供他出售，而李佳琦选择直播中的商品。李佳琦出售的商品数量之多，再加上想要与他建立工作关系的品牌阵容，这使他成为中国电子商务市场上不容忽视的力量。

直播间进行实时销售产品，马拉松直播可以持续六到八个小时。如今，李先生销售的产品从护肤品到家用电器和小吃都应有尽有。当李佳琦从 10 倒数开始时，直播用户便迫锁定冲动购买，李佳琦就在直播中宣布，上千产品在几秒钟内售罄。

但是，对于一个品牌来说，成功摆脱李佳琦如同抵达至成功之峰一样，有些品牌可能更愿意避免李佳琦的影响。

无论品牌是否喜欢，李佳琦的言论都会对销售产生巨大影响。

中国媒体 Jing Daily 于 2020 年报道，李佳琦五分钟的直播片段导致广受期待的爱马仕（Hermès）24 色唇膏系列在中国市场销售失败。

李佳琦在淘宝直播中观看爱马仕彩妆系列 Hermès line 时，他告诉 1200 万观众，这款阴影看起来“很廉价”。

“这些颜色没有灵魂，”李佳琦叹着气说。“这很不讨人喜欢，就像老母亲会使用的阴影一样。”

他在爱马仕（Hermés）现场直播的一段短片在微博上广为传播，随着标签“#李佳琦的表情”趋向流行，称赞他的诚实，尽管削减了评论。

李佳琦的直率使他在拥挤的电子商务市场中脱颖而出，赢得了忠实的支持者。

爱马仕直播发布后，一位粉丝在社交媒体上写道：“永远不要改变，佳琦。”“这就是为什么我们知道我们可以信任你的原因！”

▶ 点评：

本篇为人物财经特写，围绕“美妆主播”和“口红一哥”介绍李佳琦。新闻首段先从外貌介绍李佳琦，给予李佳琦一个普通人的形象。第二段中，新闻通过“claps and proclaims loudly”和“fans pour in”等动作描写，生动形象地描述李佳琦直播期间的火热场面。本篇财经人物特写从李佳琦的日常工作为切入点，体现李佳琦作为主播和销售形象。

（四）财经评论

财经评论是社会各界对新近发生的财经事件所发表的各种言论的总称。财经评论可以是个人的观点，也可以是某组织或团体的观点。财经评论的主要目的是向读者介绍财经信息。例文财经评论如下：

The Gig Economy's False Promise

The promises Silicon Valley makes about the gig economy can sound appealing. Its digital technology lets workers become entrepreneurs, we are told, freed from the drudgery of 9 – to – 5 jobs. Students, parents and others can make extra cash in their free time while pursuing their passions, maybe starting a thriving small business.

In reality, there is no utopia at companies like Uber, Lyft, Instacart and Handy, whose workers are often manipulated into working long hours for low wages while continually chasing the next ride or task. These companies have discovered they can harness advances in software and behavioral sciences to old – fashioned worker exploitation, according to a growing body of evidence, because employees lack the basic protections of American law.

A recent story in The Times by Noam Scheiber vividly described how Uber and other companies use tactics developed by the video game industry to keep drivers on the road when they would prefer to call it a day, raising company revenue while lowering drivers' per – hour earnings. One Florida driver told The Times he earned less than $20000 a year before expenses like gas and maintenance. In New York City, an Uber drivers group affiliated with the machinists union said that more than one – fifth of its members earn less than $30000 before expenses.

Gig economy workers tend to be poorer and are more likely to be minorities than the population at large, a survey by the Pew Research Center found last year. Compared with the population as a whole, almost twice as many of them earned under $30000 a year, and 40 percent were black or Hispanic, compared with 27 percent of all American adults. Most said the money they earned from online platforms was essential or important to their families.

Since workers for most gig economy companies are considered independent contractors, not employees, they do not qualify for basic protections like overtime pay and minimum wages. This helped Uber, which started in 2009, quickly grow to 700000 active drivers in the United States, nearly three times the number of taxi drivers and chauffeurs in the country in 2014.

The use of independent contractors is hardly an innovation. Traditional businesses like garment factories, construction companies and trucking have often misclassified employees as contractors to avoid offering benefits, paying payroll taxes and abiding by labor laws. What makes this different is that gig economy businesses are arguing that their use of the independent contractor model is in fact better for workers.

Increasingly workers, and government agencies are pushing back. Seattle passed an ordinance in 2015 allowing drivers for Uber, Lyft and other ride – hailing apps to unionize. A federal judge temporarily blocked that law on Tuesday after the U. S. Chamber of Commerce and some conservative groups filed lawsuits against the city. Workers have also sued various gig economy companies to seek overtime pay, reimbursement for expenses and other damages. Lyft recently agreed to pay $27 million to settle a class - action lawsuit brought by drivers in California.

Legislation and lawsuits might ensure that traditional labor laws are applied to the gig economy. But a few smaller companies, like Hello Alfred, which dispatches people to do household chores, and Managed by Q, which provides office maintenance and cleaning services, are taking steps on their own, by treating workers as employees. They say that this lowers turnover and improves the quality of their services. Over time even bigger companies like Uber, many of which lose money and rely on investors to keep pouring in billions of dollars of capital, might find that it pays to treat workers better and even make some of them employees.

But so far, experience with these companies shows that without the legal protections and ethical norms that once were widely accepted, workers will find the economy of the future an even more inhospitable place.

(https://www.nytimes.com/2017/04/10/opinion/the - gig - economys - false - promise.html? searchResultPosition = 5)

——The New York Times, April 10, 2017

【译文】

零工经济的虚假承诺

硅谷关于零工经济的承诺听起来很有吸引力。有人透露，其数字技术可以使零工经济从业者摆脱朝九晚五的烦琐工作，成为企业家。学生，家长和其他人可以在业余时间追求热爱之时赚取外快，甚至可以创办一家小型蓬勃发展的企业。

实际上，像 Uber，Lyft，Instacart 和 Handy 这样的公司没有乌托邦类美好愿景，零工经济从业者经常赚取低廉的工资而进行长时间的工作，永远为下一个关卡或任务准备。美国法律缺少对员工的基本保护，越来越多的证据表明这些公司可以利用软件升级和行为科学剥削守旧工人。

诺姆·谢伯（Noam Scheiber）最近在《泰晤士报》上发表的一篇报道阐述了 Uber 和其他公司利用视频游戏行业开发的策略使驾驶员在每天都喜欢的时候上路，进而增加公司收入，降低驾驶员时薪收益。一位来自美国佛罗里达州司机告诉《泰晤士报》，他一年的收入不到20000美元，其中不包括天然气和维修费用。在纽约，隶属于机械师工会的优步司机组织表示，超过五分之一的会员在扣除费用前的收入低于30000美元。

皮尤研究中心（Pew Research Center）去年进行的一项调查显示，零工经济从业者属于少数群体，他们往往比大多数人贫穷。总人口的年收入几乎是年收入低于30000美元的零工经济从业者的两倍，而40%的零工经济从业者是黑人或西班牙裔，而零工经济从业者在美国所有成年人中的这一比例为27%。大多数从业者表示，他们从在线平台上赚来的钱对家庭来说是必不可少。

大多数零工经济从业者被视为独立承包商而非雇员，因此他们没有资格获得加班费和最低工资等基本保护。从2009年开始，Uber借此在美国迅速发展的驾驶员人数达70万，这几乎是2014年美国出租车司机人数的三倍。

独立承包商几乎不再是新鲜事。制衣厂，建筑公司和卡车运输等传统企业经常将员工视为承包商，从而公司可以避免提供福利，缴纳工资税和遵守劳动法。与众不同的是，零工经济企业强调，实际上，这种独立承包商模式对员工更有利。

越来越多的工人和政府机构都在退缩。2015年，西雅图通过一项法令，该法令允许Uber，Lyft和其他打车应用程序的驾驶员加入工会。美国商会和一些保守派组织对该市提起诉讼之后，一名联邦法官于周二暂时封锁该法令。零工经济从业者也起诉了多家零工经济公司，要求支付加班费，提供费用报销和其他损害赔偿。Lyft最近同意支付2700万美元解决加州司机提出的集体诉讼。

立法和诉讼可以确保将传统劳动法适用于零工经济。但是，一些较小的公司，例如负责家务的Hello Alfred，以及提供办公室维护清洁服务的Q管理公司，正在通过将工人当作雇员来自行采取措施。这些小公司表示，该措施降低了营业额并提高了服务质量。像Uber这样的大型公司运营亏损，往往依靠投资者注入的数十亿美元资本运行，随着时间的流逝，他们可能会发现，为零工经济从业者提供更好的待遇，甚至雇用一部分从业者是值得的。

但是到目前为止，这些公司的运营状况表明，如果没有法律保护和道德规范，零工经济从业者可能面对更加荒凉的经济条件。

▶ **点评：**

本篇财经评论主要讲述各界关心的零工经济，分别从员工福利保护不完善，法律制度不健全等方面阐述零工经济中员工面临的风险。此评论中，有个人“诺姆·谢伯”和组织“皮尤研究中心”对这一事件的观点和看法。其中，还涉及法律制度对零工经济适用性的探讨。

参考文献

[1] 胡润峰．财经新闻报道与写作 [M]．上海：复旦大学出版社，2006.

[2] 邓涛．提高都市报财经新闻版的可读性 [J]．新闻战线，2004 (6)：77-78.

[3] 李本乾，李彩．英财经新闻 [M]．大连：东北财经大学出版社，2007.

[4] 孙凤毅．财经新闻报道研究 [M]．吉林：吉林教育出版社，2010.

[5] 武春河．深度影响 [N]．北京：经济日报出版社，2006.

[6] 周乃蔆．国际财经新闻知识与报道（第二版） [M]．北京：清华大学出版社，2013.

| 第三章 |

英语财经新闻的特征

第一节　英语财经新闻的词汇特征

一、概述

英语财经新闻的内容多与财政、经济、贸易、商业、金融等主题相关联。由于报道内容的特殊性，英语财经新闻中的词汇表达也颇具特色。除了经常采用专业术语和专业名词外，英语财经新闻中还常出现缩略词、新造词、对比性词汇等独具特色的词汇表达。

二、英语财经新闻的词汇特征

（一）大量使用专业词汇

英语财经新闻中会大量使用专业词汇，这些专业词汇实际上是经济领域的专业术语，这些词汇可以确保财经新闻内容的准确性和专业性。同时，这些专业词汇也一定程度上增大了人们阅读英语财经新闻的难度。例如：

The exact language of the tax hike wasn't available online until late Tuesday evening. New York was also set to raise the corporate tax rate from 6.5% to 7.25% for taxpayers with net incomes over $5 million. That move—along with a reinstatement of the capital base tax—would raise $750 million this upcoming year.

Democrats won control of the state Senate in 2018, but they gained more leverage last year by winning a veto – proof supermajority.

Cuomo expressed newfound openness to raising taxes on top – earners this year—his budget proposal included a limited, temporary tax increase on high – earners if New Yorkers didn't receive extra COVID – 19 aid.

(https://apnews.com/article/joe – biden – business – new – york – coronavirus – pandemic – manhattan – 33d68cd69256ba32fab7956d124d9c87)

▶ **点评：**

这则节选的英语财经新闻中，出现了“tax hike”（增税），“corporate tax rate”（企业所得税税率），“taxpayers”（纳税人），“net incomes”（净收入），“capital base tax”（资本基础税）及“budget proposal”（预算提案）等财经专业术语。由此可见，阅读英语财经新闻需要具备一定的专业知识，否则就有可能出现理解上的困难。

此外，需要注意的是，财经新闻中常出现一些普通名词，但这些普通名词在财经新闻中具体语境中却具有专业含义，这样的普通名词实际上也是财经专业名词。以下为几则例子：

【例 1】BEIJING/SHANGHAI, Feb 26 (Reuters) – China's soymeal futures slid nearly 5% in their sharpest decline in eight years on Friday, as investors took profit and new African swine fever outbreaks stirred concerns over demand.

—— “China's soymeal futures plunge onpig disease concerns” (*Reuters*, FEBRUARY 26, 2021)

▶ **点评：**

本句中 futures 的含义并非日常最广泛使用的“未来”，当“futures”以复数形式出现在财经新闻报道中，多是指现行的一种贸易方式，即“期货贸易”。期货交易是在现货交易的基础上发展起来的，是通过在期货交易所买卖标准化的期货合约而进行的一种有组织的交易形式。

【例 2】SAO PAULO (Reuters) – Brazilian airline Azul SA AZUL. N may forego a bailout package offered by state bank BNDES, as the company believes it will be able to get credit at more favorable terms in the private sector, the company's CEO told Reuters on Friday.

——"Brazilian airline Azul may shun government bailout, eyes private credit"(*Reuters*, AUGUST 29, 2020)

▶ **点评:**

本句中"bailout"是经济学中一个常见的专业术语，也是英语财经新闻中常出现的经济术语。所谓"bailout"指的是企业或者银行在面临倒闭的情况下，由政府或投资财团提供短期资金注入以助其渡过难关的情况，是为"救援"。"bailout"在中文新闻中多译为"救市"。

【例 3】Nearly 90% of respondents in Deutsche Bank's monthly investor survey said financial markets now had a number of price bubbles, with cryptocurrency Bitcoin and U. S. tech stocks top of the list.

——"Almost 90% see market bubbles in Deutsche Bank investor survey"(*Reuters*, JANUARY 19, 2021)

▶ **点评:**

本句中"bubbles"在日常使用中多表达为"泡沫"的意思，但在财经新闻中，"bubbles"具有其特定含义并成为专有词汇表达，指"经济泡沫"。更有专业术语"bubble economy"，表示虚拟资本过度增长与相关交易持续膨胀日益脱离实物资本的增长和实业部门的成长，金融证券、地产价格飞涨，投机交易极为活跃的经济现象。

（二）大量使用缩略词

在财经新闻中，涉及的主题信息通常并不是某个人，而是某个集团公司、国家或国际组织。这些实体一般都会有很长的英文名称，为了节省时间和空间，提高辨识度和阅读效率，使用缩写就成为了财经新闻的必然选择（皇甫俊凯，2016）。

缩略词包括缩写词和简略词两种。缩写词往往是专有名词的缩写，常使用实词的第一个字母合成，如"WTO——World Trade Organization"（世界贸易组织）等（张纯，何明霞，2010）。例如：

SINGAPORE （Reuters）——Oil prices slipped on Monday, paring strong gains made in the previous session after OPEC + agreed last week to gradually ease some of its production cuts between May and July.

——"Oil prices dip after OPEC + agree to ease output cuts"（*Reuters*, APRIL 5, 2021）

▶ **点评：**

本句中使用缩略词"OPEC +"，其为石油输出国组织的简称，"OPEC"全称为"Organization of the Petroleum Exporting Countries"。

简略词则是一些普通词汇采用截头、去尾或将两词各取部分组合而成，例子如下：

【例 4】（Reuters） – Reserve Bank of India Governor Shaktikanta Das told the Financial Times newspaper that he does not think there will be stagflation and that the consumer inflation should moderate.

——"RBI governor rules out stagflation, expects consumer inflation to moderate: Financial Times"（*Reuters*, AUGUST 31, 2020）

▶ **点评：**

该新闻中的"stagflation"一词由"stagnation"及"inflation"组合而成，表示停滞性通货膨胀，简称滞胀或停滞性通胀。在经济学，特别是宏观经济学中，特指经济停滞（stagnation），失业及通货膨胀（inflation，此处指"物价持续上涨"）同时持续增长的经济现象。

【例 5】（Reuters） – Citigroup Inc's General Counsel Rohan Weerasinghe will retire from the bank after nearly a decade in the role, Chief Executive Officer Jane Fraser told staff on Tuesday, according to a memo seen by Reuters.

Weerasinghe will retire by the end of this year and Citi will consider both internal as well as external candidates for his replacement, the memo said.

▶ **点评：**

本则新闻中，"memo"则使用去尾法，原词汇为"memorandum"，表示

"备忘录"，是商务信函中的一种，主要用于公司内部对公司的职员、部门通报信息，如会议安排、情况报告、问题处理等。此外，本条新闻中使用的缩略语"Citi"，该缩略语指代花旗银行（Citibank），其主要前身是1812年6月16日成立的"纽约城市银行"（City Bank of New York），经过近两个世纪的发展、并购，已经成为美国最大的银行之一，也是一家在全球近一百五十个国家及地区设有分支机构的国际大银行。

在词汇的使用上，英语财经新闻还有一个特点，即大量频繁地使用缩略语，如CDM（中国清洁发展机制），AIG（美国国际集团），FDI（外商直接投资），IMF（国际货币基金组织），FTA（自由贸易协定）等。

（三）大量使用新造词

由于英语财经新闻属于新闻报道，所以财经新闻必须具有时效性（杨伶俐，2004）。在经济全球化及互联网飞速发展的背景下，世界范围内经济活动的复杂程度和活跃程度相比过去都有了质的变化。世界经济变化日新月异，每天都会产生各种新的现象和信息，新的经济现象和信息需要用新的词汇来表达，这就使得财经新闻在描述某个新的经济现象和信息时必须使用新造词汇。例如：carbon footprint（碳足迹），public diplomacy（公共外交），career bottleneck（职业瓶颈），job reshuffle（换岗）等（牛书田，2014）。以下是几则新造词的例子：

【例6】The rise of carbon credits, paired with the need to restore abandoned farmland, presents companies with a new - age opportunity to address food security, ecosystem health and greenhouse gas emissions while lowering their carbon footprints.

—— "Decreasing Your Carbon Footprint Through Abandoned Farmland Restoration" (*Forbes*, APRIL 5, 2021)

▶ **点评：**

随着气候变化成为全球工商业可持续发展的重要议题，碳排放量引起全球思考。中文表达"碳足迹"一词就来源于英语"Carbon Footprint"，表示一个人或者团体的"碳耗用量"。碳是石油、煤炭、木材等由碳元素构成的自然资源，这一术语体现了一个人的能源意识和行为对自然界产生的影响。“碳足迹”的计算则是为了有效地减少温室气体的排放量并减轻其对气候和环境的不利影响。除“carbon footprint”外，与之相关联的术语还有“carbon neutrality”，即“碳中和”。

【例 7】Chimerica, the intertwined manufacturing colossus that boomed across the Pacific from the early 1990s, looked far past its prime even before the pandemic. The effect of pandemic-related shortages will deal another serious wound to the framework.

——“Chimerica Isn't Dead, but the Pandemic Grievously Wounded It”

(*The Wall Street Journal*, JUNE 8, 2020)

▶ **点评：**

本则新闻中“Chimerica”是2008年西方学者尼尔·弗格森教授将“China”和“America”进行重组合并而构成的新词，以体现中美之间“你中有我，我中有你”的经济依存关系。这一词汇主要是为了表示中美已走入经济共生时代，最大消费国（美国）和最大储蓄国（中国）应该构成利益共同体。

（四）大量使用对比性词汇

与其他类型的新闻相比，财经类新闻的一个重要特征是在文本中大量使用对比性词汇。在财经新闻中，记者需要对一些经济信息进行多种对比，以便清晰地向读者展现某些经济指标的发展势头、趋势等。同时，记者在写作财经类新闻时，记者不能掺杂个人的观点，要写具体的经济指标，要保证报道的客观性、真实性和可信度。为了更好地突出财经类新闻的客观性、真实性和可信度，记者往往频繁地使用对比性的词语。例如，在财经新闻中，jump, notch up, skyrocket, leap 等词语表示“直线上升”的意思，而 fall, drop, go down, reach a low point, fall off, decline, reduce level of 等词语则表示“下降”的意思。这些词语常常在财经新闻的同一段落中出现，或是相继出现在相邻的段落中。财经新闻中大量使用对比性词汇可以降低财经类新闻的乏味性、枯燥性，增添财经类新闻报道的趣味性、可读性，使得财经新闻变得生动形象（谢水璎，2015）。下面我们举例说明。

US technology shares slipped and European equities climbed on Tuesday, as investors backed out of pandemic winners and positioned instead for a global economic recovery.

Wall Street's tech – focused Nasdaq Composite dropped 0.1per cent to close lower for a second – straight day. The broader S&P 500 index also fell, off 0.3 per cent.

US government bonds also came under pressure. The yield on the 10 – year US Treasury hit its highest level since last January earlier in the session, rising 0.04 percentage points to more than 1.76 per cent before settling at about 1.71 per cent. The yield on the equivalent German Bund added 0.03 percentage points to minus 0.29 per cent.

The continued rise in US Treasury yields, which influences borrowing costs worldwide, has hit the valuations of growth stocks, contributing to the underperformance of the Nasdaq this year. The tech index has risen roughly 1 per cent so far in 2021.

Europe's Stoxx 600 index, which advanced 0.7per cent on Tuesday, has risen almost 8 per cent this year, following a10.5 per cent gain in the three months to last December. The European equity benchmark, which is dominated by old – economy businesses whose fortunes are pegged to rebound in global growth, is now within touching distance of its pre – pandemic record of 433.9 reached on February 19 last year.

The banks subsector of the European index has surged more than 20 per cent in the first quarter while its industrial goods and services businesses have notched up a 9 per cent gain.

"The first quarter of this year on global stock markets was as classic a cyclical rotation as you'll likely see in your lifetime" said Nicholas Colas of research house DataTrek.

The moves came as investors looked past the worsening coronavirus situation in continental Europe and bought up the bloc's globally focused businesses.

A net 30 per cent of global portfolio managers had an overweight position on European stocks in mid – March, according to a Bank of America survey, up from 20 per cent a month earlier.

Monica Defend, head of research at Amundi, said investors were also banking on European companies achieving stronger profit growth than their US peers during the next 12 months because the bloc's recovery from the pandemic and vaccine rollouts had been slower than in North America.

"The two regions are really running at different speeds," said Defend You have more recovery further out [in Europe] than you have in the US.

Germany's Xetra Dax gained 1. 3 per cent on Tuesday hitting a record high, while London's FTSE 100 closed up 0. 5 per cent, adding to an almost 5 per cent gain for the quarter.

Emmanuel Cau, head of European equity strategy at Barclays, warned that stock market trades based on recovery from the pandemic remained vulnerable to central banks reining in the huge monetary support they began applying to markets this time last year.

"There is a lot of confusion in the market," he said "If you are confident about the macro economy, then at some point you worry about the next step, which is the removal of monetary stimulus.

"Perhaps we are now in a window where you can have supportive liquidity and strong growth but we are getting close to the end of the Goldilocks phase."

—— "Wall Street slips as technology stocks sell off" (*FT News*, March 3, 2021)

▶ **点评:**

本则财经新闻采用了 slip, climb, dropped, rise, fell, rebound, surge, notch up, hit its highest level 及 closed up 等词汇细致地描述了各种经济现象的变化，增添文章的准确性客观性。如新闻的一开头就分别用"slip"（下跌）和"climb"（上涨）描绘了美国科技股票和欧洲股票的变化情况。此外，新闻中表示"下跌"的动词还有"drop"和"fall"，表示"上涨"的动词还包括"rise"和"surge"（剧增）。而"rebound"（反弹），"notch up"（达到），

"hit its highest level"（创下新高）及"close up"（接近）这些动词或动词短语都生动客观地描绘了经济现象的变化。这些动词和短语都属于财经新闻中的高频词汇和短语，英语新闻阅读者平时应多注意，多积累。

第二节　英语财经新闻的句法特征

一、简洁表达与复杂结构并存

由于财经新闻在传递信息时有准确性和时效性的要求，因而英语财经新闻的句法也呈现出复杂结构与简洁表达并存的特点。在准确性要求和财经领域信息内容本身较为复杂的背景下，财经新闻中经常会使用很多从句或修饰成分，使得句子的信息密度较高，结构复杂。但在时效性的要求下，财经新闻则需要采取尽可能简洁的方式来提高信息传递的效率，因此会避免采用复杂的名词化结构以及倒装结构，并以主谓结构作为句子的框架（皇甫俊凯，2016）。以下为几则例子：

【例 8】On Tuesday, the IMF released an updated economic forecast which boosted global growth for this year to 6%, up from a projection of 5.5% in January, with the boost coming in large part from accelerated vaccine roll-outs and the $1.9 trillion rescue package the Biden administration pushed through Congress last month.

——"Major economies support $650 billion boost in IMF resources" (*Associated Press*, APRIL 7, 2021)

▶ 点评：

此句话就体现了英语财经新闻中复杂结构与简单表达并存的特点。除去时间状语和定语从句外，此句话的主干部分只剩"the IMF released an updated economic forecast"。关系代词"which"后面的部分全部都用于修饰先行词"an update economic forecast"，即"最新的经济预测"的主要内容。此句话的翻译为"周二，国际货币基金组织发布了最新的经济预测，将今年的全球经济增长从一月份的5.5%提高到了6%，增长的很大一部分来自疫苗的加速推出及上个月拜登政府推动国会通过的1.9万亿美元救助计划”。

【例9】The meeting Wednesday of finance ministers and central bank governors of traditional economic powers such as the United States, Japan and Germany along with emerging economies such as China and India will be followed by a leaders's ummit to be held in Rome on Oct. 30 – 31.

—— “Major economies support $650 billion boost in IMF resources” (*Associated Press*, APRIL 7, 2021)

▶ **点评：**

本句同样也体现了英语财经新闻的句法特点。除去句子的修饰成分，句子的主干部分可提取为“The meeting will be followed by a leaders’ summit.”介词“of”后面的部分“finance ministers and central bank governors of traditional economic powers such as the United States, Japan and Germany along with emerging economies such as China and India”都是用来修饰“the meeting”，即交代了参会国家和参会人员。“to be held in Rome on Oct. 30 – 31”则是作为不定式修饰名词短语“a leaders'summit”，表明峰会的召开的时间和地点。此句话的翻译为“周三，美国，日本和德国等传统经济大国的财政部长及中央银行行长与中国、印度等新兴经济体将举行会议。随后，领导人峰会将于10月30日到31日在罗马举行”。

二、较多使用圆周句

英语财经新闻还较多地使用圆周句。圆周句是指把最关键的内容置于句末，读者要读懂某个句子，通常要对整个句子的结构有清晰的把握，将整个句子读完才能最终理解句子所要表达的内容。圆周句的关键信息位置靠后，所以在阅读时可以重点关注句子的后半部分信息来提高阅读效率（皇甫俊凯，2016）。下面为几则例子：

【例10】The economic growth Dimon projects the United States could see in the next two years will create opportunities to “deal with issues stemming from inequality," Dimon wrote.

—— "JPMorgan CEO Dimon sees U. S. economic boom through 2023" (*Reuters*, APRIL 7, 2021)

▶ **点评：**

本则新闻语句中，首先将新闻相关背景介绍，主语为 Dimon 所预测美国未来两年内经济发展，谓语动词为“带来机遇”，将重点放在句尾，即“为解决不平等所带来的问题带来机遇”。本句通过设置悬念来激发读者的兴趣。

【例 11】A source close to Credit Suisse said that were it not for the planned change of chairman, the bank might already have embarked on significant structural changes.

—— "Analysis: Credit Suisse in search of new map after losing way with Archegos" (*Reuters*, APRIL 7, 2021)

▶ **点评：**

本则新闻，重点内容则在宾语从句中体现，句首提出消息来源，增添新闻的真实性与可信度，在宾语从句中又使用虚拟语气，使用 if 虚拟语气的省略用法，将条件先引出，再强调结果。在这个“圆周句”中，最关键的内容被置于句末，读者不读完最后一个词，就无法理解句意。

【例 12】It's not clear that stock market authorities will stop Suez: last week French regulators criticised its use of a poison pill mechanism but declined to impose any penalties.

—— "Breakingviews - Capital Calls - Suez waste sale throws garbage at Veolia bid" (*Reuters*, APRIL 6, 2021)

▶ **点评：**

本例中，句首先提出信息“it's not clear”引起读者猜想，“it”指代后文中“stock market authorities will stop Suez”，但此时信息并不充分，后文通过“冒号”，给出具体事件，来阐释观点。本句通过把重要信息置于尾部，层层递进，帮助读者更加充分地理解文章信息。

第三节 英语财经新闻的语篇结构特征

一、概述

新闻语篇结构，即新闻语篇由几部分构成，以及每部分在新闻语篇中的位置及组篇模式。

通常，一则新闻语篇由标题（headline）、导语（lead）和正文（body）三部分组成。标题被视作新闻的“眼睛”，起猎奇和招徕的作用；导语概括全篇，通常根据信息传播的需要围绕“五 W”（when，where，who，what，why）和“一 H”（how）展开，旨在导读，被称为新闻的“灵魂”；正文则具体叙述，是新闻的“躯干”。

在一则新闻语篇中，不同的信息会被按不同的组篇模式填充到标题（headline），导语（lead）和正文（body）三个部分中。西方新闻界经过长时期探索，逐渐形成了五种典型的新闻语篇结构，即：倒金字塔结构、金字塔结构及沙漏结构。

英语财经新闻的语篇结构与常规英语新闻的语篇结构是一致的（张纯、何明霞，2010）。

二、典型的英语财经新闻的语篇结构

英语财经新闻中最常见的篇章结构为倒金字塔结构。我调查了很多英语财经新闻，调查范围包括《中国日报》《华尔街日报》以及美联社网站上刊发的财经新闻。我们发现，由于英语财经新闻十分追求时效性，绝大多数英语财经新闻的结构都是倒金字塔结构。在其他报刊上，我们常看到金字塔结构的新闻，也就是按照时间顺序来写作的新闻报道。但大部分英语财经英文都不会根据时间顺序进行报道，而是直接把最重要的信息放在开头，然后在下文慢慢补充新闻的细节，也就是说，英语财经新闻的结构最常见的是倒金字塔结构。倒金字塔结构的新闻语篇按照新闻事件各种信息的重要性逐渐递

减的次序排列相关材料。其具体结构是：导语—最精彩、最重要的支撑性材料（观点）—次要的支撑性材料（观点）—最不重要的支撑性材料（观点）—结尾。下面是一则英语财经新闻。

US jobless claims up to 744K as virus still forces layoffs

WASHINGTON（AP）— The number of Americans applying for unemployment benefits rose last week to 744000，signaling that many employers are still cutting jobs even as more people are vaccinated against COVID－19，consumers gain confidence and the government distributes aid throughout the economy.

The Labor Department said Thursday that applications increased by 16000 from 728000 a week earlier. Jobless claims have declined sharply since the virus slammed into the economy in March of last year. But they remain stubbornly high by historical standards：Before the pandemic erupted，weekly applications typically remained below 220000 a week.

For the week ending March 27，more than 3.7 million people were receiving traditional state unemployment benefits，thegovernment said. If you include supplemental federal programs that were established last year to help the unemployed endure the health crisis，a total of 18.2 million are receiving some form of jobless aid the week of March 20.

Economists monitor weekly jobless claims for early signs of where the job market is headed. Applications are usually a proxy for layoffs：They typically decline as the economy improves. Or they rise as employers retrench in response to sluggish consumer demand.

During the pandemic，though，the numbers have become a less reliable barometer. States have struggled to clear backlogs of unemployment applications，and suspected fraud has clouded the actual volume of job cuts.

By nearly all measures，though，the economy has been strengthening. During March，employers added 916000 jobs，the most since August，and the unemployment rate declined from 6.2% to 6%. In February，the pace of job openings reached its highest level on record. Last month，consumer confidence posted its highest reading in a year.

And this week, the International Monetary Fund forecast that the U. S. economy will grow 6. 4% this year. That would fastest annual pace since 1984 and the strongest among the world's wealthiest countries.

Most economists say they think the still – high level of unemployment applications should gradually fade.

"Jobless claims may bounce around week to week as the recovery takes hold, but we expect they will start to decline more consistently as the economy gains momentum," economists Nancy Vanden Houten and Gregory Daco of Oxford Economics said in a research note. "We expect the stellar March jobs report to be the first of many and look for a hiring boom in the spring and summer months."

Still, the United States still has 8. 4 million fewer jobs than it had in February 2020, just before the pandemic struck. New confirmed coronavirus cases, which had dropped sharply from early January through early March, have plateaued over the past month. In addition, the vaccination rate for elderly Americans, who are among the most vulnerable, has dramatically slowed even as the supply of vaccines has expanded.

And the data firm Womply reports that the percentage of businesses that remainedclosed last week rose from the beginning of March—from 38% to 45% for bars; from 35% to 46% for beauty shops; and from 30% to 38% for restaurants.

▶ **点评：**

该篇财经新闻就采用了典型的倒金字塔结构。该篇新闻报道的主题为受疫情影响，美国的失业人数仍在攀升。新闻的标题已经高度概括了新闻的主要内容，而新闻的导语则对标题进行了进一步补充——“上周，美国申请失业救济的人数增加至744000人，这表明即使更多的人接种了新冠疫苗，消费者信心增强，政府在经济中分配援助，许多雇主仍在裁员。”实际上，新闻的导语已经清晰地阐明了该则新闻想要表达的中心思想，而新闻的正文则详细说明了新冠肺炎疫情对美国就业市场造成的影响，例如正文的第一段就引用了美国劳工部的信息，交代了新闻的背景，即自疫情以来，美国申请失业救济人数的变化。正文的开头阐明与新闻相关的重要背景信息后，就依据新闻材料的重要性不断补充与新闻相关的各种信息。阅读整篇新闻后，我们不难发现，文章后半部分都是一些新闻背景信息的补充，其新闻价值相对较低。这就是一篇典型的倒金字塔结构的英语财经新闻。

除了倒金字塔结构的新闻外，一般情况下新闻结构还包括金字塔结构、沙漏结构等。但由于财经新闻十分追求时效性，所以大部分英语财经新闻都会采用倒金字塔的结构，将关键信息开门见山地放在开头，然后在下文对其进行补充说明。

第四节　英语财经新闻标题的特征

一、概述

标题是新闻的题目，它高度概括了新闻的内容，帮助读者挑选、阅读和理解新闻。对于新闻来说，标题十分重要（刘其中，2009：24）。英语财经新闻的标题与一般英语新闻标题一样，在版式样态和内容表述方面具有鲜明的特征。

二、英语财经新闻标题版式样态的特征

英文报纸的版面重视栏序而不重视区序，报纸的栏目较窄，各栏目依次排列，井然有序，所以英文财经新闻的标题多以多行形态出现，一般字体统一，字号统一。一个标题的排列有左对齐、居中、两端对齐、分散对齐、阶梯式和倒金字塔式等，当然也可以见到单行居中的通栏标题。另外，英文报刊标题最忌移行。由于格式上的限制，英语财经新闻的标题绝大多数都只有主标题，主标题和副标题共现的形态较为少见。

另外，英文报纸受语言形式的影响，其标题只能横排，不能竖排。

这里我们列出 China Daily 2021 年 4 月 30 日财经新闻板块、2021 年 5 月 6 日财经新闻板块及 2021 年 5 月 7 日财经新闻板块的照片。可以清楚地看出，*China Daily* 版面上几乎没有主标题与副标题同时出现的情况，也没有竖排标题的情况。

BUSINESS

JOIN THE CONVERSATION: FOLLOW US ON TWITTER · CHINA DAILY

Top cities key housing draws

Shanghai's new property projects remain popular during May 1-5

For duty-free stores in Hainan, holiday spells shopping quota peak

485 million yuan

RIGHT TRACK

Local govt bond issues to rise this year

Experts see bright future for A shares

Briefly

World's longest 'water bridge' put into use

Hongqi sees rosy sales in Jan-April

4 sci-tech innovation IPOs receive nod

China Daily 2021 年 5 月 6 日财经新闻板块

BUSINESS

FIND US ON FACEBOOK AND JOIN THE CONVERSATION · CHINA DAILY

Fiscal moves aid high-end development

China will actively provide support for key strategic tasks, says minister

15.2 percent

Chinese bicycle makers pedal away COVID blues with strong growth

Oppo releases a slew of new products

21.6 million units

Briefly

Holiday fillip for delivery companies

Transport investment up in first quarter

Gold-backed ETF holdings rise in Q1

China Daily 2021 年 5 月 7 日财经新闻板块

我们也从网络上下载具有代表性的英语财经新闻版块，如美国《华尔街日报》等。经过比对发现，英美国家的财经新闻的版块上，几乎没有主标题与副标题同时出现的情况，也没有竖排标题的情况。

DOW JONES, A NEWS CORP COMPANY

About WSJ

THE WALL STREET JOURNAL.

Subscribe　Sign In

SPRING SALE

English Edition | Print Edition | Video | Podcasts | Latest Headlines

Home　World　U.S.　Politics　Economy　Business　Tech　Markets　Opinion　Life & Arts　Real Estate　WSJ. Magazine　Search

SHARE

BUSINESS

As Amazon, McDonald's Raise Wages, Small Businesses Struggle to Keep Up

Companies forgo investment and turn down contracts as they compete with jobless benefits and wage increases at larger firms

President Biden has identified raising the minimum wage as a key goal of his administration, but economists and lawmakers disagree on the potential impact. WSJ asked two economists and a minimum-wage worker what the costs and benefits of a $15 minimum wage might be.
Photo: Bill Clark/Congressional Quarterly/Zuma Press

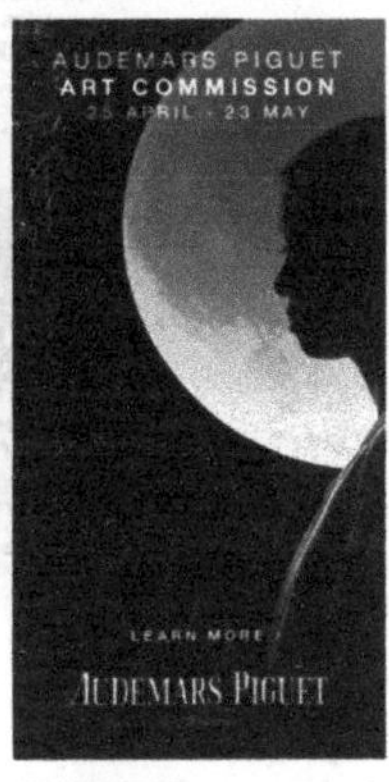

By Allison Prang
Updated May 20, 2021 5:43 pm ET

PRINT　TEXT

Ben Johnson is looking for a data analyst and a data scientist to come work for his Philadelphia-area consulting firm. The search has now stretched to Chicago.

U.S. companies of all sizes are struggling to fill jobs as surging demand and a reluctant labor force have resulted in a shortage of available workers. Some of the smallest firms said they are feeling acute pain because they have fewer people to pick up the slack and can't easily match the pay increases, benefits and other perks that larger companies are offering to fill openings. The situation is only expected to become more difficult for business owners such as Mr. Johnson, who said his 20-person company needs to double in size over the next six months to a year.

"With the growth I see in the market...in five years I'm going to be tapping out everyone in this country," said Mr. Johnson, chief executive and co-owner of Freya Systems LLC, a software and data analytics consulting firm.

More than two-thirds of small businesses reported having a hard time finding qualified workers, according to a monthly survey of 611 small firms for The Wall Street Journal by Vistage Worldwide Inc. At the same time, they are planning for their workforces to grow.

UPCOMING EVENTS

May 24 2021 — 12:30 PM - 1:00 PM EDT — Ask WSJ: A Closer Look at Biden's Tax Plans

May 26 2021 — 12:00 PM - 1:30 PM EDT — WSJ Women In: Women, Power and Equity

Jun 2 2021 — 11:00 AM - 3:00 PM EDT — WSJ Pro Cybersecurity Executive Forum

ADD TO CALENDAR

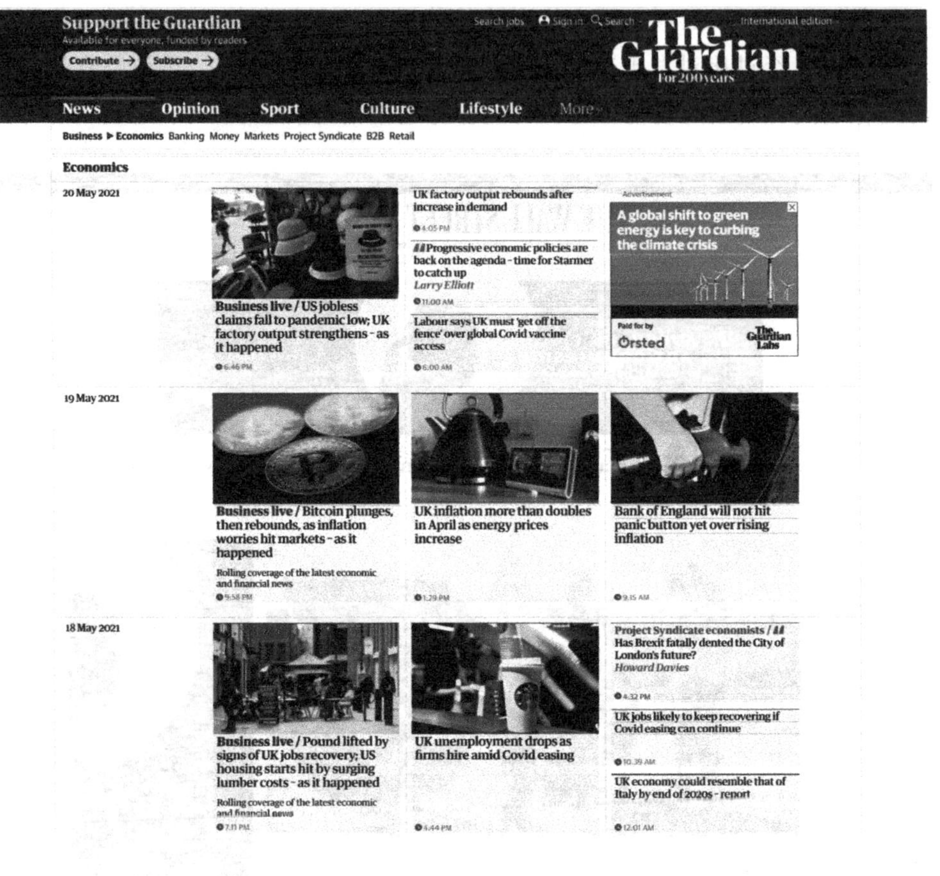
Support the Guardian
Available for everyone, funded by readers
Contribute → Subscribe →
Search jobs Sign in Search International edition
The Guardian
For 200 years
News Opinion Sport Culture Lifestyle More
Business ▶ Economics Banking Money Markets Project Syndicate B2B Retail

Economics

20 May 2021

Business live / US jobless claims fall to pandemic low; UK factory output strengthens – as it happened
6:46 PM

UK factory output rebounds after increase in demand
4:05 PM

Progressive economic policies are back on the agenda – time for Starmer to catch up
Larry Elliott
11:00 AM

Labour says UK must 'get off the fence' over global Covid vaccine access
6:00 AM

Advertisement
A global shift to green energy is key to curbing the climate crisis
Paid for by Ørsted The Guardian Labs

19 May 2021

Business live / Bitcoin plunges, then rebounds, as inflation worries hit markets – as it happened
Rolling coverage of the latest economic and financial news
9:58 PM

UK inflation more than doubles in April as energy prices increase
1:29 PM

Bank of England will not hit panic button yet over rising inflation
9:15 AM

18 May 2021

Business live / Pound lifted by signs of UK jobs recovery; US housing starts hit by surging lumber costs – as it happened
Rolling coverage of the latest economic and financial news
7:11 PM

UK unemployment drops as firms hire amid Covid easing
4:44 PM

Project Syndicate economists / Has Brexit fatally dented the City of London's future?
Howard Davies
4:32 PM

UK jobs likely to keep recovering if Covid easing can continue
10:39 AM

UK economy could resemble that of Italy by end of 2020s – report
12:01 AM

三、英语财经新闻标题内容表述的特征

英语财经新闻的标题在内容表述方面具有三个特征，即简洁性，醒目性及导读性。

（一）简洁性

所谓的简洁性是指英语财经新闻的标题一般不会过长，标题字数控制在十个单词左右，这有利于读者挑选和阅读自己感兴趣的新闻，尤其对于当今社会来说，快节奏的生活强化了人们对效率的追求，简洁的新闻标题正有助于人们节省时间，提高效率。请看以下几则英语财经新闻标题：

（1） Biden open to compromise on infrastructure，but not inaction；

（2） US jobless claims up to 744K as virus still forces layoffs；

（3） Amazon takes early lead as union vote count gets underway；

（4） Fed's Powell：US nears full reopening to "different economy"

（https：//apnews. com/hub/business）。

▶ **点评：**

以上新闻标题都选自美联社的财经新闻板块。不难发现，这些新闻标题字数都为十个单词左右，十分简洁，让读者一目了然。此外，标题中出现了"US"和"Fed"这样的缩写，都是为了让新闻标题看上去更简洁。

（二）醒目性

醒目性是指英语财经新闻的标题英语新闻一般都会选择一些具有视觉冲击力的单词或词汇作为新闻标题，让读者在浏览信息时第一眼便被牢牢吸引住，进而产生阅读欲望，并且在阅读详细全文内容的过程中始终围绕标题中的某些单词或者词汇来思考探究，试图从文章中来寻找确切的答案，这样一来便极大地提高了人们阅读新闻的有效性，充分发挥了英语新闻的价值，对于促进媒体新闻信息的快速传播而言具有十分积极的意义（韩海华，2018）。以下是几则例子：

【例 13】 Biden open to compromise on infrastructure，but not inaction

▶ **点评：**

首先，该标题以美国现任总统拜登作为主语，第一时间就抓住了读者的眼球，吸引读者继续阅读。其次，标题中的动词"compromise"（妥协）引人遐想，令人好奇，而"infrastructure"（基础设施）则交代了新闻围绕的主题。最后，标题用"but"表转折，更是激发了读者的阅读欲望。

【例 14】 IMF policy panel endorses ＄650 billion increase in resource

▶ **点评：**

该标题也是开门见山，直接以"IMF policy panel"（国际货币基金组织政策小组）作为主语，交代清楚新闻的“主人公”，吸引读者的注意力。而后，标题中出现了“$650 billion”（6500 亿美元）这样醒目的数字，同样也勾起了读者的阅读兴趣。

（三）导读性

导读性则是指因此，英语新闻的撰写者常常会使用文章的关键词来拟定标题，既是为了达到简洁明了的效果，也是为了让读者在短时间内准确把握文章的重点，并且对文章的中心思想一目了然，从而有效增强英语新闻的可阅读性（韩海华，2018）。以下是几则例子：

（1） Biden open to compromise on infrastructure，but not inaction；

（2） US jobless claims up to 744K as virus still forces layoffs；

（3） Amazon takes early lead as union vote count gets underway；

（4） Fed's Powell：US nears full reopening to “different economy”；

（5） IMF policy panel endorses $650 billion increase in resource；

（https：//apnews. com/hub/business）。

▶ **点评：**

不难看出，每一则新闻标题都交代了新闻事件的“主人公”，并以简洁明了的用词高度概括了新闻事件的主要内容，让读者能够在较短的时间内把握新闻的重点，并对新闻的中心思想一目了然，有效增强了新闻的可读性。

第五节　英语财经新闻导语的特征

一、概述

对一则财经新闻而言，导语的地位是非常重要的。财经新闻的写作者总是下很大工夫来把导语写得别具一格。因此，财经新闻导语具有鲜明的特征。财经新闻导语的鲜明特征主要从内容选择和形式表达两方面体现出来。

二、内容选择方面的特征

（一）选择内容时，对相关信息进行高度概括性

导语是新闻的起始部分。它是帮助读者阅读新闻的关键性段落，也是对新闻内容开宗明义性的宣示。新闻导语一般就是新闻中开门见山的第一段文字。它以最简练的语言把新闻中最有新闻价值的内容完整地表达出来，使读者看完这段文字以后就能获悉新闻的主要内容（刘其中，2009：25）。英语财经新闻的导语同样也具有高度的概括性，用最简洁的语言把新闻中最有价值的内容表达出来，帮助读者捕获新闻的重点。例如：

WASHINGTON（AP）— The International Monetary Fund on Thursday authorized a ＄650 billion expansion of the 190 – nation lending institution's resources with the aim of providing more support for vulnerable countries as they battle the coronavirus pandemic.

——"IMF policy panel endorses ＄650 billion increase in resource"（*Associated Press*，APRIL 8，2021）

▶ **点评：**

该则新闻导语就是十分典型的例子。上面，我们已经分析了该则新闻的标题，即"IMF policy panel endorses ＄650 billion increase in resource"，该标题已经高度概括了新闻内容。而该新闻的导语则对新闻标题中的内容进行了补充，阐明该新闻的几个关键要素："Who"，即新闻事件的主体"The International Monetary Fund"；"When"，即新闻发生的时间"Thursday"；"What"，即新闻事件的主体做了什么"authorized a ＄650 billion expansion of the 190 – nation lending institution's resources"；"Why"，即新闻事件的主体为什么要这么做"with the aim of providing more support for vulnerable countries as they battle the coronavirus pandemic"。该新闻导语以一句话就高度概括出了新闻的主要内容，开门见山地阐明了新闻中最重要的几个要素。

（二）选择内容时，注重突显主题信息

一则财经新闻的导语往往会突显重要的主题信息。也就是说，一则财经新闻的导语往往会特别强调“五 W”（when，where，who，what，why）和“一 H”（how）的一个，而省略其他的一个或几个。更具体地讲，就是在财经新闻导语中，并不一定会出现全部的“五 W”和“一 H”，而是会对某个 W 或 H 较详细地说明或描述。例如以下这则导语：

FRANKFURT，Germany（AP）— Europe's economy shrank 0.6% in the first three months of the year as slow vaccine rollouts and extended lockdowns delayed a hoped - for recovery - and underlined how the region is lagging other major economies in rebounding from the coronavirus pandemic.

——“Europe's economy shrinks in first quarter as US rolls ahead”（*Associated Press*，APRIL，30，2021）

▶ **点评：**

该财经新闻导语主要对“what”（即欧洲经济萎缩这一现象）和“why”（即导致欧洲经济萎缩的原因）这两个要素进行了说明。

三、表达形式方面的特征

为了迅速吸引读者注意力，英语财经新闻的作者都会句斟字酌地写好导语的第一句。要写好一个句子，作者往往要使句式选择多样化。英语句式选择的重要内容包括句子的开头、长句与短句的搭配、松散句与圆周句的搭配等。为了取得导语所需的特殊效果，英语财经新闻的导语在句式选择上表现出以下两个特点。

（一）灵活使用多种句型

1. 使用松散句

一般而言，“松散句”在英语表达中更常见。松散句是指主要信息和实质部分在句子的前半部分首先揭示出来，大量修饰语或补充细节附加在句子

后半部分的句式。松散句的好处在于读者子在看到最初的几个词后就知道这句话的意思，但是有时候“松散句”因为太长，包含附加信息太多，也会干扰到读者对于句子的理解，因为英语语言本来就有着“高频率使用定语从句、伴随状语等补充信息”的特点，所以“松散句”以超长定语从句结尾或者以多重伴随状语结尾的情况也很常见。例如：

China is slated to kick off nationwide Consumption Promotion Month 2021 on May 1 after an opening evening in Shanghai on Friday, the country's Ministry of Commerce said recently.

(Consumption promotion month to kick off on May 1 - Chinadaily.com. cn)

2. 使用圆周句

圆周句是指把最关键的内容置于句末，不读完最后一个词，读者就无法理解句意，而且在最后一个词出现之前，句子在语法上也是不完整的。因而在阅读这类句子的过程中，读者一直有种被吊着胃口的感觉，迫切地想捕捉句尾的重点信息。这就是“圆周句”的妙处所在——通过设置悬念来激发读者的兴趣，牢牢抓住读者的注意力，从而提升整句话的吸引力和感染力。除此之外，“圆周句”的句子结构往往显得严谨有力，通过重点信息收尾以突出整个句子的完整性。这种句子一般在正式书面文体中出现较多。例如：

WASHINGTON (AP) — From John Kennedy to Ronald Reagan to Donald Trump, American presidents have taken aim at corporate America's tax - avoidance schemes before—and mostly missed.

[Biden's corporate tax plan takes aim at income inequality (apnews.com)]

3. 使用长句

长句是指句子较长、气势恢宏、严密周详、精确明晰、委婉细腻的句式。长句结构严谨、内容丰富、逻辑性强，具有跌宕起伏、回环绵密之美。一些英语财经新闻的导语常用一个长句完成。例如：

WASHINGTON (AP) — A top Senate Democrat is urging U. S. anti - pollution standards that would follow a deal brokered by California with five automakers and then set targets to end sales of new gasoline - powered vehicles by 2035, a goal that reaches farther than President Joe Biden's climate plan.

[Carper urges tough US rules barring gas - powered cars by 2035 (apnews. com)]

ANAHEIM, Calif. (AP) — Disneyland swung open its gates to cheering visitors donning sequined Minnie Mouse ears and snapping selfies Friday, marking a dramatic turnaround in a state so overwhelmed with coronavirus cases just four months ago that patients were being treated in outdoor tents.

[Disneyland reopening marks California's COVID - 19 turnaround (apnews. com)]

4. 使用短句

短句是指句子短小精悍、简洁有力、劲健挺拔、活泼明快的句式。短句可以以简要叙述事件，表现人物的口吻，表达坚定、肯定的语气、紧张的气氛和令人震撼的内容。英语财经新闻的导语也有用短句来表达的情况。例如：

NEW YORK (AP) — Big Tech stocks are flexing their enormous strength again, after getting knocked around a bit earlier this year.

[Big Tech stocks flex muscles again after a rough winter (apnews. com)]

NEW YORK (AP) — Exxon Mobil on Friday reported first - quarter profits of $2.73 billion after a tumultuous year led to major spending reductions.

[Exxon posts $2.7B quarterly profit after unprecedented year (apnews. com)]

WASHINGTON (AP) — If you're traveling on a plane, train or bus, don't put that face mask away yet.

[US extends face - mask requirement on planes until September (apnews. com)]

(二) 句子开头丰富多彩

句子开头丰富多彩是指句子开头应避免千篇一律，只用主语开头。为了把句子写得生动活泼一点，除了用主语开头外，还可使用其他句子成分开头。例如：

用从句开头的句子：

WASHINGTON（AP）— If you're traveling on a plane，train or bus，don't put that face mask away yet.

[US extends face - mask requirement on planes until September (apnews. com)]

用介词短语开头的句子：

FUZHOU - In addition to using cash and digital payment platforms such as Alipay and WeChat Pay，participants at the fourth Digital China Summit have another payment option - the digital renminbi - if they want to buy beverages or snacks at the meeting venue.

(Digital tech spurs real economy - Chinadaily. com. cn)

参考文献

[1] 皇甫俊凯．英语财经新闻语言特点探究［J］．英语广场，2016（9）：7-9.

[2] 杨伶俐．经贸类英文报刊文章的语言特色［J］．国际商务，2004（5）：82-86.

[3] 牛书田．英美媒体英语新词来源构成分析［J］．青年记者，2014（14）：81-82.

[4] 谢水璎．英语报刊财经类新闻报道的语言风格［J］．新闻战线，2015（17）：147-148.

[5] 张纯，何明霞．财经英语新闻语言特色及阅读能力培养策略探析［J］．湖北经济学院学报（人文社会科学版）．2010（7）：182-183.

[6] 刘其中．英汉新闻翻译［M］．北京：清华大学出版社，2009.

[7] 韩海华．英语新闻标题特点探究［J］．新闻研究导刊，2018（5）：236.

| 第四章 |

英汉财经新闻的翻译原则

第一节　信

一、“信”的界定

“信”，即忠实。“信”于原文，是译者在翻译任何文本时都应遵循的首要原则。鲁迅先生曾一度提出“宁信而不顺”的主张，认为“信”是第一位的。（刘超先，1992：2）由此可见“信”的重要性。当然，如今我们所理解的“信”并非忠实于原文的字面意义，而是译文必须忠实于原文的内涵，包括意思、事实、语气、风格等方面。

财经新闻致力于传递财经信息、传播财经知识，所以，财经新闻翻译必须遵守“信”这一原则。译语准确是财经新闻翻译的首要标准，也是财经新闻传播价值和意义的第一保证。（周俊博，2014：27）

二、“信”的实现方式

财经新闻翻译的“信”主要表现在语义忠实、语气忠实和风格忠实等方面。接下来，我们结合具体例子来分析如何在不同方面实现忠实。

（一）语义忠实

财经新闻具有很强的专业性，有很多的专业术语和专有名词。它们本来作普通词汇使用时，语义多元，但用于财经语境中，则成为专业术语或专业术语的一部分，词义单一。翻译这类词汇时，译者要考虑其所处的专业语境，译出其专业含义，确保译语准确。（周俊博，2014：27）

【原文】Wen Bin, chief researcher of China Minsheng Bank, also said that from the perspective of major exchange rate changes, the US dollar index strengthened in February, the appreciation rate reached 0.8%, the euro weakened and the yen strengthened. In consideration of exchange rate conversion factors, the portion of China's foreign exchange reserves that is denominated in currencies other than US dollars is converted into US dollars to form valuation losses. In terms of asset prices, the yield on U.S. 10 - year Treasury bonds fell to 1.13% from 1.51% at the end of January; the hedged global bond index denominated in US dollars rose 1.2%; the stock index fell significantly, and the S&P 500 index fell 8.4%; the Eurozone Stoke 50 Index fell 8.6% and the Nikkei 225 Index fell 8.9%. Taking into account the effects of exchange rate translation and changes in asset prices, changes in valuations have led to a reduction in the size of foreign exchange reserves this month. He also said that real trade will be a drag on the formation of foreign exchange reserves in February. Affected by the epidemic, domestic restart of work is delayed, and the smoothness of the industrial chain and supply chain is affected. Foreign trade companies face difficulties such as resumption of work, transportation, contract compliance, poor international logistics, and trade barriers. Fluctuations in foreign trade are inevitable.

【译文】中国民生银行首席研究员文斌也表示，从重大汇率变动来看，2月份美元指数走强，升值幅度达到0.8%，欧元走弱，日元走强。考虑到汇率折算因素，我国外汇储备中以美元以外的货币计提的部分折算为美元，形成估值损失。资产价格方面，美国10年期国债收益率从1月底的1.51%降至1.13%；以美元计价的对冲全球债券指数上涨1.2%；股指大幅下跌，标准普尔500指数下跌8.4%；欧元区斯托克50指数下跌8.6%，日经225指数下跌8.9%。考虑到汇率折算和资产价格变化的影响，本月估值变化导致外汇储备规模减少。他还表示，实际贸易将拖累2月份外汇储备的形成。受疫情影响，国内开工时间推迟，产业链和供应链畅通受到影响。外贸公司面临复工、运输、合同履行、国际物流不畅、贸易壁垒等困难。对外贸易的波动是不可避免的。（见文末链接3）

【分析】原文中的词汇 changes，strengthened，weakened，denominated，valuation，rose，fell，translation 分别被译为"变动""走强""走弱""计提""估值""上涨""下跌""折算"。这些表述是财经新闻中常见的专业表达方式，还成为专业人士认可的表达方式，具有专业性、权威性。这样的表述可以准确地把词语在原文中的语境意义翻译出来，这样的译文在语义层面是忠实于原文的。

【原文】It's no secret what kind of stocks Buffett likes. He prefers reliably profitable companies with strong balance sheets and sustainable competitive advantages，which he calls economic moats. Buffett is a conservative value investor，and he wants stocks that will deliver predictable returns.

【译文】巴菲特喜欢什么样的股票已经不是什么秘密了。他更喜欢可靠盈利的公司，这些公司拥有强大的资产负债表和可持续的竞争优势，他称之为经济护城河。巴菲特是一个保守的价值投资者，他希望股票能够带来可预测的回报。

【分析】balance sheets 是财经新闻中一个常见的专业术语，虽然可以译作"资产负债表"，但是根据《柯林斯高阶英语学习词典》的解释，这个词语还有另外一个意思，它还可以指公司的"整体财务状况"（general financial state of a company）。因此，此处若译为"这些公司拥有良好的财务状况……"似乎更加贴切原文的语义。

（二）语气忠实

财经新闻致力于传播客观存在的财经事实，以便读者做出正确的经济决策，因此其语气多是客观的。译者在翻译财经新闻时必须忠实于原文的语气，不能破坏财经新闻的客观性。请看下例：

【原文】The International Air Transport Association（IATA）said on the 5th that major airlines may lose \$63 billion to \$113 billion in global passenger revenue in 2020. The scale of the specific loss will depend on the spread of the new crown pneumonia epidemic. Brian Pierce, chief economist of the International Air Transport Association, said that the last time the global aviation industry faced such a large - scale impact was during the 2009 global financial crisis.

Affected by this, aviation stocks fell sharply. According to statistics from the International Air Transport Association, the stock price of airlines has fallen by nearly 25% since the outbreak. The impact of this decline on industry revenue is also far greater than previously estimated.

The US Global Aviation Exchange Traded Fund (ETF) has fallen more than 32% since February 12. The Dow Jones Transportation Average and the Dow Jones Industrial Average also fell nearly 20% and more than 10% respectively over the same period. The share prices of American Airlines Group, Delta Air Lines, and Southwest Airlines fell 14.4%, 14.5%, and 13.2% over the same period, while United Airlines'stock prices fell more than 30%.

The sharp decline in American Airlines stocks has caused many investors to suffer losses. According to reports, well - known American investor Warren Buffett has lost about $3 billion in the past few weeks. According to reports, Buffett's Berkshire - Hathaway company began to gradually build up aviation stocks in the third quarter of 2016. From the end of 2016 to February 12, 2020, except for the share price of American Airlines Group, which has fallen by nearly 35%, the share prices of several airline operators such as Delta have risen to varying degrees. Market Watch website reports that Berkshire - Hathaway is the largest shareholder of Delta Air Lines and held 70.91 million shares of Delta Air Lines as of December 31 last year. Berkshire - Hathaway also holds 42.5 million shares of American Airlines Group, 53.65 million shares of Southwest Airlines and 21.94 million shares of United Airlines. It is the second largest shareholder of these three companies.

It's not just the American aviation industry that is suffering the cold winter. The British Broadcasting Corporation (BBC) reported on the 5th that Frieby Airlines, the main British regional airline operator, entered bankruptcy management procedures that day, and could lose 2000 jobs.

IATA Chairman and Chief Executive Officer Alexander de Junielk said many airlines are cutting capacity and taking urgent steps to reduce costs. He called on governments to note that airlines are doing their best to help themselves. When the government introduces stimulus measures, it must consider the reduction and exemption of airline - related taxes and flight schedules.

【译文】国际航空运输协会（IATA）5日表示，2020年，各大航空公司可能会损失630亿美元至1130亿美元的全球客运收入。具体损失的规模将取决于新冠肺炎疫情的蔓延。国际航空运输协会（International Air Transport Association）首席经济学家布莱恩·皮尔斯（Brian Pierce）表示，全球航空业上一次面临如此大规模的冲击是在2009年全球金融危机期间。

受此影响，航空股大幅下跌。据国际航空运输协会统计，自新冠肺炎疫情暴发以来，航空公司股价已下跌近25%。这一下降对行业收入的影响也远大于此前的估计。

自2月12日以来，美国全球航空交易所交易基金（ETF）已下跌逾32%。同期，道琼斯运输平均指数和道琼斯工业平均指数也分别下跌了近20%和10%以上。美国航空集团、达美航空和西南航空的股价同期分别下跌14.4%、14.5%和13.2%，而美国联合航空的股价跌幅超过30%。

美国航空公司股票的大幅下跌使许多投资者蒙受损失。据报道，美国著名投资者巴菲特（Warren Buffett）在过去几周损失了约30亿美元。据报道，巴菲特旗下的伯克希尔哈撒韦公司在2016年第三季度开始逐步积累航空股。2016年底至2020年2月12日，除美国航空集团股价下跌近35%外，达美航空等多家航空运营商股价均有不同程度上涨。市场观察网站报道称，伯克希尔哈撒韦是达美航空的最大股东，截至去年12月31日，该公司持有达美航空7091万股股份。伯克希尔哈撒韦还持有美国航空集团4250万股，西南航空5365万股，联合航空2194万股。它是这三家公司的第二大股东。

遭受寒冬折磨的不仅仅是美国航空业。英国广播公司（BBC）5日报道，英国主要地区航空公司弗里比航空公司当天进入破产管理程序，可能失去2000个工作岗位。

国际航协主席兼首席执行官亚历山大德朱尼尔克（Alexander de Junielk）表示，许多航空公司正在削减运力，并采取紧急措施降低成本。他呼吁各国政府注意，航空公司正在尽最大努力自救。政府在推出刺激措施时，必须考虑减免与航空公司有关的税收和航班时刻表。

（来源：http：//www. qqenglish. com/bn/39549. htm）

【分析】原文主要介绍了新冠肺炎疫情对美国航空业的打击，运用大量的间接引语和数据支持这一事实。文章语义清晰，语气客观。译文也应以客观的语气传达原文的信息。如，According to statistics from the International Air Transport Association，the stock price of airlines has fallen by nearly 25% since the outbreak. 被译成“据国际航空运输协会统计，自新冠肺炎疫情暴发以来，航空公司股价已下跌近25%。”译文采用直译的翻译方法，保留原文的间接引语，语气客观，体现了译文的语气忠实。

当然，有些财经新闻为了引起读者注意、说服读者采取行动也会带有一些感情色彩。比如企业推出新产品、新服务的新闻消息，其主要目的就是吸引更多的消费者，因此，其所传递的信息固然要尽量客观真实，但是原文的一些信息（如强调新产品服务部分）也会以极富感情色彩的方式表达，以发挥一定的推介宣传作用。译者在翻译这样的信息时，也需要忠实于原文的语气。请看下例：

【原文】Sanya city signed a strategic cooperation agreement with Chinese Cultural Group（CMC Inc）and Merlin Entertainments Group（MEG）in Beijing on Sept 6 to establish a Legoland Park & Resort，a world - leading family entertainment theme park.

It will be the second Legoland Park in China after Shanghai's，which is under construction and anticipated to open in 2021.

The park，blending Lego elements with the tropical scenery of Sanya，is expected to become a world - class tourist resort with water park features. It will provide children ages 2 to 12 with a variety of engaging and educational interactive experiences and will serve as a great family holiday destination.

A premier educational toy brand known around the world，Legoland Park offers children an enjoyable and educational experience at its eight popular theme parks built in countries including the United States, the United Kingdom, Denmark, Germany and Japan.

As a colossal and renowned media and entertainment group, CMC is active in developing various culture and entertainment businesses, including film and television program productions, online and offline entertainment products, and internet media platforms and technologies. Its recreation products have a broad influence in the global market.

MEG ranks second only to Disney as a live entertainment development company. It owns Legoland Park, Legoland Discovery Centre, Madame Tussaud's, the London Eye, Sea Life and the Dungeons, and attracts more than 60 million visitors each year.

Joining hands with these two world – famous cultural giants, the tourism industry in Sanya will grow at a faster speed and serve as a demonstration for the country's tourism culture.

【译文】9月6日，三亚市与中国文化集团（CMC Inc.）、梅林娱乐集团（MEG）在北京签署战略合作协议，建立世界领先的家庭娱乐主题公园乐高乐园。

这将是继上海之后中国第二个乐高乐园，上海乐高乐园正在建设中，预计2021年开放。

该公园融合了乐高元素和三亚的热带风光，有望成为具有水上公园特色的世界级旅游胜地。它将为2岁到12岁的儿童提供各种各样的参与和教育互动的体验，并将作为一个巨大的家庭度假目的地。

乐高乐园是世界知名的教育玩具品牌，在美国、英国、丹麦、德国和日本等八个受欢迎的主题乐园中，为孩子们提供了愉快的教育体验。

作为一家庞大而知名的传媒娱乐集团，中集集团积极发展各类文化娱乐业务，包括影视节目制作、线上线下娱乐产品、互联网媒体平台和技术等。其娱乐产品在国际市场上具有广泛的影响力。

作为一家现场娱乐开发公司，梅格的排名仅次于迪斯尼。它拥有乐高乐园、乐高乐园探索中心、杜莎夫人蜡像馆、伦敦眼、海洋生物和地牢，每年吸引6000多万游客。

与这两大世界文化巨头携手，三亚旅游业将以更快的速度发展，为国家的旅游文化做示范。（见文末链接6）

【分析】原文是一篇关于乐高将在三亚建立家庭娱乐主题公园乐高乐园的介绍，其中的 a world – leading family entertainment theme park、a world – class tourist resort、premier、enjoyable、popular 等词明显带有感情色彩，主要是为了吸引顾客。译者分别将其译为"世界领先的家庭娱乐主题公园""世界级旅游胜地""知名的""愉快的""受欢迎的"，保留了原文的感情色彩，同样具有吸引宣传作用，体现了译文语气的忠实。

（三）风格忠实

财经新闻属于专业应用文体范畴，词汇专业，句型多变，语法规范灵活，都体现了财经新闻独特的文体风格。因此，译者在翻译财经文本时需要根据原文语篇的特色来塑造译文的风格，做到风格忠实。

【原文】Walmart had a blockbuster 2020 in large part thanks to its booming e – commerce business buoyed by its large network of stores from where it could ship orders more quickly and from where customers could retrieve them faster.

Yet despite that success—Walmart's U. S. business saw e – commerce grow 79%, making it the No 2 online retailer in 2020—the big box store remains far behind its longtime rival, Amazon, and will continue to be so this year, according to a forecast released on March 29 by eMarketer.

The research firm expects Amazon to ring in sales of $367. 2 billion this year, nearly six times more than the $64. 6 billion it forecasts Walmart U. S. will rake in. What's more, eMarketer expects Amazon, which already generates almost 40% of all e – commerce stateside, to win more market share.

Walmart has hardly been idle in its battle with Amazon. It has launched an express delivery service for groceries, one area of e – commerce where it has a clear upper hand over Amazon, as well as Walmart +, a subscription service similar to Amazon Prime.

"We've got a unique opportunity because of our stores. We've got all of the things available to us related to ecommerce growth," Walmart CEO Doug McMillon told Wall Street in February.

Despite Amazon's growing dominance, a number of big box stores thrive D during the pandemic. Target, for one, saw e – commerce more than double last year, helped by its popular store brands and vastly improved grocery offering that curbside delivery for those wary of going into stores made easier to buy.

Kroger, despite its massive size, is still not a Top 10 U. S. e – retailer, but eMarketer thinks that changes this year. In 2020, Kroger benefited enormously from its partnership with tech firm Ocado, whose automation and artificial intelligence, make the grocer much better at filling online order.

In contrast, Macy's, long on the Top 10 list fell out of the list last year and isn't likely to return. The department store's e – commerce business is formidable but the pandemic set it back very far.

Best Buy and Home Depot, two of the pandemic's big retail winners, are also expected to have strong years online. （见文末链接 7）

【译文】2020 年，沃尔玛（Walmart）大获成功，这主要源于该公司庞大的门店网络为其电商业务的蓬勃发展提供了强大的支撑，门店送货快，顾客从门店取货方便、快捷。

据 eMarketer 于 3 月 29 日发布的一项预测，尽管沃尔玛 2020 年在美国的电商业务取得了成功，销售额增长了 79%，使其成为美国第二大电商，但沃尔玛仍然远远落后于其老对手亚马逊（Amazon），而且今年仍将如此。

该研究公司预计，今年沃尔玛在美国的电商业务销售额将达到 646 亿美元，而亚马逊则是其六倍之多，达到 3672 亿美元。此外，eMarketer 预计，尽管亚马逊已经拥有近 40% 的美国电商业务份额，但其将会赢得更多市场份额。

实际上，沃尔玛这些年也没有闲着，一直都在采取各种方式与亚马逊展开竞争。沃尔玛推出了一项杂货配送服务，沃尔玛在此电商领域明显比亚马逊有优势。此外，沃尔玛还推出了一项订阅服务 Walmart +，对标亚马逊 Prime 服务。

“我们有绝对的市场先机，因为我们拥有庞大的门店网络。我们还拥有发展电商业务的一切条件。”沃尔玛的首席执行官董明伦（Doug McMillon）于今年 2 月向华尔街表示。

尽管亚马逊日益占据主导地位，但在此次新冠肺炎疫情期间，一大批零售商飞速发展。例如，塔吉特（Target）去年的电商业务增长了一倍多，这得益于其广受欢迎的自有品牌和明显改善的杂货配送服务，对那些不愿意进店选购商品的人来说，配送服务是一个不错的选择。

克罗格（Kroger）虽然规模庞大，但仍然未能进入美国十大电商之列，不过 eMarketer 预计这一情况今年会有所改变。2020 年，克罗格在与科技公司 Ocado 的合作中获益匪浅，在 Ocado 的自动化和人工智能技术支撑下，其电商业务进行得非常顺利。

相比之下，一直位列前十的梅西百货（Macy's）去年跌出了榜单，而且不太可能重返榜单。梅西百货的电商业务实力一直十分强大，但此次疫情使其倒退了很远。

百思买（Best Buy）和家得宝（Home Depot）是此次疫情期间的两大零售赢家，预计其电商业务也将保持强劲增长。（见文末链接 8）

【分析】这篇财经新闻在风格方面呈现三个鲜明特征。一、句子长，句式多变。英语财经新闻多使用长句，句式灵活多变，修饰语多后置。汉语译文中多短句，修饰语多前置，符合汉语的表达习惯。例如，原文 Target, for one, saw e - commerce more than double last year, helped by its popular store brands and vastly improved grocery offering that curbside delivery for those wary of going into stores made easier to buy 被译为“塔吉特（Target）去年的电商业务增长了一倍多，这得益于其广受欢迎的自有品牌和明显改善的杂货配送服务，对那些不愿意进店选购商品的人来说，配送服务是一个不错的选择。”二、多用数字。财经新闻中一般会出现大量数字，直观、清晰准确地向读者传达了相关信息。但英汉语言在数字表达方面存在较大差异，如英语多用三进位制，如 1000，1000000。而汉语多用二进位制，如一百、一万等。所以译者在翻译财经新闻时，需要准确、恰当地转换数字有关的信息。也就是说，把英语数字转换成汉语时，要尽量使其符合汉语的表达方式，如“646亿美元”。三、多用专名、品牌名、人名、机构名，如沃尔玛（Walmart）、亚马逊（Amazon）、塔吉特（Target）等。译文在风格上实现了对原文的忠实。

第二节　达

一、“达”的界定

“达”，即译文表达要通顺、流畅、自然，符合目的语的表达习惯。这一翻译原则是对译文在语言方面的要求，旨在通过通俗易懂的表达增强译文的可读性。译文的“达”主要通过对原文语言进行恰当得体的翻译表现出来。

“达”是汉语新闻语言的基本要求。对汉语财经新闻而言，更为重要，因为财经新闻具有抽象性的特点，财经新闻中经常会出现专业术语或专有名词，使得财经新闻的语言晦涩难懂。这就需要财经新闻的译者化抽象为具体，内容上专业，表现形式上通俗，将抽象的财经信息贴切的表达出来（贯丽丽，2016：43）。此外，英汉财经新闻在词汇运用和句法特征上有着明显的差异，译者在翻译财经新闻时需要考虑汉语的表达习惯，灵活处理，尽量以通畅顺达的语言向读者传达正确的信息。

二、“达”的实现方式

总的来说，我们可以从两个方面来实现财经译文通顺畅达的效果。其一，恰当地释译专名，即对一些重要的专名进行增译。其二，流畅地转换句法结构，即译文要尽力摆脱原文句型束缚，使译文句法结构清明，语义衔接流畅。下面，我们结合具体实例来体会财经新闻翻译如何实现“达”的要求。

（一）恰当地释译专名

【例 1】In 2019, both Uber and Lyft gave veteran drivers cash grants to buy a small allocation of pre – IPO shares, but both stocks performed poorly in the months that followed.

【译文】2019 年，网约车服务商 Uber 和 Lyft 不约而同地为资深司机提供现金补贴，以资助他们购买一小部分上市前股票，但两只股票在随后几个月都表现不佳。

【分析】此例中的 Uber 和 Lyft 为公司名，是美国两家提供打车服务的供应商。译者此处使用增译法，增加了“网约车服务商”来说明这两家公司的主要业务，避免了对这两家公司不熟悉的读者产生困惑，增加了译文的连贯性和可读性。

【例 2】While it was “marginally encouraging” that Boeing reported a net rise in orders in March for the second month in a row, the 29 aircraft deliveries last month were “lacklustre”, Cowen analyst Cai von Rumohr said in a note.

【译文】投行考恩（Cowen）的分析师卡伊·冯鲁莫尔（Cai von Rumohr）在一份简报中表示，尽管波音在 3 月连续第二个月报告订单净增长“有点令人鼓舞”，但该月 29 架飞机的交付量是“低迷的”。

【分析】原文中的 Cowen 是一个以人名命名的投行机构名称，在英语中，以某人名字命名某研究中心、某大学、某地名的现象非常普遍。然而，汉语读者对这一点并不熟悉。如果直译，会令汉语读者产生困惑或歧义。因此，翻译时，可以采用增译法。本例的译者就增加了“投行”这一修饰语来说明 Cowen 是一个投行机构名称。

【例 3】Facebook is making a push into audio, launching a suite of new features that will allow users to host audio conferences and podcasts, in a dash to compete with up – and – coming apps such as Clubhouse.

Mark Zuckerberg, chief executive of the world's largest social media company by users, said on Monday said that over the next three to six months it planned to roll out live audio rooms as well as new tools allowing users to search for, listen to and create podcasts. In addition, its live audio rooms, which will be available on the main platform and its Messenger app, can be saved and turned into podcasts.

Zuckerberg also announced the launch of a feature called "Soundbites", where users can post or listen to short audio clips that will be showcased in a continuous feed, in a similar way to its Reels video feed in Instagram.

Facebook plans to allow users to earn money from the podcasts and audio rooms they create—for example, by allowing users to charge for access to a room by purchasing it individually or as part of a subscription.

"We think that audio is of course also going to be a first - class medium," Zuckerberg said in a live interview with tech journalist Casey Newton on Monday. He added that audio "allows for longer form discussions and exploring ideas" but was also "accessible because you can multitask".

The move is Facebook's latest effort to copy popular products from its rivals, after it raced to introduce new videoconferencing features last April following the rise of Zoom and Google Hangouts as ways to host meetings and socialise from home.

Audio products tap into so - called "Zoom fatigue" — a frustration with endlessly having to be on camera—butalso provide entertainment - starved professionals with new ways to network while the conference circuit remains closed because of the coronavirus pandemic.

In particular, the Facebook launch could hurt the audio start - up Clubhouse, which became the fastest - growing social media app in the world this year by providing a platform to discuss topics such as entrepreneurship, politics and the latest news events.

Clubhouse has topped 14m downloads, according to data from App Annie, but has suffered outages as its servers have struggled under the influx of users.

Over the weekend, Clubhouse announced that it had secured a new round of financing led by Andreessen Horowitz, with new investors DST Global and Tiger Global. The fundraising gives the start - up, which only launched its product a year ago, a valuation of $4bn, according to two people familiar with the situation, up from $1bn this January.

Facebook is also taking aim at Twitter, which rolled out its Clubhouse clone "Spaces" this month and discussion forum Reddit, which previewed its forthcoming "Reddit Talk" feature on Monday. Twitter previously tried to acquire Clubhouse for $4bn, though the discussions stalled, according to a recent report from Bloomberg.

Facebook is currently facing antitrust lawsuits from federal and state officials in the US, which include accusations that it clones or buys up rivals.

Facebook said on Monday that it had been investing in audio technologies, including voice morphing and speech - to - text transcription capabilities as part of the move.

Zuckerberg also said that the company was working on a partnership with Spotify dubbed Project Boombox to make it easier for users to listen to or share Spotify tracks without leaving the platform.

The shift towards live audio, such as livestreaming, brings with it content moderation challenges given its real - time nature, at a time when Facebook is already under fire from US regulators over its perceived content policing failures.

【译文】Facebook 正准备进军音频领域，将推出一系列新功能，允许用户召开音频会议和发布播客，以此与Clubhouse 等后起之秀展开竞争。

全球用户数量最多的社交媒体企业 Facebook 的首席执行官马克·扎克伯格（Mark Zuckerberg）周一表示，该公司计划在未来三到六个月内推出"音频直播室"（live audio room），以及允许用户搜索、收听和创建播客的新工具。音频直播室将在 Facebook 主平台及其旗下的Messenger 应用上推出，可以保存并转化为播客。

扎克伯格还宣布要推出一种名为"Soundbites"的功能，用户可以发布或收听以连续方式展现的短音频片段，类似于其旗下Instagram 上名为Reels 的视频模式。

Facebook 计划允许用户通过他们所创建的播客和音频直播室赚钱——例如，它会允许用户对进入其直播室的人收取费用，通过单独购买或是作为订阅的一部分。

扎克伯格周一在接受科技记者凯西·牛顿（Casey Newton）的现场访谈中表示："我们认为，音频肯定也会成为一流的媒介。"他补充称，音频"可以进行更长时间的讨论和探讨想法"，但也"便于使用，因为你可以同时处理多项任务"。

此举是Facebook模仿竞争对手热门产品的最新努力。去年4月，在Zoom和谷歌（Google）的Hangouts兴起、成为在家举行会议和进行社交的方式后，Facebook赶紧推出新的视频会议功能。

在会议线路仍因疫情而处于关闭状态时，音频产品利用了所谓的"Zoom疲劳"（Zoom fatigue）——因不得不无休止地出现在镜头前而感到的一种疲劳——也为急需娱乐的专业人士提供了新的交际方式。

Facebook推出这些新功能尤其可能会对音频初创公司Clubhouse造成影响。Clubhouse通过提供一个讨论创业、政治和新闻时事等话题的平台，而成为今年全球增长最快的社交媒体应用程序。

根据App Annie的数据，Clubhouse的下载量已经突破1400万次，但由于其服务器难以应对大量涌入的用户，该应用遭遇了宕机事件。

上周末，Clubhouse宣布获得新一轮融资，由Andreessen Horowitz领投，新投资者为DST全球（DST Global）和老虎环球（Tiger Global）。据两位知情人士透露，此次融资使这家一年前才推出产品的初创企业的估值从1月份时的10亿美元升至40亿美元。

Facebook还瞄准了Twitter和论坛Reddit，前者本月推出了Clubhouse的克隆产品"Spaces"，后者则在周一展示了其即将推出的功能"Reddit Talk"。彭博社（Bloomberg）最近的一则报道称，Twitter此前曾试图以40亿美元收购Clubhouse，但谈判陷入了僵局。

Facebook目前正面临美国联邦和州政府官员的反垄断诉讼，其中包括指责其模仿或收购竞争对手的指控。

Facebook周一表示，它一直在投资音频技术，包括语音转换和语音文本转换功能。

扎克伯格还表示，Facebook正在与Spotify合作一个Boombox项目，目的是让用户无须离开Facebook平台就能更便捷地收听或分享Spotify的歌曲。

考虑到实时性，向直播等实时音频功能的转变会使 Facebook 面临内容审查方面的挑战。目前，Facebook 就因被认为对内容监督不力而受到美国监管机构的抨击。

（来源：https：//mp. weixin. qq. com/s/C6ohTgB－lhyzS07POQcswA）

【分析】英语财经新闻中往往包含许多人名、机构名、产品名等专有名词，译者在翻译时要结合上下文恰当地翻译这类专名，使读者能准确地理解原文的意思。比如，本例中就出现了 Facebook、Clubhouse 和 Zoom 等社交公司名，Mark Zuckerberg 和 Casey Newton 等人名，Soundbites、Reels 和 Hangouts 等产品服务名称。译者对这些专有名词分别采用了不同的翻译方法，比如，对于 Facebook 和 Clubhouse 等公司名，译者直接保留了其英文名称；在翻译 Mark Zuckerberg 等人名时，鉴于已有读者普遍接受的译名，译者采用音译法并在括号中保留其英文原名。

（二）流畅地转换句法结构

【例 4】James Cox, who teaches corporate and securities law at Duke University, said the Securities and Exchange Commission should take action to deal with such misinformation, which can distort stock prices.

【译文】杜克大学（Duke University）的公司法和证券法教师詹姆斯·考克斯表示，美国证券交易委员会（Securities and Exchange Commission）应当采取措施，处理这种可能导致股价扭曲的假新闻。

【分析】英语较长的定语常常位于所修饰词的后面，而汉语中的定语，无论长短，一般都放在所修饰词的前面。这是英汉句法构成的明显差异。因此，汉译时需要把英语中的后置定语放在所修饰词的前面，这样处理可以避免“欧式汉语”，使译文符合汉语的表达习惯，读起来通顺畅达。上例译文就把 who 和 which 引导的后置定语提前，考虑到了汉语的行文习惯。

【例 5】This is a bigger deal than you might think: A national digital *currency could* reduce reliance *on commercial banks as the principal interface* for money management and increase optionality for consumers, many of whom are beyond the reach of physical bank branches or excluded from the financial system due to poor credit or lack of funds.

【译文】这件事可能比你想象的更加重要：目前货币管理主要由商业银行负责，然而许多消费者超出了实体银行分支机构的覆盖范围，或者由于信用欠佳或资金不足无法获得金融服务。国家数字货币可以减少这种依赖性，增加消费者的选择。

【分析】英语为形合语言，汉语为意合语言，这是英汉语言最重要的一个区别。英语句子注重显性衔接，常常借助各种衔接手段连接词、语、分句或从句，形成复杂的长句；而汉语注重隐形连贯，不常使用形式连接手段，多短句。这一特点在英语财经报道中尤为突出。因此，在翻译财经新闻时，对于英语长句要通过拆分、重组等手段对其进行灵活处理。上例译文对原文进行了拆分重组，重组后的译文逻辑性强，语义连贯，明白易懂。

【例 6】With so few players on the cutting edge of the industry, TSMC has been left to satisfy a significant proportion of advanced demand, which is why its \$100 billion investment might not be replicated by other players.

【译文】由于业内有能力生产高端芯片的厂商少之又少，因此台积电需要满足对高端芯片的绝大部分需求，所以其他厂商可能不会效仿台积电投资 1000 亿美元。

【分析】在这个例子中，原语句子中的画线部分为被动语态，而译者翻译时考虑到汉语的表达习惯，将其调整成了主动语态。如果不调整语态，直译为“由于业内有能力生产高端芯片的厂商少之又少，因此台积电被要求满足对高端芯片的绝大部分需求。所以台积电投资 1000 亿美元的行为可能不会被其他厂商效仿”，则不符合汉语的表达习惯，读起来别扭且不易于读者理解。

【例 7】Internet retails' expansion into smart production and e – commerce platforms' digital connection with each part in the industrial chains significantly boost efficiency in the supply chains and industrial transformation and upgrading.

【译文】互联网零售正在向自动化生产拓展，电商平台与产业链各环节正在实现数字化对接，这两点极大地提升了供应链及产业转型升级的效率。

【分析】英语中名词的使用频率较高，而汉语中动词明显用得较多。英语的名词化问题往往导致表达的抽象化，这也是英语财经新闻翻译的难点之一，需要译者采取词类转换的方式，使抽象概念具体化。上例译文将 expansion 和 connection 分别转换为汉语动词"拓展""对接"，既准确传达了原文的语义，又使译文符合译入语的表达习惯，读起来更加通顺流畅。

第三节　快

一、"快"的界定

"快"就是译者以最快的速度把财经新闻的新信息翻译出来。时效性是财经新闻的生命力，包括"新"和"快"两大要素（白翔云，2000：43－45）。全球财经新闻是日新月异的，翻译过于陈旧的财经新闻意义不大。因此，财经新闻的翻译要"快"，要及时、快速地为读者提供新的全球财经信息，这也是读者最感兴趣的部分。

二、"快"的实现方式

（一）摘译

摘译快速传播简明信息，就是只译标题、中心的意思，常以消息形态出现。

【例 8】

Bitcoin surges past ＄60000 for first time

Cryptocurrency Bitcoin has risen for the first time above ＄60000 (￡43100), continuing its record－breaking run.

Bitcoin－which has more than tripled in value since the end of last year－has been powered on by well－known companies adopting it as a method of payment.

But some analysts said this latest surge came in part due to the huge US stimulus package approved this week.

Bitcoin's total market value last month exceeded \$1tn.

However, Bitcoin has a track record of wild price swings and has fallen sharply a number of times since it was created in 2009.

The recent spikes have been fuelled by big companies.

In February, Elon Musk revealed that his electric carmaker Tesla had bought \$1.5bn worth of Bitcoin and would be accepting it as payment for its cars in future.

Mastercard also plans to accept certain cryptocurrencies asa form of payment while BlackRock, the world's largest asset manager, is exploring ways it can use the digital currency.

The Covid–19 pandemic has also played its part in Bitcoin's price rise, as more people go online for shopping, moving further away from physical coins and notes.

Critics argue Bitcoin is less of a currency and more of a speculative trading tool that is open to market manipulation.

There is also concern over its environmental impact, with huge amounts of energy needed to conduct transactions. （见文末链接 1）

外媒：比特币 3 月 18 日以来首次突破 6 万美元

参考消息网 4 月 2 日报道 据英国广播公司（BBC）消息，加密货币比特币的价格继续创新高，自当地时间 3 月 18 日以来首次突破 6 万美元。3 月 13 日比特币的价格曾短时突破 6 万美元。

报道称，自去年年底以来，比特币的价值已经增长了三倍多。一些分析师认为最新涨幅部分是由于本周美国批准了庞大的经济刺激计划。

【分析】参考消息网报道的本篇文章是从 BBC 摘译的新闻，通过对比原文和译文，不难发现译文仅摘取了原文标题、导语以及传达新闻核心话题的前两个段落，实现了快速传播新闻的目的。（见文末链接 2）

（二）编译

编译快速传播核心信息，核心信息指重要信息，分布在不同段落。

【例 9】

China and Brazil have world's greenest central banks, activists say

FRANKFURT (Reuters) – China has the world's greenest central bank, followed by Brazil, both beating richer countries thanks to concrete steps such as lower interest rates on loans for pollution – fighting projects, an activist group said on Wednesday.

The UK – based campaign group Positive Money ranked the central banks and financial supervisors of G20 countries based on how much theyare doing to fight climate change.

Only three of them got a pass: China, Brazil and France.

The results may surprise some as China, which got the highest rating in the report, is one of the world's top polluters and Brazil has faced criticism for destroying parts of the Amazon's rainforest.

But the authors of the study said financial policymakers in both countries acted earlier precisely because they faced larger environmental threats.

"This makes environmental impacts and risks more immediately visible and relevant for their central bankers and supervisors, and may result in a greater impetus to green their policymaking processes," Positive Money said.

For example, the People's Bank of China's first green initiative dates back from 1995 and banks are now required to offer cheaper loans on environmentally friendly projects, the report said.

Brazil stands out for restricting financing for crop expansion in the Amazon and other vulnerable regions.

France, which largely derives its monetary policy and financial regulation from the European Union, narrowly beat its EU peers to the third place thanks to extra points earned through its own climate stress test of large banks and insurers.

This comes on top of steps taken by the European Central Bank, which has started demanding that banks take climate change into account when making loans and is considering adopting a green bias in its bond purchases.

The report mainly focuses on official policy and does not reflect efficacy in implementation.

NO CONSENSUS

Central banks' role in fighting climate change is the object of an increasingly lively global debate but so far there is no consensus on the way forward.

A report by a group of 89 institutions published last week found all policy options, such as skewing central bank funding to benefit green issuers or punishing polluters, have drawbacks.

A key issue is that engaging in climate policy would raise questions on two sacred cows of the past three decades: central bank independence from politics and its single - minded focus on inflation, coupled in some countries with employment.

Indeed, the Chinese central bank is not independent of its government while Brazil's has only just been granted autonomy.

Positive Money advocated throwing such qualms to the wind because the costsof inaction would be more severe, and called for choking off funding to polluters.

"Targeting the most high risk and environmentally harmful assets—such as those linked to fossil fuel extraction— for exclusion from monetary policy operations and limits or penalising factors in prudential policy would be an important first step," it said in the report. (见文末链接4)

英机构报告称：中国央行是全球最环保央行

参考消息网 3月31日报道 据路透社法兰克福消息，英国"积极财富"机构对20国集团中央银行进行调查后在当地时间31日发布的排行榜说，中国拥有全球最环保的央行，其次是巴西和法国。这几个国家的央行通过降低利率和增加贷款等金融措施为全球环保做出的贡献超越了一些发达国家。

这家致力于研究各国金融机构的英国机构说，他们的排名可能会让某些人感到意外，但他们是根据各国央行为环保所做贡献的各种数据进行的分析，最后只有三个国家通过他们的标准。

"积极财富"的调研人员说，中国和巴西的金融政策制定者很早就开始采取行动应对各种挑战。

【分析】众所周知，英语新闻多采用倒金字塔结构的方式写作，即按照新闻的价值大小或新闻事实的重要程度依次将新闻事实写出。通过对比本例中的原文和编译版本，不难发现译者仅选取了原文中的前五个段落，也就是新闻的核心信息段落，进行翻译，而省去了那些仅对源语读者有用，但对译语读者可有可无的信息。(见文末链接5)

第四节 活

一、"活"的界定

现今，世界上每天都会发生新的事件，产生新的成果，相应地，新闻的内容也会涉及人类认知范围的方方面面，新闻也会用多种形式向读者呈现各类信息，满足了各类读者的多样化需求。

译者在翻译财经新闻时，应该遵循"活"的原则。"活"就是译者在翻译财经新闻时使用灵活的方法，在译文中把原文的内容以新颖活泼的形式展现给读者。财经新闻主要向人们提供经济、金融方面的信息。阅读财经新闻的读者对各类财经信息的渴望度、理解全面性大相径庭。因此，译者在翻译财经新闻时，要考虑满足不同读者的需要，翻译时应该使用新颖奇特、灵活多样的形式，对原文中的各类信息进行选择、重组，用读者易于接受的方式呈现出来。也就是说，财经新闻的译语在形式和内容方面可以与原语新闻完全一样，也可以部分相近，也可以完成不同。

二、"活"的实现方式

(一) 灵活转换词汇信息

从词汇层面讲，"活"就是把原文词汇隐喻表达的信息用言简意赅、通俗易懂、符合规范的汉语词汇表达出来。在英语财经新闻翻译过程中，词汇隐喻的翻译就是要剥开原语词汇中难以理解的东西，并把这些难以理解的东西用汉语读者能够理解的词汇表达出来。这就要译者用灵活的翻译方法翻译这些词汇。也就是，巧妙地选用汉语词汇来转换英文词汇所含信息。

【例 10】

【原文】…its F – 150 pickup truck – the nation's top – selling vehicle and the company's biggest moneymaker.

【译文】F150 皮卡是美国最畅销的汽车，也是福特的“摇钱树”。

▶ 点评：

本句出自参考消息网，主要对于福特将暂停北美工厂，对于 F150 皮卡减量进行了大篇幅描述，本句则是增补的背景信息，向读者表明 F150 皮卡在福特的重要性，而选择一个接地气的词“摇钱树”，不仅体现了该款车型对于福特公司的重要性，也使译文变得灵活起来。

【例 11】

【原文】A shorter expansion may also limit how high the Federal Reserve can lift interest rates from their current setting near zero before having to cut them to combat a recession.

【译文】扩张时间缩短还可能限制美联储将利率从目前接近零的水平提高的幅度，之后将不得不降低利率以对付衰退。

▶ 点评：

“A shorter expansion”名词形式灵活地处理为“扩张时间缩短”主谓结构的短语，补充了“expansion”隐含信息，这样处理，使读者能够清晰理解本句所传达的内容。

同时，在财经新闻中不可避免会出现有关组织机构的名称，专有名词的信息对英语读者来说是不言自明的常识性知识，但对大多数中国读者而言，则会感到陌生费解。对于这样的内容，就需要译者加上适当的注释，以减少读者的阅读负担。加注释时，应以注释位置符合译文的最佳通顺度为原则。同时，翻译方法要根据具体的语境进行恰当选择。

【例 12】

【原文】Consulting firm AlixPartners estimates the chip shortage will cut $60.6 billion in revenue from the global automotive industry this year.

【译文】咨询公司艾睿铂估计，芯片短缺将使今年全球汽车行业的营收减少 606 亿美元。

【原文】According to the latest statistics from Auto Forecast Solutions… So far, the shortage of chips has caused a cumulative reduction of 1.157 million vehicles in the global automotive market.

【译文】据 AutoForecast Solutions 最新统计，截至目前，芯片短缺已致全球汽车市场累计减产 115.7 万辆。

▶ **点评：**

第一句中 "Consulting firm AlixPartners" 直接译为 "咨询公司艾睿铂"；第二句中 "AutoForecast Solutions" 则直接保留原文。前者是由于 AlixPartners 在中文里已经存在其名称，同时在翻译中保留其解释 "咨询公司" 则减少了读者的阅读困惑。而后者，由于中文中没有其固定的名称，直接保留原文，这种处理方式也十分灵活，从而避免对 "AutoForecast Solutions" 的误解。但也可以在英文后加入注解，说明其性质，这样会实现更好的阅读效果。另外，如果在译文中不能直接删去，则会影响引用数据的可靠性。

（二）灵活转换句法信息

从句法层面讲，"活" 就是把英语中灵活多变的语言形式进行适当的处理。英语中句子长、分句多、段落短、篇幅大、信息量大，而汉语中则一般句子较短、分句（或修饰成分）较少、段落较长、篇幅短小，但其信息量（从总体上讲）并不因之减少。但刘其中在《英汉新闻翻译》一书中呼吁 "把新闻译文的句子、段落译得简短些"，从而让读者阅读更加轻松。

【例 13】

【原文】The U.S. economic recovery from the pandemic collapse is starting off a lot hotter but could end up cooling much sooner than the record 10 - 1/2 - year long upswing that preceded it.

【译文】经历这场大流行病带来的崩溃后，美国经济复苏的起步比以前快得多，但最终降温的速度可能远高于之前创纪录的10年半的经济回升。

▶ 点评：

原文是一句长难句，信息含量大，包括美国经济复苏背景，现在经济状态以及未来走向，而在译文中，选择对信息进行拆分，按照中文读者的阅读习惯，将信息用三个短句译出，是信息内容信息展现在读者面前。

【例14】

【原文】Fed Chair Jerome Powell has played down concerns by former Treasury Secretary Lawrence Summers and others that the big bounce - back will cause the economy to overheat, arguing that strong global disinflationary forces will keep price rises from getting out of hand.

【译文】美联储主席杰罗姆·鲍威尔对前财政部长劳伦斯·萨默斯等人的担忧不屑一顾，后者认为大幅反弹将导致经济过热，但鲍威尔辩称强劲的全球通货紧缩力量将阻止价格上涨失控。

▶ 点评：

原文中出现了两个人物以及他们所对应的观点，信息含量大，但却可以利用主从句来排列信息；译文则采用重复人物名字，引出新的信息，但通过“后者”“但”原文内容有逻辑地展示给读者。

（三）灵活转换语篇信息

从语篇层面讲，“活”就是根据不同的读者，不同的媒介可以采用不同的翻译方法，提供灵活多样的翻译语篇。例如，如果全文语篇过长，内容过于分散，可以选用摘编的方法。如以下案例：

Hotter U. S. Economy Risks Faster Cooldown as Biden Pushes Plan

(Bloomberg) —The U. S. economic recovery from the pandemic collapse is starting off a lot hotter but could end up cooling much sooner than the record 10 - 1/2 - year long upswing that preceded it.

With a surge of government spending already in train and President Joe

Biden's promise on Wednesday of yet more to come, gross domestic product is primed to skyrocket—beginning with what some economists see as a double-digit annualized rise in the second quarter.

U. S. manufacturing growth roared ahead in March at the fastest in more than 37 years, and government job-market data out on Friday are expected to show the first in a series of outsized monthly increases in payrolls that could reach as high as one million.

"This is a huge, fiscally-fueled recovery, the fastest recovery in the history of the U. S. over the next two years," said Ethan Harris, Bank of America Corp.'s head of global economic research.

But the rapid rebound is not without its pitfalls, some economists say. While Biden's latest program may well boost productivity over time, there's still a risk that the exuberant expansion will pump up inflation and spur excessive leverage, laying the groundwork for the upswing's eventual demise.

"It pulls forward the day of the next recession," said Mark Zandi, chief economist for Moody's Analytics. He hypothesized that the current expansion could end sometime in the middle of decade, well short of the run the economy enjoyed after the 2007-09 financial crisis.

That has implications for investors and policy makers. In a 62-page report in March, Morgan Stanley advised its clients to be prepared to rotate out of investments that have done well early in the economic cycle, like emerging market equities, into those like Japanese stocks that might fare better later in an upturn.

A shorter expansion may also limit how high the Federal Reserve can lift interest rates from their current setting near zero before having to cut them to combat a recession. "It means that you can never quite break out of that lower for longer world," said Morgan Stanley chief U. S. economist Ellen Zentner.

Infrastructure Spending

Fresh off winning congressional approval of a $1.9 trillion economic rescue package, Biden unveiled an additional $2.25 trillion spending proposal on Wednesday aimed at rebuilding and refashioning the economy after the pandemic.

"It will generate historic job growth, historic economic growth, help businesses to compete internationally and create more revenue as well," Biden said in a speech in Pittsburgh touting the plan.

The four - part, eight - year proposal dedicates $620 billion for transportation, $580 billion for strengthening American manufacturing and $400 billion to address improved care for the elderly and people with disabilities.

Unlike the rescue package, this one will be paid for, with increased taxes on corporations, but over a 15 - year time horizon. That means the plan will modestly add to the federal government's already mammoth budget deficit in the early years, pushing the economy further up against its limits.

Productivity Boost

Biden administration officials portrayed the program partly as an effort to boost the economy's capacity to grow without overheating by promoting faster productivity growth.

"Well - designed public investment can spur innovation and can spur productivity and it can spur job growth all around America," Brian Deese, director of the National Economic Council, said on Bloomberg Television Wednesday.

While the program could indeed help increase productivity growth, those gains are likely to be years in the making, outside economists said.

The current recovery is already looking a lot different from the last one.

A year after suffering the deepest quarterly decline on record as the pandemic struck, the economy is poised to regain its previous peak in less than half the time it took to achieve that goal after the 2007 - 09 financial crisis.

U. S. manufacturing is a bright spot, expanding in March at the fastest pace since 1983, catapulted by the firmest orders and production readings in 17 years, according to Institute for Supply Management data released Thursday.

Treasury Secretary Janet Yellen sees the U. S. returning to full employment next year—something that didn't occur in the last expansion until 2018, when the jobless rate fell below 4%.

The drawdown of a massive accumulation of savings since the start of the pandemic will bolster consumption, as will sizable wealth - effects from rising real estate and equity markets. Both factors should push output higher and sustain above - trend growth over a longer horizon.

It's not only fiscal policy that's revving up growth. Fed policy is too, with a preponderance of officials forecasting they'll keep interest rates pinned near zero through 2023 even as the economy roars ahead.

Fed Chair Jerome Powell has played down concerns by former Treasury Secretary Lawrence Summers and others that the big bounce - back will cause the economy to overheat, arguing that strong global disinflationary forces will keep price rises from getting out of hand.

Some economists are not so sure. Ex Fed official Peter Hooper sees at least a one - in - five possibility of inflation rising to 3% or more over the next few years, markedly above the Fed's average 2% target.

The $1.9 trillion rescue plan Congress passed last month is already set to push the economy toward the limits it can grow without overheating, according to Hooper. And that's before taking account of any meaningful increase in spending by households running down the stash of savings they built up while shut in during the pandemic.

If inflation rises to 3% and looks to be persistent, "the Fed will get uncomfortable enough to start acting more aggressively and have more of a disruptive impact on financial markets and the economy," Hooper, who is now global head of economic research for Deutsche Bank AG, said.

High Leverage

There's another way the current upswing is different that might make it more vulnerable, Zandi said. Normally recessions end up purging the economy of excesses, forcing households and companies to reduce leverage and put their finances in better shape.

That didn't happen this time, especially when it comes to corporations. Thanks in part to a since – ended emergency program from the Fed, even some of the riskiest companies have been able to ramp up borrowing.

"High levels or rapid increases in leverage can represent a financial vulnerability, leaving the economy more exposed to a future severe downturn in activity or a sharp correction in asset prices," International Monetary Fund officials Adolfo Barajas and Fabio Natalucci wrote in a March 29 blogpost.

The past three expansions have lasted on average just under nine years. Given the way this one is starting, it may end up more in line with the 64 – month – long, post – World War II average.

"We could be going back to some of the earlier cycles," Zentner said. The current expansion may end up "closer to the five year smark than the 10 years one."（见文末链接3）

【例 15】

美媒：拜登连续撒钱或致经济过热

【来源】经济参考网

彭博社网站4月1日刊载题为《在拜登推行其计划之际，美国经济越热，降温可能越快》的文章，作者系里奇·米勒，文章称，尽管拜登的最新计划很可能会随着时间的推移提高生产率，但这种迅猛的扩张有可能会加剧通胀并导致过高的杠杆，从而为这种上涨的终止埋下隐患。全文摘编如下：

经历这场大流行病带来的崩溃后，美国经济复苏的起步比以前快得多，但最终降温的速度可能远高于之前创纪录的10年半的经济回升。

随着政府开支即将大幅增加以及拜登3月31日承诺会继续增加开支，国内生产总值将大幅飙升，而一些经济学家认为第二季度将达到两位数的年化增长率。

美国银行有限公司全球经济研究部门的负责人伊桑·哈里斯说："这是一场由财政手段推动的大规模复苏，是未来两年美国历史上最快的复苏。"

但一些经济学家说，这种快速反弹并非没有风险。尽管拜登的最新计划很可能会随着时间的推移提高生产率，但这种迅猛的扩张有可能会加剧通胀并导致过高的杠杆，从而为这种上涨的终止埋下隐患。

穆迪分析公司首席经济学家马克·赞迪说："这将把下一次衰退的日子提前。"

他猜测，目前的经济扩张可能会在今后10年当中的某个时间结束，远短于2007～2009年金融危机后美国经济快速发展持续的时间。

扩张时间缩短还可能限制美联储将利率从目前接近零的水平提高的幅度，之后将不得不降低利率以对付衰退。

刚刚赢得国会对其1.9万亿美元的经济救助计划的支持后，拜登3月31日又推出了另外一项2.25万亿美元的开支计划，目的是在疫情后重建和重塑经济。

与救助计划不同，此次的开支计划的资金将来自对企业增加的税收，但将在15年的时间内完成。这意味着最初几年，这一计划将小幅增加联邦政府已经庞大的预算赤字，推动经济进一步走向极限。

目前不仅仅是靠财政政策促进增长。美联储的政策也在发挥这种作用，许多官员预测，即使经济快速发展，他们仍会把利率保持在接近零的水平，直到2023年。

美联储主席杰罗姆·鲍威尔对前财政部长劳伦斯·萨默斯等人的担忧不屑一顾，后者认为大幅反弹将导致经济过热，但鲍威尔辩称强劲的全球通货紧缩力量将阻止价格上涨失控。

一些经济学家对此并不那么肯定。美联储前官员彼得·胡珀认为，未来几年，通胀率至少有五分之一的可能性会上升到3%或更高，明显高于美联储2%的平均目标。

赞迪说，目前的回升趋势还有另外一个不同之处，可能使得这种回升变得更加脆弱。通常情况下，衰退最终会清理掉经济中过剩的部分，迫使家庭和企业减少杠杆，改善他们的财务状况。

但这一次并未发生这种情况，尤其就企业来说，连一些风险最高的公司也得以增加借款。

国际货币基金组织官员阿道夫·巴拉哈斯和法比奥·纳塔卢奇在3月29日的一篇博文中写道："高杠杆率或杠杆的迅速增加可能代表着金

融脆弱性，使经济更容易受到未来经济活动严重下滑或资产价格大幅调整的影响。”

美国此前三次经济扩张平均持续了不到9年。鉴于这次扩张的起步方式，它的持续时间最终可能更接近二战后平均持续64个月的水平。

明晟公司首席美国经济学家埃伦·曾特纳说，当前的经济扩张持续的时间可能最终“更接近5年而不是10年大关”。(见文末链接2)

▶ **点评：**

本篇是对彭博社网站4月1日刊载题为《在拜登推行其计划之际，美国经济越热，降温可能越快》的摘编，对新总统拜登推行的新的经济计划进行分析，推断其可能造成的后果。原文先对当前美国的经济发展做了总述，然后分三部分：基础设施支出，生产力提升，和高杠杆比率进行分析。本文则灵活地保留了总述部分，对于具体分析的三部分进行了选择删减，主要留下了高杠杆率部分。一方面，这种处理对文章的篇幅进行了控制；另一方面，保留了重点信息，减轻了读者的阅读负担。另外，本文对于直接引语和间接引语的保留提高了文章的可读性、可靠性。

第五节　切

一、“切”的界定

“切”就是译者在翻译财经新闻过程中，用适当的方式处理原语—译语的转换中涉及的语言、思维、文化问题。从宏观层面讲，英汉两种语言存在差异，英汉民族的思想、文化也存在差异。译者在翻译财经新闻过程中，也就是在把原语文本转换成译语文本的过程中，会涉及英汉两种语言转换问题，也涉及英汉民族不同思维方式的转换问题，也涉及英汉两种文化的转换问题。译者在翻译财经新闻过程中，如果语言、思维、文化任何一个方面的问题没有处理好，都可能影响翻译效果，也就是说，译者也许不能完成英汉财经新闻宏观层面的翻译转换。所以，译者在翻译英汉财经新闻时，在宏观层面上要采取恰到好处的方式，处理原语—译语转换中涉及的语言、思维、文化问题，以使译文能够符合汉语读者的阅读习惯。

译者在翻译财经新闻过程中，可以根据我国学者胡庚申提出的生态翻译学理论，来遵循“切”的原则。根据生态翻译学理论，译者在翻译过程中既要适应，又要选择。“适应”是指译者对翻译生态环境的适应；“选择”是指译者以翻译生态环境的“身份”实施对译文的选择。根据生态翻译学理论，译者在翻译时要实现原文—译文之间的“三维”转换，即实现语言维、文化维和交际维的适应性选择转换。

英语财经新闻具有句子长、分句多、段落短、篇幅大、信息量也大的特点，在同样的情况下，汉语新闻一般句子较短、分句（或修饰成分）较少、段落较长、篇幅短小，但其信息量（从总体上讲）并不因之减少。译者在英汉翻译过程中，要面对专业词汇翻译、词类转换、适当增删、变换句式等翻译问题。

二、“切”的实现方式

首先，在翻译实践过程中遇到了一些问题，如：英语财经新闻常出现一些财经专业词汇，译前准备不充分或专业背景了解不够都会导致词汇翻译的生搬硬套；数字在财经新闻报道中出现特别频繁，是传达信息的重要依据，也是“忠实”这一翻译标准的重要部分，对于频繁出现的数字一定要反复核查，以免失之毫厘，谬以千里；在英语财经新闻中的“say”一般情况下会被直接翻译成“说”，而一篇好的译文要想表达生动，则需根据语境将“say”相应翻译为“宣称”“感慨道”“惊叹道”等。

其次，英语的语法逻辑和语义逻辑与汉语不同，英语财经新闻的翻译在句法层面也遇到一些典型性问题，如：句子冗长，应将其中出现的关系副词或关系代词引导的定语从句、同位语、插入语等恰当放置，并进行适当的语序调整或长句拆分；句序紊乱，这需要正确把握句意以及各成分间的逻辑关系，在翻译此类句子时，应先理顺句意，然后按汉语表达习惯，对句子的语序进行适当调整，必要时添加适当的逻辑连接词或对一些词进行词类转换；英语财经新闻常用到被动句，或是由于上下文联系的需要，或是由于讲话人故意回避动作的施动者，或是信息来源掌握不全，或是不便透露，这就需要根据具体情况将英语中的被动句转换为相应的被动句或主动句。

最后，新闻编译是经过翻译和编辑的手段，将用原语写成的新闻转化、加工成为译语语言新闻的翻译方法。编译而成的新闻保留了原语新闻的中心思想和主要信息，但其内容却更加集中，更加精炼，更加可读，更适合在译语国家或地区进行二次传播，也更适合于译语语言读者们阅读和理解。原语新闻一般篇幅较长，内容多有重复，而新闻媒体的版面不多，若要在新的环境中进行二次传播，就必须对其进行“增”删、压缩或综合。

Luckin Coffee to pay $180 million penalty to settle accounting fraud charges – U. S. SEC

(Reuters) – Luckin Coffee Inc has agreed to pay a $180 million penalty to settle accounting fraud charges for "intentionally and materially" overstating its 2019 revenue and understating a net loss, U. S. regulators said on Wednesday.

1. The U. S. Securities and Commission (SEC) fine on the China – based rival to Starbucks comes after it said earlier this year that much of its 2019 sales were fabricated, sending its shares plunging and sparking an investigation by China's securities regulator and the SEC.

2. The SEC said it found that Luckin "intentionally and materially overstated its reported revenue and expenses and materially understated its net loss in its publicly disclosed financial statements in 2019."

3. Luckin has not admitted or denied the charges, the SEC said. The company has agreed to pay the penalty, which may be offset by certain payments it makes to its security holders in connection with its provisional liquidation proceeding in the Cayman Islands.

4. "This settlement with the SEC reflects our cooperation and remediation efforts, and enables the company to continue with the execution of its business strategy," Dr. Jinyi Guo, Chairman and Chief Executive Officer of Luckin Coffee said in a statement.

5. "The Company's Board of Directors and management are committed to a system of strong internal financial controls, and adhering to best practices for

compliance and corporate governance," Guo added.

6. The transfer of funds to the security holders will be subject to approval by Chinese authorities.

7. "Public issuers who access our markets, regardless of where they are located, must not provide false or misleading information to investors," SEC Director of Enforcement Stephanie Avakian said in a statement.

8. "While there are challenges in our ability to effectively hold foreign issuers and their officers and directors accountable to the same extent as U. S. issuers and persons, we will continue to use all our available resources to protect investors when foreign issuers violate the federal securities laws," she said.

9. Founded in June 2017, Luckin had one of the most successful U. S. IPOs by a Chinese company last year, attracting interest from prominent U. S. investors, including long – only funds and hedge funds.

10. But Luckin said in early April that as much as 2.2 billion yuan ($310 million) in sales last year were fabricated by its Chief Operating Officer Jian Liu and other staff, who had been suspended while the company carried out its investigation.

11. The falsified numbers equate to about 40% of Luckin's annual sales projected by analysts, according to Refinitiv IBES data.

12. The Xiamen – headquartered company, which delisted from Nasdaq at the end of June due to the accounting scandal, used related parties to create false sales transactions through three separate purchasing schemes, the SEC alleged.

13. "Luckin employees attempted to conceal the fraud by inflating the company's expenses by more than $190 million, creating a fake operations database, and altering accounting and bank records to reflect the false sales," the agency found.

14. Further, the SEC alleges that during the period of the fraud, Luckin raised more than $864 million from debt and equity investors. （见文末链接 3）

瑞幸将支付 1.8 亿美元罚款给美国证交会

美国证券监管部门 16 日表示，瑞幸咖啡同意支付 1.8 亿美元罚款，以就其受到的财务欺诈指控达成和解，这是迄今为止中概股遭遇的美证券监管机构最大罚单。美国证监会当天在纽约提起的诉讼指控瑞幸违反美国联邦证券法。在不承认或否认指控的情况下，经法院批准之后，瑞幸同意达成和解，同意遵守美国市场永久性禁令，并支付罚款。

今年早些时候，美国证券交易委员会称该机构发现瑞幸咖啡曾在其公开披露的2019财报中蓄意并大幅夸大其报告的收入和开支，并大幅少报其净亏损。瑞幸在今年4月“自曝”其去年多达22亿元人民币的销售收入为伪造，并在6月底因该财务丑闻从纳斯达克退市。我国的财政部和国家市场监督管理总局也对此展开调查。9月和10月，国家市场监督管理总局先后对涉案公司处以6100万元人民币和200万元人民币罚款。（见文末链接2）

▶ **点评：**

本篇主要讲瑞幸咖啡由于受到财务欺诈的指控向美国证交会支付1.8亿美元。相比来源于路透社的原文，本文进行了大篇幅的删减，其中包括直接间接引语，背景信息。瑞幸咖啡是一家来自中国的企业，所以中国读者比较熟悉，因此没有必要赘述相关背景介绍。

译文导语部分整合了第一段和第三段内容，客观陈述，并且加入“这是迄今为止中概股遭遇的美证券监管机构最大罚单”，提供给读者本事件的严重性，引起读者的兴趣。但是导语部分过于冗长，信息提供比较密集，可以适当进行划分，会更符合“切”的原则。

译文第二段在原有的信息基础上添加了新的信息，即中国相关机构如何对此进行处理。一方面，满足中国读者对于事件主要内容的获取；另一方面，也提供了中国对于瑞幸咖啡的处理方法，符合读者的阅读要求。

第六节　显

一、“显”的界定

“显”就是译者在翻译财经新闻时，把原文中有价值的内容转换成译语，并根据译文媒介的需求、译文读者的需求、译文时效需求，把相关信息凸显出来。

财经新闻毕竟不是一般的社会新闻，其重点在提供给读者有关经济活动、现象、决策等信息。同时，不同的财经新闻媒介有不同的风格，有的偏好发表某些专业主题的财经新闻，有的则偏好发表综合性的财经新闻，有的则偏好发表评论性的财经新闻。不同读者也会偏爱阅读不同类别、不同风格的财经新闻，不同读者也会经常阅读某类财经新闻，获取自己偏爱的财经信息。另外，财经新闻中的信息也会有时效价值，一些信息对一些读者而言可能已成昨日黄花，毫无价值，但对另一些读者而言却是初次相见，非常重要。财经新闻中的信息也会因读者的认知能力不同，表现出独特的价值，一些信息是通过非常简洁的方式呈现出来的，对一些读者而言这些信息显而易见，通俗易懂，但对另一些读者而言却是不易认知，枯涩难懂。因此，译者在翻译财经新闻时，译者应该根据译文媒介的需求、译文读者的需求、译文时效需求，在译语文本中把相关财经信息凸显出来。

二、“显”的实现方式

（一）显化主题信息

按汉语文本结构，凸显主题信息；从不同原文篇章中摘取有用的信息，按主题排列相关信息。“对新闻事件中的人、事等信息进行排序，保证逻辑的合理性。”（佘达文，2018）之所以采用编译的方式是因为原文语篇有众多信息而且译文语篇或版面有限或为了把最主要的信息呈现给读者，所以要凸显主要信息。一时讲不清楚且对新闻文稿主题影响不大的信息或背景介绍可以不译、不编。而有时则可以适当地增加一些背景性的信息或解释性的话语，以利于帮助读者阅读和理解，或有利于上下文的连接。

Pandemic fears, online deals thin U. S. Black Friday crowds

By Melissa Fares

NEW YORK (Reuters) – Masked shoppers turned up in smaller numbers at major U. S. retailers including Macy's Inc, Walmart Inc and Best Buy

Co Inc on Black Friday as early online deals and worry about the spike in COVID - 19 cases dulled enthusiasm for trips to the mall.

Retailers overhauled the traditionally busy shopping day that comes the day after Thanksgiving. Walmart opened stores at 5 a. m. on Friday, directing shoppers to turn right upon entering and proceed along main aisles to shop deals before paying at registers surrounded by plastic barriers.

Best Buy opened at 5 a. m. , employing workers in can't miss orange vests to serve as traffic cops. Others offered temperature checks and "grab - and - go" merchandise, including toys, bikes and kitchen appliances to discourage lingering in store aisles.

Bill Park, a partner at Deloitte & Touche LP, estimated traffic at the King of Prussia mall outside of Philadelphia was down about 20% ~30% compared to last year.

"I'm surprised at the traffic. It's down a little bit but heavier than I thought," he said but noted shoppers were not loaded down with packages.

Elsewhere, shoppers with empty carts lined up a socially - distant six feet apart before the Walmart in LaGrange, Kentucky opened, but crowds appeared down overall. Stores selling popular computer game consoles had some of the longest lines as gamers tried to land Sony Corp's PlayStation 5.

Brothers - in - law Gabriel Rojas, 24 and Juan Cabrera, 24 were waiting inline at GameStop in New ork's Bronx borough, since 2 a. m. on Friday, hopeful to snatch up a PS5. They were unsuccessful as there were some 20 people ahead of them and the retailer only had two left in stock, they said.

"We're bummed" said Rojas. "But that's ok. "

Some had better luck.

Roger Mustafa, 37, walked out of a Manhattan GameStop with a PS5 in a plastic bag and a huge smile on his face. It cost him $544 and a lot of sleep.

"I've been waiting outside of GameStop for two days," said Bronx resident Mustafa. "Now I'm going to go home and get some sleep. "

At Macy's New York flagship, Asuncion Peralta, 77, said she was not afraid to shop because she had COVID – 19 antibodies.

“I've been waiting for this day for a long time to buy towels and sheets, everything else that I need,” said Peralta. “These prices are not Black Friday prices. I came here two days ago and the deals were better.”

DEALS ONLINE

During this pandemic – ridden year, retailers from Target Corp to Kohl's Corp and Walmart rolled out online winter holiday promotions in October to capture any holiday – related spending as early as possible.

Upscale department store operator Nordstrom, which has seen its sales tumble in the pandemic, offered customers a $15 gift card if they picked up packages curbside at their stores.

Overall, the National Retail Federation (NRF) forecasts U. S. holiday retail sales will increase between 3. 6% and 5. 2% over 2019, for a total of $755. 3 billion to $766. 7 billion. That compares with an average annual increase of 2. 5% over the past five years.

On Nov. 19, the Center for Disease Control and Prevention (CDC) deemed “going shopping in crowded stores just before, on, or after Thanksgiving” as a high – risk activity.

Target employee Seth Schaffer, 22, from Lufkin, Texas, said shoppers in his store appeared less concerned about taking precautions to prevent the spread of COVID – 19.

“Deep east Texas isn't the type of place where you'll see everyone respecting mask policies or avoiding close contact.”

Adobe Analytics expects Black Friday and Cyber Monday 2020 to still become the two largest online sales days in history, with Black Friday online sales between $8. 9 billion and $10. 6 billion.

Melissa Bloss, who works at a bank in Rapid City, South Dakota, said she plans to do all her shopping online this year.

“Most companies have been having sales throughout the month. I really don't have a need to rush out when I can get the same deal a week later,” she said.

Reporting by Melissa Fares in New York; Additional reporting by Richa Naidu inChicago, James Davey in London and Aishwarya Venugopal in Bengaluru; Editing by Vanessa O'Connell, Louise Heavens and Nick Zieminski.（见文末链接4）

【译文】

美国感恩节假期购物人数低于去年同期

2020－12－02 18：46：32 来源：新华网

新华社华盛顿12月1日电（记者熊茂伶 高攀）美国全国零售商联合会1日发布数据显示，11月26日至11月30日感恩节假期期间，美国购物总人数较去年有所下滑，平均消费金额也低于去年同期水平。

数据显示，今年感恩节假期美国约有1.864亿人购物，略低于2019年同期的1.896亿人。消费者在礼物、装饰品等与假日相关商品上平均花费311.75美元，较去年同期的361.90美元大幅下降。

新冠肺炎疫情持续肆虐，美国假日购物季消费者转向线上购物的趋势明显。数据显示，感恩节假期期间，只进行网购、未去实体店购物的消费者人数同比增长44%。"黑色星期五"当天，在线购物人数首次突破1亿，同比增长8%；而在实体店购物的人数则同比下跌37%。

宾夕法尼亚大学沃顿商学院市场营销教授大卫·雷布斯坦对新华社记者说，在经济遭重创、失业率高企、收入下滑的当下，消费者想要寻找好的折扣。与实体店消费相比，线上消费更有利于消费者货比三家，而零售商只好提供更大力度的折扣。"对大多数零售商而言，这将是一个艰难的假日购物季。"（见文末链接3）

▶ **点评：**

导语对标题进行补充，向读者展现出本篇新闻的主要内容，即美国感恩节购物总人数相较去年比较少，第二段、第三段则提供出具体的数据，例证导语内容"美国感恩节假期购物人数低于去年同期"，最后一段则提出原因。由此，可看出信息排列是按照与导语的相关重要性，逐渐降低，最重要的内容放在最突出的位置。对比原文路透社的报道，本篇新闻去除了很多背景信息和不同人的观点意见，篇幅虽短，却凸显了主题重点。

（二）显化专业信息

财经新闻逻辑强，可以用简洁的语言指出背景、资讯隐藏的核心影响。这种简洁需要包含很多财经专业术语和专业信息内容。但简洁不等同于简短，信息含量低，还是要对重点内容，进行专业的解释、补充，凸显其专业性，也就是说对某专业术语、某公司进行解释性翻译，如补充相关信息等。如原文只是一个公司名，译文可能在公司名前增加“美国＊＊领域巨头”。这样不仅有画龙点睛之用，而且对于相关财经知识薄弱的普通读者，也能获得有效的信息。

【例 16】美国《福布斯》双周刊网站 4 月 29 日发表文章《“大炮与黄油”时代回归，通胀随之而来》，作者是美国佩金—哈迪—斯特劳斯财富管理公司联合首席执行官亚当·斯特劳斯。

▶ **点评：**

本句是对文章作者背景进行了补充说明，主要是突出原文作者的可靠性，从而体现出文章的专业性，以及可读性。

【例 17】

【原文】Billionaire Warren Buffett warned people not to think investing is an easy way to make a fortune as he answered a variety of questions at Berkshire Hathaway's annual meeting Saturday.

【译文】据美联社美国奥马哈 5 月 1 日报道，亿万富翁沃伦·巴菲特 5 月 1 日在伯克希尔—哈撒韦公司年会上回答了各种各样的问题，他提醒人们不要以为投资是轻松致富的方式。

▶ **点评：**

本句逐词翻译，没有凸显导语的专业信息，如果可以省略“回答了各种各样的问题”，则会有更好的效果。因为原文中这部分只是背景，而且在从句中，并非重要内容，如果译出，反而削弱了导语的主要内容。

改译：据美联社美国奥马哈 5 月 1 日报道，5 月 1 日在伯克希尔—哈撒韦公司年会上，亿万富翁沃伦·巴菲特提醒人们投资并非轻松致富的方式。

（三）显化隐性信息

财经新闻背后还蕴藏着很多隐性背景信息、隐性目的信息，可能是相应的政治、经济的目的。例如，通过展示量与价的关系，指引价格趋势，预估未来市场方向和政策指向。因此，在译文中，要突出相关内容，使读者能够获得相对应的启发，实现财经新闻的阅读价值。

The Guns And Butter Era Has Returned,
Bringing Inflation With It

In response to the coronavirus pandemic, the U. S. government embarked on an unprecedented surge of fiscal spending and monetary easing that has continued unabated ever since. One year later, as the economy is starting to open up, inflation pressures are rising, although it is still unclear whether these pressures will be transitory or not.

While finding appropriate historical analogies is always tricky, the current economic environment seems most reminiscent of the mid – 1960s. Those years represented an inflection point, much like today, when fiscal spending accelerated. The Federal Reserve financed that spending with low – interest rates, assuming that historically low inflation levels experienced in the early 1960s would continue. To be sure, inflation worsened considerably in the 1970s, but the foundation for accelerating inflation was built during the mid – to – late 1960s.

Upon his swearing – in, President Lyndon Johnson pursued an agenda that included an ambitious level of fiscal spending, following a significant tax cut that was passed in 1964. U. S. commitments in fighting the Vietnam War escalated even while domestic spending increased under the auspices of various Great Society programs that were intended to reduce minority unemployment and income inequality. Economists often refer to the era of the late 1960s as the "Guns and Butter" era, as that administration chose to pursue several ambitious goalR s at once, all of which required significant and sustained increases in fiscal spending along with an expanding budget deficit. The average year – over - year growth rate of government spending increased from 5.5% per annum from 1960 through 1964 to 10.8% per annum from 1965 through 1969.

Reminiscent of President Johnson's 1964 tax cuts, President Trump signed a large tax cut in 2017, even while the economy was growing at a reasonable rate and unemployment was low. President Trump also oversaw the most significant fiscal expansion in U. S. history in 2020. The Federal deficit reached an estimated $4 trillion, representing a year - over - year increase in government spending of 43%. With a new administration in place, President Biden has communicated his intention to pursue multiple sweeping goals simultaneously. These goals include but are not limited to providing support for individuals and groups who have been economically harmed by the pandemic, combating climate change, making infrastructure investments, and providing Social Security and Medicare benefits to a growing population of retirees. Given the Biden administration's plans, it is not unreasonable to assume that the budget deficit could remain around $3 - 4 trillion per year between 2021 and 2025, representing a fiscal expansion similar in magnitude to the one undertaken in the late 1960s.

Early on in the Johnson administration, President Johnson met the Federal Reserve Chairman at the time, William McChesney Martin, and famously tried to intimidate him into keeping interest rates low and monetary policy accommodative. After the Federal Reserve raised interest rates in 1965, Johnson said to the Chairman, "Martin, my boys are dying in Vietnam, and you won't print the money I need." Although Martin was a strong proponent of an independent Federal Reserve and an anti - inflation hawk early in his career, he complied with President Johnson's demands. Ultimately, Chairman Martin decided to provide monetary accommodation to fund the U. S. government's spending plans, despite the inflation risk. The average year - over - year growth rate in the monetary base, which was 1.8% between 1960 and 1964, tripled to 6.0% between 1965 and 1969 (see chart below). Chairman Martin confessed his regret in acquiescing to President Johnson's demands years later, saying, "to my everlasting shame, I finally gave in to him." He stepped down from his position in 1970, but only after he had let the inflation genie out of the bottle.

Similar to what occurred in the 1960s, the current Federal Reserve's independence has weakened considerably during the past year due to the current war on the coronavirus and the need to finance multi – trillion dollar annual fiscal deficits. The choice of former Federal Reserve Chair Janet Yellen as Treasury Secretary is somewhat symbolic of the marriage that seems to have occurred between the Federal Reserve and the U. S. Treasury Department. Relatedly, the Federal Reserve is determined to protect the nominal value of financial assets and especially the value of U. S. Treasuries. Not doing so would likely have catastrophic consequences on the housing market, the stock market, and U. S. tax receipts, all of which are increasingly reliant on low – interest rates. Even while the Consumer Price Index is likely to exceed 3% during Q2 2021 for the first time in years, current Federal Reserve Chairman Jerome Powell has communicated his view that the current inflationary pressures are transitory, assuming, like Chairman Martin, that inflation remains well – contained. While Chairman Powell may well turn out to be correct, four trillion dollars a year in fiscal deficit spending facilitated by a 0% Federal Funds rate and a skyrocketing money supply is likely to be a recipe for inflationary acceleration.

The spending during the Guns and Butter era created inevitable inflationary pressures that continued through the 1960s. During the early 1960s, inflation was well – contained, with the Consumer Price Index fluctuating in a relatively tight range of 1. 1% to 1. 6%. With increasing fiscal commitments and money supply in the late 1960s, however, inflation accelerated. In 1966, the Consumer Price Index increased by 3. 0%, and by 1969, the Consumer Price Index increased by as much as 5. 8%. Similarly, in the past five years, inflation has been low and contained, comparable to the inflation rate of the early 1960s. The average year – over – year increase in the Consumer Price Index was just 1. 8% from 2016 through 2020. Looking forward over the next several years, it would be unsurprising to see a CPI acceleration that rhymes with the late 1960s.

Important similarities exist between the late 1960s and the current era, but there are also important differences. The dollar is no longer pegged to the gold price, and the trade deficit has expanded significantly. Because U. S. government debt is currently so large relative to GDP, the Federal Reserve's options are limited by the necessity of keeping debt service costs reasonable, regardless of the Fed's inflation outlook. China has developed into a geopolitical and economic foe of the United States, and cheap imports from China have had a deflationary impact on the United States over the past twenty years. Finally, while the Biden administration is planning enormous fiscal spending initiatives, significant income tax increases would dampen their inflationary impact. Put more simply, many similarities seem to exist between the current era and the mid – 1960s, but the situation is complex and dynamic with many moving parts.

The 1970s are well known for being a period when inflation accelerated further even compared to the late 1960s. At some point, it may well be worth comparing the 1970s to the current era. Before inflation reaches the 10% inflation rates of the 1970s, however, it must first reach the 5% inflation rates of the late 1960s, and for this reason, the 1960s seem to offer a more applicable comparison for the next couple of years.

Having discussed the macroeconomic backdrop of the 1960s, let us now examine what happened to the primary asset classes during the five years beginning on January 1, 1965:

Stocks: Adjusted for inflation, the S&P 500 Index generated a total return of 0. 3% per year. Earnings increased by 0. 6% per year adjusted for inflation. However, as is often the case when inflation increases, the P/E ratio of the S&P 500 Index contracted, from 18. 8x to 15. 8x, and the dividend yield increased from 2. 9% to 3. 5% between the beginning of 1965 and the beginning of 1970. Today, the S&P 500 Index is currently trading with a P/E ratio of 33.7x and a dividend yield of 1.5% . The P/E ratio is extremely high compared to history, and the dividend yield is extremely low compared to history. Unfortunately, increasing inflation generally results in a contraction of P/E ratios and an expanding dividend yield. Accelerating inflation today could result in a significant downward re – rating of P/E ratios, which might make it difficult for the stock market to keep up with inflation.

Bonds: In 1965, the yield to maturity on 10 – year Treasury bonds was 4.2% ; by the time the decade ended, the yield – to – maturity on that same bond, with five years remaining until maturity, was 8.2%. The total return of that 10 – year Treasury bond was an estimated – 33.1% , or – 7.7% per annum, adjusted for inflation. Bonds woefully underperformed other asset classes during the late 1960s, as one might expect in any environment where bond yields are rising to compensate investors for increasing inflation expectations. The yield – to – maturity on 10 – year Treasury bonds is currently 1.7% , which means that the downside risk of a rise in bond yields is greater today than it was in 1965. For this reason and others, it probably makes sense to seek out substitutes for bonds in your investment portfolio.

Home prices: Housing performed better than bonds in the late 1960s but still did not keep up with inflation. Home prices increased by 3.3% per year, but home prices declined by a slight – 0.6% per year adjusted for inflation. Houses tend to keep up with inflation due to increases in wages, land costs, and construction costs, all of which occurred during the late 1960s. In recent months, land prices, construction costs, and wages are rising, all of which support rising home prices. It seems likely that home prices should approximately keep pace with inflation, as they did in the late 1960s.

Gold: During the Johnson administration, the dollar was pegged to gold at $35/ounce, and it was not yet legal for Americans to own physical gold during that period. However, demand for gold among Europeans increased significantly; during the 1960s, U. S. gold reserves dropped by 38% , from

15800 tonnes to 9800 tonnes as undervalued U. S. gold flowed to Europe. After the dollar/gold peg was removed in 1971, gold's return was spectacular during the following decade as investors sought to sell dollars to invest in gold as a store of value. While not an investment option in the late 1960s, it's probably a good time to own gold, which will likely serve as an excellent long – term store of value should inflation continue to increase.

Looking back at how these asset classes performed in the late 1960s, the results seemed to coincide with the era's inflationary circumstances. Housing and stocks were the relative winners, generating returns that kept up with, but did not exceed, inflation. The clear loser of the late 1960s Guns and Butter era was the bond market, which suffered from increasing bond yields and gradual erosion of purchasing power. It probably makes sense to be wary of bonds today and to seek out reasonable bond substitutes. It also makes sense to own reasonably priced stores of value, such as gold. （见文末链接6）

【例 18】　美媒：美国倒退回“大炮与黄油”时代

参考消息网5月7日报道　美国《福布斯》双周刊网站　4月29日发表文章《“大炮与黄油”时代回归，通胀随之而来》，作者是美国佩金—哈迪—斯特劳斯财富管理公司联合首席执行官亚当·斯特劳斯。全文摘编如下：

为应对新冠肺炎疫情，美国政府掀起一波前所未有的财政支出和货币宽松浪潮，之后也不曾减弱力度。一年后，随着经济开始开放，通胀压力也在增大，目前尚不清楚这些压力是否是暂时性的。

当前的经济环境似乎最像20世纪60年代中期。那个年代是个拐点，很像财政支出加速增长的今天。美联储以低利率为工具为当年的支出提供资金，它假定20世纪60年代初的历史性低通胀现象将持续下去。诚然，通胀是在20世纪70年代大幅加剧的，但通胀加速的“根基”是在20世纪60年代中后期“埋下”的。

2017年，美国时任总统特朗普签署了一项大规模减税法案，尽管当时经济正以合理的速度增长，失业率也很低。这让人联想起1964年时任总统约翰逊推行减税政策。特朗普还在2020年见证了美国历史上幅度最大的财政扩张。联邦赤字估计达到了 4 万亿美元，这代表政府开支同比增长 43%。

现任总统拜登表示，他打算同时设法实现多个广泛目标。这些目标包括但不限于：向因疫情而遭受经济损害的个人和组织提供支持、抗击气候变化，进行基础设施投资以及向越来越多的退休人员提供社会保障和医疗保险。有鉴于此，认为 2021 ~2025 年预算赤字可能保持在每年 3 万亿 ~4 万亿美元并非没有道理，这一财政扩张规模也与 20 世纪 60 年代末的情况类似。

同样与 20 世纪 60 年代的情况类似的是，由于当前需要抗疫和为年度财政赤字提供资金，美联储的独立性在过去一年间被大大削弱。美联储前主席珍妮特·耶伦被选中担任财政部部长，这在一定程度上象征着，美联储和财政部之间似乎已经“联姻”。与此相关的是，美联储决心保护金融资产的名义价值，尤其是美国国债的价值。如果不这样做，很可能会为住房市场、股市和美国的税收带来灾难性后果，所有这些都越来越依赖低利率。尽管消费价格指数可能会在 2021 年二季度超过 3%（那将是多年来的首次），但美联储现任主席杰罗姆·鲍威尔的观点是，目前的通胀压力是暂时的。尽管到头来鲍威尔很可能是对的，但每年 4 万亿美元的财政赤字支出很可能会导致通胀加速。

20 世纪 60 年代末“大炮与黄油”时代的明显输家是债券市场，它因债券收益率上升和购买力逐渐减弱而受损。

如今，对债券保持警惕并寻找合理的替代品或许是有道理的。持有定价合理的价值储存品（比如黄金）也是有道理的。(见文末链接 5)

▶ 点评：

本文通过对原文内容的筛选，显化了隐性信息，缩小了篇幅，同时减轻读者的阅读负担。相比于原文《“大炮与黄油”时代回归，通胀随之而来》，译文很明显删去了大部分背景知识，大篇幅的内容很明显是贴近时事，突出当前美国的财政状况，提供了过去特朗普的政策，和现在拜登的政策，无形中形成了对比。读者可以迅速抓取他们所需要的财经内容，避免大篇幅阅读有关的背景历史知识。

第七节 简

一、“简”的界定

“简”，顾名思义，即简洁。简作为财经新闻翻译原则之一，也是译者在翻译过程中必须时刻铭记于心的标准。

有些英文财经新闻的特征之一便是篇幅较长，段落短，段落数量多。专业人士写的财经评论往往有这样的特征。这样的财经新闻，会给译语读者增加了阅读难度。这样的语篇对汉语读者而言，会显得外在形式上很繁复、不凝练。另外，刊载财经新闻的媒体也会因为版面的原因，对译文的字数有特定的要求。因此，译者在财经新闻的英译过程中需要提供语义简洁、篇幅恰当的译文。一般地，译者需要遵循“简”的原则，删减原文中不必要的冗余信息，在译文中突出核心内容及中心思想，使译文简洁明了，达到为读者传递财经信息的目的。

二、“简”的实现方式

在具体操作上，有两种方式可以实现财经译文的简洁效果。其一，整合段落，即把多个段落合并成一个段落或数个段落。其二，删减次要信息，即把对目标语读者而言次要的信息进行选择性删减。

（一）整合段落

原有英文财经信息内容较长，段落分布较多，且有些信息对于汉语的新闻阅读者来说并不是熟知的内容或者不是新闻内容的关键信息时，在翻译的时候可以进行段落整合，让汉语的受众读起来更流畅。

（二）删减次要信息

请看下面一则例子：译者就对英语新闻的内容进行了整合并删除了原文

中表述的中国读者熟悉的信息、普通读者可能不感兴趣或较难理解的信息、次要信息。

Biden wants to build a national EV charging system under $2 trillion infrastructure plan, but it won't be easy

[1] Charging stations for electric vehicles will be part of a $2 trillion infrastructure bill being pushed by the Biden administration.

[2] It's going to take more than government support to successfully expand EV infrastructure.

[3] AlixPartners estimates $300 billion will be needed to build out a global charging network to accommodate the expected growth of EVs by 2030, including $50 billion in the U. S. alone.

[4] President **Joe Biden** is prioritizing a national EV charging network under his $2 trillion infrastructure bill, promising to have at least 500000 of the devices installed across the U. S. by 2030.

[5] The Biden administration is rolling out Wednesday a $174 billion plan to spur the development and adoption of electric vehicles that includes money to retool factories and boost domestic supply of materials, tax incentives for EV buyers, and grant and incentive programs for charging infrastructure.

[6] But it's going to take more than government support to successfully expand EV infrastructure. There aren't enough EV drivers to make it a viable business yet, and building a network of chargers is far more complex than it sounds. It takes a mix of private - public partnerships that can involve local municipalities, businesses and utility companies as well as automakers and an emerging group of EV charging companies. It's not as simple as having a gas station at every corner.

[7] "As electric vehicles become more primary vehicles for people, certainly it's not like we're going to replace the gas station with the charging station and that's it," said Mark Wakefield, a managing director and global co - leader of the automotive and industrial practice at AlixPartners.

[8] AlixPartners estimates $300 billion will be needed to build out a

global charging network to accommodate the expected growth of EVs by 2030, including $50 billion in the U. S. alone. Costs for EV chargers vary based on the "level" of charger. The higher the level, the quicker the charge and the more expensive it is to install.

[9] "It is a big pill to swallow for anybody," Wakefield said. "These are really, really expensive, especially these fast chargers" that some automakers are promising will take as little as 10 minutes to charge upcoming EVs about 80%. That compares with lower-level chargers, including home outlets, that take several hours. Level three chargers cost $12000 to $260000 installed on average, according to AlixPartners. "These are not cheap."

[10] But demand for the networks isn't quite there yet. Plug-in vehicles, which include EVs and hybrid electric vehicles with traditional engines, only accounted for about 2% of the more than 17 million new vehicles sold domestically in 2019, according to the Energy Department. But many believe now is the beginning of the end of gasoline vehicles.

[11] "It's no longer a matter of if, and it's no longer a matter of when, it's now the question is how fast? Because we know that the automakers have put the money into the retooling," said Jonathan Levy, chief commercial officer of EV charging company EVgo.

[12] While automakers like General Motors and Volkswagen are heavily investing in improving performance and lowering prices of EVs to catch up to Tesla, they're far less interested in building, owning and operating their own charging networks. The profit margins and amount of effort involved to maintain them just doesn't make sense. Tesla, an early leader in the industry, built its own charging network out of necessity and, in part, to help sell its cars.

[13] Most automakers are partnering with third-party companies to provide charging stations. Their strategy, combined with enthusiasm from Wall-Street for EVs, has driven investor demand for charging companies such as ChargePoint and EVgo. ChargePoint went public through a reverse merger with a special purpose acquisition company, or SPAC, in March. EVgo plans to do

the same in the second quarter.

[14] There are about 41400 EV charging stations in the U. S. , according to the Department of Energy. Fewer than 5000 are fast chargers. That compares with more than 136400 gas stations, according to GasBuddy.

[15] "The answer is not one size fits all," ChargePoint CEO Pasquale Romano told CNBC. "You're going to need an entire universe of charging infrastructure that is easy to use and accessible for the different scenarios to kind of play out."

[16] Charging suppliers and operators have largely focused infrastructure at destination points in urban and suburban areas such as grocery stores and other places where people regularly shop. Businesses consider it a draw for EV owners. There's also a growing call for additional fast chargers between major cities to enable faster and longer trips for EVs. Tesla has been building out such a network for its owners for nearly a decade.

[17] GM has committed to releasing 30 or more EVs through 2025 <u>under a $27 billion investment</u> in electric and autonomous vehicles. It also is one of many companies to focus on EVs following the success of Tesla. Volvo has announced plans to become an all – EV company by 2030, while Volkswagen has a mission of being the world's largest manufacturer of electric vehicles.

[18] "We're moving into this year at a tipping point for EVs and really an inflection point on sustainability, inclusion, and growth," GM CEO Mary Barra said Thursday during a JPMorgan Securities conference.

[19] Public chargers are needed to power those vehicles, but companies such as EVgo need the demand for charging to be there to justify their business. Many have described it asa "chicken and egg" scenario regarding which is needed first. Levy, who served as deputy chief of staff at the Department of Energy under the Obama administration, characterizes it as "peanut butter and jelly" instead.

[20] "It's not 'chicken and egg' because we're not starting from scratch," he said. "We have charging, we have EVs. It's not what comes

first. It's peanut butter and jelly, in that we need to build these things out in a complementary way."

[21] About 30% of Americans don't have access to home or workplace charging that they may need in the future, according to Levy.

[22] As for 2020, IHS Markit reports EVs were only 1.8% of new light – duty vehicle registrations in the U. S. AlixPartners expects there to be 18 million EVs on U. S. roadways by the end of 2030.

[23] EVgo, which plans to go public in the second quarter through a $2.6 billion SPAC deal, owns and operates more than 800 charging locations in 67 major markets across 34 states. The company's business model is different than ChargePoint, which sells stations to businesses and other establishments and then charges them subscription fees to be a part of their network.

[24] "We're essentially crowdfunding for the driver one business at a time, the largest network of EV chargers in the area for them and they see it all as one network through our mobile application," ChargePoint's Romano said. "It all says ChargePoint, we don't own any of it. It's just all looks like we own it to the driver and that's what we want is to create a model where each business does their part."

[25] Charge Point is Cowen's "top pick" for the recharging market, which the investment firm believes will be a total addressable market of about $27 billion by 2040. The company went public March 1 through a SPAC deal with Switchback Energy Acquisition Corp.

[26] While largely new to public investors, Cowen believes "the sector is poised for tremendous growth and value creation, underpinned by a large, strong unit economics, and recurring revenue," according to a report on EV charging earlier this month.

[27] But that growth needs to come with EV sales as well as incentives and investments from several sources, including the federal government, according to officials.

[28] "Right now you absolutely need government funding at some lev-

el," Wakefield said. "The reality of it is that the automakers don't have the money. Utilities havesome of the money, but the business case isn't there. It's so expensive."（见文末链接1）

拜登要建50万充电站，美媒不兴奋

【来源】环球时报　2021－04－02 08：40

［1］美国总统拜登3月31日公布一项规模达2.3万亿美元的基础设施计划，其中包括建设50万座电动汽车充电站。对此，美国媒体普遍比较谨慎，认为拜登的新能源之路并不平坦。

［2］据美国CNBC网站3月31日报道，拜登在其超过2万亿美元基建计划中把建设电动汽车充电网络排在优先位置，承诺到2030年在全美建设至少50万座充电站。

［3］建设充电站，成本是大问题。CNBC称，根据咨询公司"阿利克斯合伙"的数据，三级快速充电桩的平均安装成本为12万～26万美元。但目前，美国并没有对充电网络产生足够需求。美国能源部的数据显示，2019年全美销售的1700多万辆新车中，纯电动汽车和混合动力汽车仅占2%左右。美国大约有4.14万座电动汽车充电站，其中快充站不到5000座。相比之下，传统加油站超过13万座。虽然通用和大众等汽车制造商正在投入巨资，以提高电动汽车的性能并降低价格，但他们对建设、拥有和运营自己的充电网络并不感兴趣。因为投入回报不成比例。特斯拉有自己的充电网络，但部分是为了销售自己的汽车。

［4］彭博社4月1日援引乔治·华盛顿大学环境与能源管理研究所可持续能源部门主任斯科特·斯克拉尔的话说："美国政府是巨大的客户，他们的参与可能会推动美国电动汽车行业超过中国，成为世界领先者。"不过，也有人质疑拜登的计划规模不足以让消费者从燃油车转向电动汽车。特朗普政府前顾问汤姆·派尔表示，50万座充电站连加州一半的需求都满足不了。

［5］相比之下，彭博社统计显示，2019年，仅北京的公共充电桩数量就跟全美国一样多，而全中国的数量为美国的8倍。仅在去年12月，中国就安装11.2万个公共充电桩，超过美国全国数字。

［6］"在奥巴马时代，民主党就在搞充电桩等新基建，但最后人走

政息，特朗普执政后开了倒车。现在，拜登又开始往回扳，觉得要加把劲。”汽车行业分析师钟师4月1日接受《环球时报》记者采访时表示，“公共基础设施还是需要政府支持，不能仅靠市场解决。从目前来看，拜登这么做只是弥补过去的功课，但做得好或坏跟中国关系不大，没什么直接影响，因为中国已经走在前面了”。(见文末链接2)

评析：该篇新闻是关于美国总统拜登计划在美建设电动汽车基础设施的报道。原文共有28个段落，而译文只有6个段落。这说明译者在翻译新闻时对原文内容进行了整合。如：原文第2、6、27、28段都涉及了同样的信息：建设电动汽车基础设施需要政府的财政支持，译文将这些信息整合在第6段。

原文第10、12段的内容融合至译文第3段：电动汽车数量少，消费者对充电桩的需求并不大。各大汽车制造商如通用、大众等对建设充电网络并不感兴趣。

原文第13～15段以及第23～25段对ChargePoint和EVGo等充电公司的相关报道被删减。

【例19】再如下面的新闻，我们用下划线标出被删除的信息，并进行分析。

XIAOMI WILL INVEST 10 BILLION YUAN + $10 BILLION IN SMART ELECTRIC VEHICLE BUSINESS IN THE NEXT 10 YEARS

[1] Today, Xiaomi issued a voluntary announcement confirming that the board of directors had formally approved the establishment of the smart electric vehicle business.

[2] Xiaomi said that it plans to establish a wholly - owned subsidiary to be responsible for the smart electric vehicle business. The first phase investment is 10 billion yuan ($1.52 billion). But the investment is expected to reach $10 billion in the next 10 years.

[3] According to the announcement, Lei Jun will concurrently serve as the CEO of the smart electric vehicle business.

[4] <u>In fact, previously, we have heard that Xiaomi will start making cars. But there has been no official confirmation. Even the head of Xiaomi's public relations department has repeatedly denied it categorically.</u>

评析：该段落讲述此前小米就已经开始造车，但这一消息并未得到证实。该信息与这篇新闻的主旨并无任何直接关系，且讲述的是发生过的事，属于次要信息，故译者删除了这一信息。

[5] However, prior to this, Lei Jun disclosed the so - called 'Xiaomi $10 billion big project'. At that time, many were thinking this could only refer to the car business. The latest financial report shows that Xiaomi's 2020 annual revenue is 245.9 billion yuan ($37.41 billion), and its cash reserves exceed 100 billion yuan ($15.21).

评析：该段落内容为小米总裁雷军此前披露造车计划，以及小米2020年的营收状况。由于下文第九段介绍了小米公司2020年年底的现金余额，表明小米完全有经济能力启动造车计划，故此处的营收状况是没有必要再赘述的。

[6] On January 15, Lei Jun said that they began to research and build cars. 'I have visited Musk twice before, and I am very optimistic about the electric vehicle industry. I have also invested in nearly 10 electric vehicle industry companies in the past.'

LEI JUN WILL SERVE AS THE CEO OF XIAOMI's SMART ELECTRIC VEHICLE BUSINESS

[7] Lei Jun revealed that in the past 75 days, there have been 85 industry visits, in - depth exchanges with more than 200 automotive industry veterans, 4 internal management discussions, and 2 formal board meetings.

评析：该段落讲述小米公司为启动造车计划所做的准备工作：考察、交流、讨论等。前期准备相比于计划的实施情况而言是次要信息，故译者将其删除。

[8] 'With high - quality smart electric cars, users around the world can enjoy ubiquitous life,' Lei Jun said. This is the original intention of Xiaomi to build cars.

评析：电动汽车为用户带来的方便，这并非小米汽车的独特之处，故删除。

[9] Lei Jun said frankly that he is very aware of the risks in the automotive industry. Also, the investment of tens of billions of dollars will take 3 - 5

years to be effective. But he also said that Xiaomi now has accumulated, and the company has a cash balance of 108 billion yuan by the end of 2020. Moreover, the company has a research and development team of more than 10000 people. They also have the world's top three smartphone businesses and the world's best smart ecosystem. So the company can afford to lose money. These are important supports for the Xiaomi car business.

[10] He added that ‘this will be the last major entrepreneurial project in his life. And he is willing to suppress all his reputation and fight for Xiaomi. One day, Xiaomi will succeed. As long as you are willing to wait, you must live up to expectations and bring Xiaomi cars to everyone as soon as possible.’(见文末链接3)

评析：该段落是雷军对于小米启动造车计划的看法和观点，属于个人主观信息，不是实质性内容，故删除。

【译文】

小米未来10年　将投资100亿美元造车

【来源】环球时报　2021-03-31 08：39

[1] 30日，中国智能手机厂商小米集团在港交所发布公告，宣布小米智能汽车业务正式立项。公告称，公司拟成立一家全资子公司负责有关业务，小米CEO雷军将兼任智能电动汽车业务的CEO。

[2] 在30日举行的发布会上，雷军也宣布，小米正式进军智能电动汽车行业。公司计划在未来10年投资100亿美元到智能电动车业务中，首期投资为100亿元人民币。雷军表示，自2013年以来，他对新能源汽车产业非常看好。在过去七八年时间里，他曾对十多家有关公司进行投资。他非常清楚汽车行业的风险和巨大投入，但“今日的小米，不再是当年的小米”，小米集团2020年年底现金余额为1080亿元人民币，“小米亏得起”。另据路透社26日报道，小米汽车正在和长城汽车密切接触，计划用长城汽车的工厂生产电动汽车，双方或在本周签署合作造车计划。

评析：上面这个例子表明，译文呈现出“简”的效果。首先，译文的段落数远远少于原文段落数。原文一共有10个段落，译文则有2个段落。其次，原文的字数远远少于原文字数。原文一共，译文则只有 345 个汉字。最后，译文呈现的信息比原文少，且表述精炼。原文与译文的核心信息都是"小米智能汽车业务正式立项"。与原文相比，译文的信息更加凝练，只列出"小米拟成立一家全资子公司智能电动汽车业务""小米 CEO 雷军将兼任的 CEO""公司的投资计划和原因"。

译文将原文中第 4，5，7，8，10 段的信息全部删除。

原文第 4 段讲述此前小米就已经开始造车，但这一消息并未得到证实。该信息与这篇新闻的主旨并无任何直接关系，且讲述的是发生过的事，属于次要信息，故译者删除了这一信息。

原文第 5 段内容为小米总裁雷军此前披露造车计划，以及小米 2020 年的营收状况。由于下文第九段介绍了小米公司 2020 年年底的现金余额，表明小米完全有经济能力启动造车计划，故此处的营收状况是没有必要再赘述的。

参考文献

[1] 白翔云. 论新闻的真实性和时效性. 宝鸡社会科学，2000 (1)：45 - 47.

[2] 贯丽丽. 英语财经报道翻译分析 [J]. 黑龙江教育 (理论与实践)，2016 (3)：43 - 44.

[3] 刘超先. 温故而知今：鲁迅翻译思想的教益 [J]. 中国翻译，1992 (1)：2 - 6.

[4] 刘其中. 英汉新闻翻译 [M]. 北京：清华大学出版社，2009.

[5] 佘达文. 新媒体时代网络新闻写作的技巧分析 [J]. 新闻研究导刊，2018，9 (24)：162 - 164.

[6] 周俊博. 财经新闻英汉翻译教程 [M]. 湖北：武汉大学出版社，2014.

[7] https：//finance. huanqiu. com/article/419BeaXRrDh.

[8] https：//finance. huanqiu. com/article/42WhX8wEqa8.

[9] https：//finance. huanqiu. com/article/42YMS5Nz0V8.

[10] https：//mp. weixin. qq. com/s/C6ohTgB - lhyzS07POQcswA.

[11] https：//www. bloomberg. com/news/articles/2021 - 03 - 31/u - s - heads - for - hotter - shorter - upswing - as - biden - pushes - new - plan.

[12] https：//www. cnbc. com/2021/03/31/us - ev - charging - system - a - priority - under - bidens - 2 - trillion - infrastructure - plan. html.

[13] https：//www. forbes. com/sites/adamstrauss/2021/04/29/the - guns - and - butter -

era – has – returned – bringing – inflation – with – it/? sh = 13809ec27354.

[14] https://www.gizchina.com/2021/03/30/xiaomi – will – invest – 10 – billion – yuan – 10 – billion – in – smart – electric – vehicle – business – in – the – next – 10 – years/.

[15] https://www.newsbreak.com/news/2193070985488/despite – its – best – efforts – walmart – s – e – commerce – is – still – a – fraction – of – amazon – s.

[16] https://www.reuters.com/article/us – climate – change – central – banks – idUSKBN2BN01K.

[17] https://www.reuters.com/article/us – usa – holidayshopping – black – friday – idUSKBN28710B.

[18] https://www.reuters.com/article/us – usa – sec – luckincoffee/luckin – coffee – to – pay – 180 – million – penalty – to – settle – accounting – fraud – charges – us – sec – idUSKBN28Q34P.

[19] http://www.cankaoxiaoxi.com/finance/20210403/2439432.shtml.

[20] http://www.cankaoxiaoxi.com/finance/20210507/2442561.shtml.

[21] http://www.cankaoxiaoxi.com/finance/20210331/2439059.shtml.

[22] http://www.cankaoxiaoxi.com/finance/20210402/2439329.shtml.

[23] http://www.fortunechina.com/shangye/c/2021 – 03/31/content_388043.htm.

[24] http://www.qqenglish.com/bn/40088.htm.

[25] http://www.qqenglish.com/bn/39549.htm.

[26] http://www.qqenglish.com/bn/36371.htm.

[27] http://www.qqenglish.com/bn/39552.htm.

[28] http://www.xinhuanet.com/fortune/2020 – 12/02/c_1126813691.htm.

[29] www.bbc.com/news/business – 56390409.

| 第五章 |

英汉财经新闻的常用翻译方法

第一节　直译法

一、直译法的界定

直译法指的是译者在翻译时尽量保持原作的语言形式的翻译方法。一般的，直译法是译者最可能选用的方法，也是译者最常用的翻译方法，当然，也是译者最方便的翻译方法。具体而言，翻译者要对原文的词汇、句子结构、修辞手段等进行直接转换。直译法要求译者呈现的语言自然流畅、清晰明确、通俗易懂。

在翻译财经新闻时，译者用直译法把原文本中的词汇、句子结构、修辞手段转换成汉语文本，可以令读者领略原文本在词汇、句子结构、修辞手段的独特风姿。

下面，我们用实例来分析如何通过直译法来翻译财经新闻的词汇、句子结构、修辞手段。

二、直译法的具体应用

（一）词汇的直译

新诞生的、可能会受到广泛关注的、与汉语构词法相似的词汇应尽量直译，这样词汇译文容易被译语受众理解和接受，促进词汇译文的流行和应用。

【例 1】

【原文】"Equivalent VIII" by Carl Andre was a minimalist sculpture bought by Britain's Tate Gallery in 1972. The Tate described the work as "a rectangular arrangement of 120 firebricks... altering the viewer's relationship to the surrounding space". The public called it a pile of bricks. A few years later newspapers execrated the gallery for having wasted brick - shaped wads of cash on the avant - garde work.

【译文】卡尔·安德烈的《平衡 8 号》是一件极简主义雕塑，于 1972 年被英国泰特美术馆买下。泰特美术馆将这幅作品描述为"一个由 120 块防火砖组成的矩形结构……改变了观者与周围空间的关系"。公众则称其为"一堆砖头"。几年后，报纸谴责美术馆在这种前卫的作品上浪费了大量的砖形钞票。

原文 & 译文链接：http://kekenet.com/menu/202103/625570.shtml

【分析】这里译文对原文里的一些重要名词，如"rectangular arrangement""firebricks""a pile of bricks"等词都采用了直译的方法，这样可以让读者直接捕捉到新闻报道的重点，更容易接受新闻信息，准确把握原文信息。

【例 2】

【原文】China is the clear frontrunner. On February 17th it concluded the third big test of its digital currency, handing out 10m yuan ($1.5m) to 50000 shoppers in Beijing. It has announced a joint venture with SWIFT, an interbank - messaging system used for cross - border payments. Sweden, another champion, has extended its pilot project.

【译文】中国显然是领跑者。2 月 17 日，它结束了对其数字货币的第三次大型测试，向北京的 5 万名购物者发放了 1000 万元数字人民币。中国已宣布与用于跨境支付的银行间报文系统 SWIFT 成立合资公司。另一个冲在前头的国家瑞典已延长了其试点项目。

原文 & 译文链接：http://www.kekenet.com/menu/202103/624955.shtml

【分析】这里译文将原文新闻中的重点信息"digital currency"作了直译处理，方便读者更直接迅速掌握新闻主体信息和关注焦点，采用直译的方法，使得译语读者更容易理解原文信息。

（二）句子结构的直译

与汉语句子结构相同或相近的句子结构是适合用直译法翻译的。经过长时间的发展，新闻语篇已形成了特定的模式。新闻记者在写新闻语篇时会按照特定的模式来填充相当的信息，新闻编辑在编辑新闻语篇时会按照特定的模式来修改润饰，新闻读者在阅读新闻语篇时也会按照特定的模式去搜寻有价值的信息。比如，一则消息往往是一个陈述句，而一个新闻语篇的导语则往往是囊括五个 W 一个 H 的长句子。在英语新闻语篇中，无论是展示一则消息的陈述句，还是位于新闻开头、充当导语的、囊括五个 W 一个 H 的长句子，其结构都是清明简洁的。这样的句子结构是适合用直译法翻译的。

【例 3】

【原文】

GM，Ford cutting more North American production due to chip shortage

WASHINGTON（Reuters） – General Motors Co and Ford Motor Co both said on Thursday they will cut more vehicle production due to a semiconductor chip shortage that has roiled the global automotive industry.

The White House plans a summit on the chip shortage issue next Monday that is expected to include GM Chief Executive Mary Barra and Ford Chief Executive Jim Farley and top technology firm executives.

A U. S. auto industry group this week urged the government to help and warned that a global semiconductor shortage could result in 1. 28 million fewer vehicles built this year and disrupt production for another six months.

President Joe Biden wants at least $50 billion to help boost U. S. semiconductor production, but that will not address short – term needs. "This is something that there is a great deal of focus at the highest level across government," White House spokeswoman Jen Psaki said.

The largest U. S. automaker said it will cut production for two weeks at its Spring Hill assembly plant that makes popular SUVs starting on Monday, and cut a week of Chevrolet Blazer production at its Ramos plant in Mexico and its

Lansing Delta Township factory in Michigan.

GM's Lansing Grand River Assembly will extend its downtime through the week of April 26, while its CAMI Assembly (Canada) and Fairfax Assembly plants will extend production shutdowns through the week of May 10.

Ford, the second - largest U. S automaker, said it will cancel production next week at its Chicago Assembly Plant, its Flat Rock Assembly Plant and part of its Kansas City Assembly Plant. It will also operate its Ohio Assembly Plant on a reduced schedule.

Ford said it will operate more plants this summer during traditional shutdown weeks to make up for lost production.

GM said the latest cuts have been factored into its forecast that the shortage could reduce this year's profit by up to $2 billion.

GM said it has not taken downtime or reduced shifts at any of its more profitable full - size truck or full - size SUV plants due to the shortage.

【来源】https://www.reuters.com/article/us-gm-semiconductors-idUSKBN2BV21N

【译文】

英媒：通用福特因“缺芯”继续减产

据路透社华盛顿4月8日报道，美国通用汽车和福特汽车均在4月8日表示，由于半导体芯片短缺，将进一步削减汽车产量。“芯片荒”已经令全球汽车业大受影响。

白宫计划12日就芯片短缺问题召开会议，预计通用汽车首席执行官玛丽·巴拉、福特汽车首席执行官吉姆·法利和大型科技公司的高管们将参加会议。美国一个汽车行业组织本周敦促政府施以援手。该组织警告称，全球半导体供应短缺可能导致今年汽车产量减少128万辆，并将在未来六个月继续干扰生产。

美国总统拜登希望拿出至少500亿美元来帮助提振美国半导体生产，但这无法满足短期需求。白宫发言人普萨基说：“政府最高层对这个问题给予高度关注。”

报道称，通用汽车表示，斯普林希尔装配厂将减产两周；墨西哥拉莫斯工厂和密歇根州兰辛德尔塔工厂的雪佛兰开拓者车型将减产一周。

通用汽车位于兰辛的另一家装配厂停工时间将延长至 4 月 26 日当周。CAMI 装配厂（加拿大）和费尔法克斯装配厂停产将延长至5 月 10 日当周。

福特汽车表示，下周将取消芝加哥装配厂、弗拉特罗克装配厂以及一部分堪萨斯城装配厂的生产；其俄亥俄州装配厂也将减产。

【来源】http：//www. cankaoxiaoxi. com/finance/20210411/2440112. shtml

【分析】在这篇新闻报道中，其导语就是采用了直译的方法翻译了导语部分，新闻六要素，即五个“W”和一个“H”全都包含在内了，对其进行直译可以完整且清晰的将原文信息传递给读者。

【例 4】

【原文】

The number of billionaires spiked by 30% during the pandemic

The total number of billionaires exploded over the course of the coronavir-uspandemic—and they individually became extraordinarily wealthier during the last 12 months.

That's according to a new report from Forbes, which does one of the most complete analyses each spring about the state of the billionaire class across the globe. Tracking the net worths of the wealthy is painstaking work that requires sifting through arcane filings; the end results are not perfect, but the estimates offered by Forbes represent one of the best stabs at covering the scale of income inequality in the world. And while it's easy to lose track of the numbers or to see the figures as old news — "Billionaires continue to be billionaires" — the scale matters for anyone who wants to get a grasp on how much of a problem wealth inequality truly is.

The world isnow home to 2755 billionaires, a world record and a startling 30 percent increase from Forbes's accounting last year of the world's uber - rich. And 86 percent of those billionaires are richer than they were a year ago. The list does paint an exaggerated picture of some of the pandemic gains because it compares today's net worths to Forbes's last analysis in mid - March

2020, when the market had yet to recover from the early pandemic - inspired sell - off.

The pandemic has reinvigorated the debate over inequality, with nations like Argentina adopting a wealth tax and other similar proposals gaining a foothold in the United States. In the US, many Americans have more personal income and savings than they had before the pandemic, thanks in part to unprecedented government stimulus measures. But at the same time, demand for food pantries smashed records and the economy shed about 10 million jobs. Billionaire philanthropists have played center stage in America's recovery.

Perhaps no statistic better encapsulates the scale of the yawning inequality than that MacKenzie Scott, the former wife of Jeff Bezos and one of the wealthiest people in the world, probably gave more money away directly to nonprofits in 2020 than any person has in a single year ever before. Yet because of Amazon's surging stock price, she actually ended the year richer, Forbes reports.

Forbes finds that the tech set, like Scott, fared particularly well. Six of the world's 10 richest people made their money in tech, and the total assets controlled by alltech billionaires globally measures $2.5 trillion, far more than any other industry. Neither of those figures includes Tesla and SpaceX founder Elon Musk, who is classified by Forbes as in the automotive industry but has ridden Tesla's extraordinary bull run to become the second - richest person in the world.

That's all to say that the debate over wealth inequality isn't going anywhere, even when the pandemic fades away. Check out Recode's recent coverage of how the coronavirus has made America more reliant on billionaires and our exclusive polling on how ordinary Americans feel about these central characters in American society.

【来源】https://www.vox.com/recode/2021/4/6/22370351/billionaires-forbes-inequality-pandemic

【译文】

美媒：全球亿万富翁人数在疫情期间增加30%

美媒援引《福布斯》一份新报告称，在新冠肺炎疫情期间，全球亿万富翁的总人数激增。

美国沃克斯网站4月6日发文称，《福布斯》报告每年春天都会对全球亿万富翁的情况进行全面的分析。追踪富人的净资产需要筛查秘密文件，而且最终的结果并非完美的。但这对了解财富不平等问题到底有多严重而言至关重要。

根据报告，疫情期间，全球亿万富翁增加了2755名，这一数字同比增加30%。

疫情重新引发关于不平等的讨论。

贝索斯前妻麦肯齐·斯科特在2020年向非营利组织捐款的数额比以往任何人一年向非营利组织捐款的数额都要多。然而，据《福布斯》报道称，由于亚马逊的股价飙升，斯科特在这一年结束时实际上更加富裕了。

而疫情期间，人们对食物站的需求打破纪录，经济衰退缩减了大约1000万个就业岗位。

【来源】http：//www.cankaoxiaoxi.com/finance/20210409/2440026.shtml

【分析】这篇报道并非将原文信息完整翻译，而是节选了重要信息，但仍采用的是直译的方法。这样可以保证读者迅速掌握新闻重点，并了解当前亿万富翁人数的基本情况。

（三）修辞手段的直译

新闻报道中也会采用一些修辞手段吸引人们的关注，在翻译时，采用直译的翻译方法可以很好地保留使用修辞手段来吸引关注的这一特点，吸人眼球。

【例5】

【原文】Success in manufacturing depends on physical things：creating the best product using the best equipment with components assembled in the most efficient way. Success in the service economy is dependent on the human element：picking the right staff members and motivating them correctly. If manufacturing is akin to science, then services are more like the arts.

【译文】制造业的成功取决于物质因素：使用最好的设备，以最有效的方式组装部件，才能创造出最好的产品。服务经济的成功取决于人的因素：挑选合适的员工并正确地激励他们。如果说制造业类似于科学，那么服务业更像是艺术。

原文 & 译文来源：http：//www. kekenet. com/menu/202101/623679. shtml

【分析】原文采用比喻的修辞手段将制造业和服务业的性质描述的十分到位，译文保留了这种修辞手段使得读者更容易把握两者之间的区别和各自特质，这时采用直译的方法保留了原文的语言风格，使读者更容易理解原文内涵。

【例 6】

【原文】In the autumnof 2010 le tout Paris of business braced for the sad, if predictable, end of an era. After 173 years and six generations, Hermès, a purveyor of handbags to bankers and neckties to their husbands, was to become part of LVMH. The champagne - to - evening - gowns mastodon, home to Louis Vuitton and Christian Dior, among many others, had disclosed a stake of 17% and rising. Bernard Arnault, LVMH's boss, with a knack for closing in on companies he admires, had only to pick off a few Hermes heirs ready to cash out. Bankers assumed the "wolf in cashmere" would take mere weeks to gobble up his elegant prey.

【译文】2010 年秋季的巴黎商业圈生意悲惨，不出所料还见证了一个时代的落幕。爱马仕是一家为银行家们提供手袋，为丈夫们提供领带的公司。经过 173 年六代人的努力，这家公司准备加入酩悦·轩尼诗 - 路易·威登集团（LVMH）。LVMH 这家奢侈品巨头业务广泛，从香槟到晚礼服，名下还拥有路易威登和迪奥等众多品牌，这家公司已经披露持有爱马仕 17% 甚至更多的股份。LVMH 的老板贝尔纳·阿尔诺很擅长接近自己欣赏的公司，他只需要接近几位准备接手爱马仕的继承人即可。银行家们认为这匹“披着羊皮的狼”只需几周就能吞下优雅的猎物。

原文 & 译文来源：http：//www. kekenet. com/menu/202009/618216. shtml

【分析】原文采用隐喻的修辞手段将 LVMH 老板面对要收购公司的狠辣

和奸诈，带有一种幽默色彩，译文保留了这一修辞手段，采用直译的翻译方法也就保留了这一幽默特性，吸引读者的好奇心和关注。

第二节　意译法

一、意译的界定

意译指的是译文形式不同于原文形式，但内容信息保持一致。意译的翻译方法不受原文词语的限制，不拘泥于原文的句子结构，用译语语言的组织形式及习惯性表达方法将原语信息更为流畅的表达出来。意译主要体现在词汇、语句和语篇这三个方面。下面，我们用实例来分析如何通过意译法来翻译财经新闻的词汇、句子结构和语篇结构。

二、意译法的具体应用

（一）词汇的意译

在财经新闻翻译时，译者需要用意译法翻译以下词汇：（1）按照独特英语构词法产生的词汇，（2）已有约定俗成意译名的专业词汇。用意译法翻译这样的词汇，可以使词汇译文容易被译语受众理解和接受，使译文流畅自然。

【例 7】

【原文】From monthly rentals to circular product swapping, more retailers are catering the whims of shoppers who are inclined to invest in what they fantasize their homes and lives to be for occasions, but not forever. Rent The Runway spotlighted this purchasing proclivity with its recent expansion into reusable home furnishings through a partnership with West Elm.

【译文】有些购物者的消费旨趣往往在于不时翻新家居和生活，而非经年不变。为迎合这类购物者的心血来潮，越来越多的零售商采用按月租赁或产品循环交换使用的销售方式。Rent The Runway（RTR）公司最近与 West Elm 公司合作，将业务扩张到了重复使用家居用品，此举令这一消费趋势备受关注。(《英语世界》, 2019 (6), 55)

【分析】这篇译文对部分专业词汇进行意译，使原文内容更加清楚明白。原文的“fantasize”原意为“幻想”，“home”意为“住房”，因此“who are inclined to invest in what they fantasize their homes and lives”直译版本应为“他们倾向于投资能够用于幻想住房和生活的东西”，显然直译显得呆板且表意不明。而译文则采用了意译的方法，将“fantasize their homes and lives”翻译为“翻新家居和生活”，“fantasize”译为“翻新”，“home”的意义被具体化，意译为“家居”，并且“将 inclined to invest”翻译为“消费旨趣”，使译文更符合原文语境，同时完美的表达了原文的隐藏含义，清晰易懂。

【例 8】

【原文】And it's lucrative. The resale market alone is expected to generate ＄41 billion by 2020, while the sharing economy is projected to reach ＄335 billion by 2025. Those projections borrow from the belief that sharing, renting and swapping will extend into a variety of categories, such as the large home furnishings sector.

【译文】这种模式还有利可图。到 2020 年，仅转售市场的产值就有望达到 410 亿美元，而到 2025 年，共享经济产值预计将高达 3350 亿美元。这些预测源自这样一种理念，即共享、租赁和交换将扩展到大型家具等多种商品类别（《英语世界》, 2019 (06), 57）。

【分析】该段译文也采用了意译的方法。原文为“generate ＄41 billion”，直译版本应为“产生 410 亿美元”，而译文基于整个新闻背景，将其意译为“转售市场的市值就有望达到 410 亿美元”，运用财经术语“转售市场的市值”，使译文的语言更加符合财经新闻的用词要求。

（二）句子结构的意译

英语财经新闻中常有许多符合英语思维表达方式却与汉语思维表达方式不一样的句子结构。对于这一类句子结构，译者也应对其采取意译的翻译方法，从而使译文避免翻译腔，能够满足目标读者的阅读习惯，符合目标读者的思维表达方式。

【例 9】

【原文】What is consistent across all of these services is users have the option to own what they rent. But even then, shoppers should think about their product's next life. Because somewhere, there will likely be a service or merchant prepared to re - enter these items into the economy, to be refurbished, rented or shared without the commitment of ownership. No sale, or experience, will be final.

【译文】上述所有这些服务的共同点是，用户有权选择购进自己租用的商品。但即便如此，购物者还是应该考虑所购商品一旦用完要如何处理。因为在某个地方，很可能会有某个服务公司或商家准备将这些商品重新投入市场，在不固定所有权的前提下翻新、租赁或共享。未来，将不再有一锤子买卖或体验了（《英语世界》，2019（06），59）。

【分析】本段最后一句采取意译方法。首先译者在翻译“be final”套用了中国的俗语“一锤定音”，避开了“be final”的原有意义，使译文富含新闻特点的同时带有幽默色彩。其次，译者改变了原句结构，将原句中的主语“no sale or experience”变成了译文中的宾语部分，并且添加上“未来”一词，使译文时间线更加明确。

【例 10】

【原文】China's Economy

Asnorthern China struggles, the south surges ahead.

"Don't invest beyond Shanhaiguan" is a popular quip in China, referring to a pass in the Great Wall that leads to the north - eastern rust belt. Online pundits have updated the maxim to "don't invest outsidethe Southern Song", a dynasty that fell almost 750 years ago whose territory was roughly the same as China's southern half today. The joke has a nub of truth: China's southern provinces are outperforming the north in nearly every economic dimension.

Figures released on January 18th showed that China's GDP grew by 2. 3% in 2020. The recovery was unbalanced, with factories at full throttle but consumption subdued. That should improve after the pandemic ends. The north -

south imbalance, though, is likely to outlast it.

The south's share of GDP has risen to a peak of 65%, from 59% in 2015. Some of that is down to luck. The north, home to China's largest coal mines and oil reserves, was caught out by falls in commodity prices after 2013. It also boasts big industrial firms; China's shift from construction - fuelled growth towards consumption and services has hurt.

Northern officials have tried harder to goose up growth, to the region's detriment. In 2013, the peak of China's building frenzy, investment in assets suchas roads and factories reached an eyewatering 66% of GDP in the north versus 51% in the south. Southern officials have been more hands - off. China's two most dynamic regions are in the south, anchored by Shanghai and Shenzhen. The south also makes the smartphones and sofas lapped up globally. Its foreign - trade surplus last year was about 7% of GDP. The north ran a 2% deficit.

To add insult to injury, the north has also been disrupted more by sporadic covid - 19 outbreaks. Geography is part of the problem: a harsher winter makes the virus more transmissible. The north is stuck out in the cold.

【译文】

在中国北方挣扎之际，南方却奋起直追

“不要投资山海关以外的地方”在中国是一个很流行的讽刺语，说的是通往东北铁锈地带的长城关隘。网络权威人士将这则格言更新为“不要投资南宋以外的地方”，南宋是一个朝代，在大约750年前就灭亡了，其领土大致相当于今天中国的南半部。这个笑话有一点道理：中国南方省份在几乎所有经济领域的表现都优于北方省份。

1月18日公布的数据显示，2020年中国GDP增长了2.3%。经济的复苏是不平衡的，工厂马力全开，但消费受到抑制。新冠肺炎疫情结束后情况可能会有所改善，但是，南北方之间发展的不平衡可能会持续更久。

南方占GDP的比重从2015年的59%上升到65%的峰值，这在一定程度上要归功于运气。2013年之后，拥有中国最大煤矿和石油储量的北方受到了大宗商品价格下跌的影响。北方还拥有大型工业企业，中国经济增长从建筑驱动型向消费和服务驱动型的转变已对其造成损害。

北方官员一直在努力刺激经济增长，但这对该地区不利。2013 年，中国的建筑热潮达到顶峰，在公路和工厂等资产上的投资达到了令人瞠目的 GDP 的 66%，而在南方则是 51%。南方官员则更加不干涉。中国最具活力的两个地区位于南部，以上海和深圳为中心。南方还生产风靡全球的智能手机和沙发。中国去年的对外贸易顺差约为 GDP 的 7%，北方有 2% 的赤字。

雪上加霜的是，北方也更多地受到了零星暴发的新冠肺炎疫情的影响。地理位置也是问题的一部分：严冬令病毒更具传染性，而北方寒冷刺骨。

原文 & 译文链接：http：//www. kekenet. com/menu/202102/624277. shtml

【分析】该篇译文不仅在词汇翻译方面多次运用意译法，在句子翻译层面也多次使用了意译。如“The north, home to China's largest coal mines and oil reserves, was caught out by falls in commodity prices after 2013.”原句中“home to China's largest coal mines and oil reserves”作为插入语与主句衔接，这种句子安排方式在汉语中并不常见。译文“2013 年之后，拥有中国最大煤矿和石油储量的北方受到了大宗商品价格下跌的影响”将原句中的插入语成分意译成了定语成分，同时改变了原句中的时间“after 2013”，将其放在句首翻译，从而符合汉语中将时间状语放在句首的习惯，满足了目标语读者的阅读习惯。

（三）语篇结构的意译

语篇结构的意译是指把原语本文中的段落衔接方式用译语文本常见的段落衔接方式。英语财经新闻中，常有多个段落依照“主—述”句相互串接的方式来呈现段落衔接。汉语读者往往会感觉这样的语篇结构呈现的信息是碎片式的，语篇意义不连贯。所以，译者有翻译财经新闻时，可以把原文的几个段落整合成一个段落，减少整个语篇的段落数，并且在不同的段落中突显不同的主题信息。这样做，从语篇层面讲，其实也可以看作是一种语篇结构的意译。

【例 11】

【原文】

In the rich world the era of sharp - edged capitalism is giving way to a golden age for labour.

In the popular imagination the past four decades were wonderful for the owners of capital and miserable for labour. The rich world's workers endured competition from trade, relentless technological change, more unequal wages and tepid recoveries from recessions. Investors and companies enjoyed expanding global markets, liberalised finance and low corporate taxes. Even before covid - 19, this caricature of broken labour markets was mistaken. Today, as the economy emerges from the pandemic, a reversal of the primacy of capital over labour beckons—and it will come sooner than you think.

It might seem premature to predict a wonderful world of work only a year on from a labour - market catastrophe. But America is showing how rapidly jobs can come back as the virus recedes. In the spring of 2020 the country's unemployment rate was nearly 15%. Now it is already just 6% after a year containing five of the ten best months for hiring in history. Public perceptions of how easy it is to find a job have already recovered to levels that it took nearly a decade to reach after the global financial crisis. And even in Europe, which is suffering a third wave of infections, the labour market is beating forecasts as economies adapt to virus - containment measures.

As the labour market recovers, two deeper shifts are unfolding, in politics and in technology. Start with the political environment, which is becoming friendlier to workers than it has been for decades. An early sign of change was the surge in minimum wages during the previous economic cycle. Relative to average wages, they rose by more than a quarter in the OECD, a club of mostly rich countries, weighted by population. Now governments and institutions are falling over themselves to chum up to workers. President Joe Biden hopes to use his planned infrastructure splurge to promote unionisation and to pay generous wages. Central banks are worrying ever more about jobs and less about inflation. It was not a prank when on April 1st the IMF, once famed for its austerity, floated the idea of one - off solidarity taxes on the rich and on companies. In his letter to shareholders this week, Jamie Dimon, the boss of JPMorgan Chase, Wall Street's biggest firm, called for higher wages—and he wasn't talking about CEOs.

The second big shift in the labour market is technological. In the pandemic doomsayers have doubled down on predictions of long - term labour - market woes. Robots will create armies of the idle, precarious jobs are displacing stable ones and even prosperous workers chained to emails and screens know in their hearts that their "bullshit jobs" are pointless. But as our special report this week explains, these ideas were never supported by evidence and do not look as if they are about to be now. In 2019 nearly two - thirds of Americans said they were completely satisfied with their job security, up from less than half in 1999; a lower share of German workers felt insecure than in the mid - 2000s. Countries with the most automation, like Japan, enjoy some of the lowest unemployment.

【来源】http://www.kekenet.com/Article/202104/626582.shtml

【译文】

在发达国家，尖锐的资本主义时代正在退位让贤于劳动大军的黄金时代。

在公众心目中，过去四十年对资本所有者来说是美好的，但对劳动者来说却是痛苦的。贸易竞争、无休止的技术革新、工资不平等加剧以及经济衰退后的复苏乏力一直折磨着富裕国家的打工人们。而投资者和公司却享受着全球市场的扩张、金融的自由化和较低的企业税。甚至在新冠肺炎疫情之前，这种对崩溃的劳动力市场的滑稽描述也是错误的。如今，伴随全球经济从疫情中复苏，资本优先于劳动力的局势正在逆转，而且其到来将远比你想象的快。

预测打工人将迎来美好的职场似乎还为时过早，毕竟现在距离劳动力市场困境只有一年的时间。但美国正在展示随着新冠肺炎疫情的消退，他们能以多快的速度迅速恢复就业机会。在 2020 年春天，美国的失业率接近 15%。一年后（在有史以来招聘情况最好的 10 个月中，有 5 个月涵盖在这一年里）的美国失业率如今仅为 6%。公众对找工作有多容易的看法，已经恢复到全球金融危机后近十年才达到的水平。即使是在正遭受第三波感染冲击的欧洲，随着各经济体逐渐适应病毒控制措施，劳动力市场的情况也在超出预期。

伴随劳动力市场复苏，两个更深层次的转变开始在政治层面和技术层面展开。首先是政治环境的改变。与过去几十年相比，政治环境对打工人来说越来越友好。该变化的一个早期迹象就是上一个经济周期中最低工资的激增。在主要由富裕国家组成的经合组织（OCED）中，相较于平均工资，其最低工资按人口加权增长超过四分之一。如今，各国政府和机构都在竭力拉拢打工人。拜登总统希望利用他计划的大量投资基础设施建设来促进工会组织的建立，并支付丰厚的工资。各国央行对就业的担忧与日俱增，对通货膨胀的担忧却越来越少。4 月 1 日，曾靠经济紧缩打天下的国际货币基金组织（IMF）提出了对富人和企业征收一次性团结税的想法，这并非玩笑。华尔街最大的公司摩根大通（JPMorgan Chase）的老板杰米·戴蒙本周在致股东的信中呼吁涨薪，但他并不是在谈论给高层涨薪。

劳动力市场的第二大转变是技术。在此次疫情期间，因为预测到劳动力市场会面临长期困境，悲观主义者已经翻倍。机器人将创造出劳动力闲置大军，不稳定的工作岗位取代稳定的工作岗位，即使是那些受电子邮件和屏幕羁绊的富裕员工心里也知道自己的工作毫无意义。但正如我们本周的特别报道所解释的那样，这些观点从未得到证据支持，而且看起来也与当前实际情况有出入。2019 年，近三分之二的美国人表示，他们对自己的工作保障完全满意，相较于 1999 年不到一半的满意度有所上涨；与 2000 年代中期相比，对工作没有安全感的德国员工的比例有所下降。日本等自动化程度最高的国家失业率最低。

【来源】http：//www. kekenet. com/Article/202104/626582. shtml

【分析】

在这篇译文中，译者多次添加衔接词，以体现语篇内的衔接性。

原句“In the popular imagination the past four decades were wonderful for the owners of capital and miserable for labour”中，两个小句虽然是用“and”连接起来，但两个小句之间却存在着资本家和打工人之间的对比关系，因此译文“在公众心目中，过去四十年对资本所有者来说是美好的，但对劳动者来说却是痛苦的”中用“但”一词将语句内暗含的对比关系表现了出来，实现了语句之间的完美衔接。

原句“It might seem premature to predict a wonderful world of work only a year on from a labour - market catastrophe”中的“only a year on from a labour - market catastrophe”是时间状语，用于说明“现在这个时间不适合进行这些预测”。为了体现这层深层意思并使译文通顺连贯，译文“预测打工人将迎来美好的职场似乎还为时过早，毕竟现在距离劳动力市场困境只有一年的时间”将原句分为两小句翻译，并用“毕竟”引出下文给出的原因，从而将译文顺利衔接，也由此体现了语篇的意译。

【例 12】

【原文】

Pentagon Gives Company Control of Massive Unused Internet Space

The U. S. Department of Defense has given a private company control over a massive part of its unused internet space.

The Florida - based company, identified in news reports as Global Resource Systems, now controls more than 175 million IP addresses belonging to the military. An IP address is a number given to each computer when it is connected to the internet.

The addresses have long been owned by the Defense Department, but were not being used by the agency.

Experts in the computer networking industry had been wondering about the change, which happened the day President Joe Biden was sworn into office in January. Military officials made no official announcement about the move.

The huge number of IP addresses involved has been estimated to be about 1/25th the size of the current internet. It is also thought to be more than twice the size of the internet space actually used by the Pentagon.

"It is massive. That is the biggest thing in the history of the internet," expert Doug Madory told The Associated Press. He is the director of internet analysis at Kentik, a company that designs and operates computer networks.

The Defense Department confirmed the change in a statement by Brett Goldstein, chief of the Pentagon's Defense Digital Service, which is running the project.

The military hopes to "assess, evaluate and prevent" the "unauthorized use" of agency IP address space, the statement said.

It added that the "pilot project" also aims to identify possible "vulnerabilities" that could lead to internet attacks by international groups attempting to break into U. S. networks.

In addition to attempted attacks, the Defense Department has also experienced problems with outside groups or individuals taking over and using its internet space without permission. This happened, in part, because there has been a shortage of first – generation internet addresses since 2011.

Kentik's Madory said advertising the address space will make it easier to get rid of unauthorized users. It should also permit the military to "collect a massive amount of background internet traffic for threat intelligence," he added.

Some cybersecurity experts have suggested the Pentagon may be using the newly advertised space to create so – called "honeypots." These are machines set up with vulnerabilities to draw in internet attackers, or hackers.

The project could also be the start of a new system of software and servers set up to search internet traffic for suspect activity, the experts say. "This greatly increases the space they could monitor," Madory said.

A Defense Department spokesman did not comment on why the military chose Global Resource Systems to oversee the IP addresses. The company, which operates an office in Plantation, Florida, did not return phone calls or emails from The Associated Press seeking information.

A Defense Department spokesman told the AP that even with the current shortage of IP addresses, the Pentagon has no interest in selling any of its unused space.

I'm Bryan Lynn.

【来源】 http://www.kekenet.com/broadcast/202105/626668.shtml

【译文】

私企接管美国防部大量闲置互联网 IP 地址

美国国防部已经授权一家私企接管其大量闲置的互联网空间。

新闻报道称,这家位于佛罗里达州的公司名为"全球资源系统有限公司",目前该公司控制着超过 1.75 亿属于美国军方的 IP 地址。IP 地址是每台计算机连接互联网时被分配的一组数字。

这些地址一直归美国国防部所有,但是该机构并未使用这些地址。

计算机网络行业的专家对这种措施表示不解,这一变动发生在拜登总统 1 月份宣誓就职当天。军方官员并未对这一举措发表任何官方声明。

据估计,这些大量的 IP 地址约占到目前互联网规模的 4%。它也被认为是五角大楼实际使用互联网空间的两倍多。

专家道格·马杜里(Doug Madory)对美联社表示:"它的规模非常庞大,这是互联网历史上最重大的事件。"马杜里是 Kentik 公司的互联网分析主管,这是一家设计和运营计算机网络的公司。

美国国防部通过布雷特·戈德斯坦发布的一份声明证实了这一变化,戈德斯坦是负责该项目的五角大楼国防数字服务部负责人。

这份声明表示,军方希望评估、评价和防止未经授权使用国防部的 IP 地址空间。

声明还补充称,这一"试点项目"旨在发现潜在的漏洞,这些漏洞可能导致试图入侵美国网络的国际组织发起网络攻击。

除了攻击企图,国防部还遇到过外部组织或个人未经批准接管和使用其互联网空间的问题。发生这种情况的部分原因是 2011 年以来,第一代互联网地址一直短缺。

Kentik 公司的马杜里表示,展示这些 IP 地址空间将更容易摆脱未经授权用户。他还表示,这还将允许美国军方"收集大量的后台互联网流量,以获取威胁情报"。

一些网络专家提出，五角大楼可能是在利用这些新展示的互联网空间来制造所谓的“糖衣炮弹”。这些机器设置存在漏洞，旨在吸引互联网攻击者或黑客。

专家们表示，这些项目也可能是开始建立新的软件或服务器系统，用于搜索从事可疑活动的互联网流量。马杜里表示：“这将大大增加他们可监控的空间。”

国防部发言人并未对军方为何选择全球资源系统有限公司来接管这些IP地址发表评论。这家公司在佛罗里达州普兰泰申市设立了办事处，但是该公司并未回复美联社寻求获得更多信息的电话或邮件。

国防部发言人对美联社表示，即使目前IP地址短缺，五角大楼也无意出售其任何闲置网络空间。

【来源】http：//www.kekenet.com/broadcast/202105/626668.shtml

【分析】

首先原文中三次引用他人话语：（1）“It is massive. That is the biggest thing in the history of the internet,” expert Doug Madory told The Associated Press. 专家道格·马杜里（Doug Madory）对美联社表示：“它的规模非常庞大，这是互联网历史上最重大的事件。”（2）It should also permit the military to “collect a massive amount of background internet traffic for threat intelligence,” he added. 他还表示，这还将允许美国军方“收集大量的后台互联网流量，以获取威胁情报。”（3）“This greatly increases the space they could monitor,” Madory said. 马杜里表示：“这将大大增加他们可监控的空间。”

很明显，原文语句均是先给出话语内容，再引出说话人。然而这种衔接方式却并不符合汉语读者的阅读习惯，容易导致汉语读者阅读混乱。因此译文都将其改成了先点明说话人是谁再引出说话内容的模式。译文由此显得更加流畅，脉络也更加清晰。

此外译文还注重段落之间的衔接情况。

如原文“The Defense Department confirmed the change in a statement by Brett Goldstein, chief of the Pentagon's Defense Digital Service, which is running the project. The military hopes to “assess, evaluate and prevent” the “unauthorized use” of agency IP address space, the statement said. It added that the “pilot project" also aims to identify possible "vulnerabilities" that could lead to internet attacks by international groups attempting to break into U. S. networks. " 原文中这三句话各成一段，但都与美国国防部发的一个声明相关。然而，这三句话之间的衔接性却不明显。于是，译者在译文中做出部分改动，使其中的衔接性更加鲜明。与原文对应的译文为"美国国防部通过布雷特·戈德斯坦发布的一份声明证实了这一变化，戈德斯坦是负责该项目的五角大楼国防数字服务部负责人。这份声明表示，军方希望评估、评价和防止未经授权使用国防部的 IP 地址空间。声明还补充称，这一"试点项目"旨在发现潜在的漏洞，这些漏洞可能导致试图入侵美国网络的国际组织发起网络攻击。"该译文中第一句的"一份声明"、第二句开头的"这份声明表示"与第三句开头的"声明还补充称"使这三段内容完美衔接，前后连贯，降低了阅读难度，使文章层次更加清晰。这是篇章意译的一个体现。

第三节　节译法

一、节译的界定

方梦之（2019：320）在《应用翻译研究》一书中提到，节译，或称选译，即有选择地翻译全文的一部分或大部分。其中节译主要有两种方式，一个是选择全文的主要信息，删去枝节；另一个是选择读者感兴趣的信息。

节译的原则有：一，针对性，节译的内容和含量根据读者的需要而定；二，客观性，节译的译法跟全译一样，对所译部分要确切传达原意，不得加入译者个人的思想；三，简明性，既然是节译，目的就是剪枝裁叶，删繁就简，简单明了。(方梦之，2019：320 - 321)

二、节译的具体应用

（一）挑选重要信息进行节译

对读者而言，阅读新闻的目的就是想要迅速掌握最新时事消息。因而在翻译财经新闻时，译者常常会直接节选新闻报道中的重要信息进行节译，这样方便读者捕捉最重要的新闻信息。

【原文】

World food price index rises in March for 10th month running – FAO

ROME (Reuters) – World food prices rose for a 10th consecutive month in March, hitting their highest level since June 2014, led by jumps in vegetable oils, meat and dairy indices, the United Nations food agency said on Thursday.

The Food and Agriculture Organization's food price index, which measures monthly changes for a basket of cereals, oilseeds, dairy products, meat and sugar, averaged 118. 5 points last month versus a slightly revised 116. 1 in February. The February figure was previously given as 116. 0.

The Rome – basedFAO also said in a statement that worldwide cereal harvests remained on course to hit an annual record in 2020, adding that early indications pointed to a further increase in production this year.

FAO's cereal price index fell 1. 7% month on month in March, ending eight months of consecutive gains, but still 26. 5% higher than the same period last month.

Among major cereals, wheat export prices dropped the most, declining 2. 4% on the month, reflecting good supplies and encouraging production prospects for the 2021 crops, FAO said.

FAO's vegetable oil price index surged 8. 0% on the month to reach its highest level since June 2011, lifted by higher prices for palm, soy, rape and sunflower oils. Dairy prices rose for a 10th month running, registering a 3. 9% increase. FAO said one of the drivers in the sector was milk powder, which *was boosted by a surge in imports in Asia*, especially China, due to concerns over short – term supplies.

The meat index climbed 2. 3%, but unlike all the other indices, it was still slightly down on a year – on – year basis. FAO said poultry and pig meat quotations increased, underpinned by a fast pace of imports by Asian countries, mainly China.

Sugar prices dropped 4.0% month on month, but was still up 30% on the year. March's decline was fuelled by prospects of large exports from India, FAO said.

FAO raised its forecast for the 2020 cereal season to 2.765 billion tonnes from a previous estimate of 2.761 billion, pointing to a 2.0% increase year on year.

Looking ahead, FAO said it expected global cereal production to increase for a third consecutive year in 2021.

Global wheat production was seen hitting a new high of 785 million tonnes this year, up 1.4% from 2020 levels, driven by an anticipated sharp rebound across most of Europe and expectations of a record harvest in India, FAO said.

Above - average outputs were also expected for maize, with a record harvest forecast for Brazil and a multi - year high predicted for South Africa.

For the current 2020/21 marketing season, global cereal utilisation was forecast at 2.777 billion tonnes, 2.4% up on the previous year, driven largely by higher estimates of feed use of wheat and barley in China, where the livestock sector is recovering from African swine fever.

【来源】https://www.reuters.com/article/global - economy - food - idINKBN2BV1BB

【译文】

外媒：全球食品价格连涨10个月

据路透社罗马4月8日报道，联合国粮农组织当地时间周四表示，在植物油、肉类和乳制品价格指数大涨的带动下，今年3月全球食品价格连续第10个月上涨，达到自2014年6月以来的最高水平。

报道称，粮农组织的食品价格指数衡量多种谷物、含油种子、乳制品、肉类和糖类的月度价格变化。今年3月，该指数的平均值为118.5，而2月的修正后数值为116.1（修正前数值为116.0）。

总部设在罗马的粮农组织在一份声明中说，2020年全球谷物收成将创年度纪录，而且初步迹象表明，今年的谷物产量将进一步增加。

今年3月，谷物价格指数环比下降1.7%，结束了连续8个月的上涨幅，但仍比去年同期高出26.5%。

粮农组织说，在主要谷物中，小麦的出口价格跌幅最大（为2.4%），这反映出供应状况良好，且2021年谷物产量前景乐观。

报道还称，受棕榈油、大豆油、菜籽油和葵花籽油价格上涨的提振，植物油价格指数3月上涨8.0%，达到2011年6月以来的最高水平。乳制品价格连续第10个月上涨，涨幅为3.9%。粮农组织说，奶粉是推动价格上涨的因素之一。由于对短期供应感到担忧，亚洲（尤其是中国）奶粉进口激增。

【来源】http://www.cankaoxiaoxi.com/finance/20210410/2440062.shtml

【分析】

原文中，路透社将各类全球食品价格的涨幅都进行了具体描述，还对整体价格涨幅作了一些预期判断和分析，而译文中只节选了整体涨幅和有关谷物价格的涨幅以及植物油类的价格进行了翻译。对中国读者而言，他们更关心的就是整体性的涨幅和谷物类价格，因而译者选取相比更重要的信息进行了节译。

（二）针对特定读者进行节译

不同读者会选择不同的新闻网站选择自己需要了解的新闻信息，因而，在进行财经新闻翻译时，译者常常会针对自己所在网站的一些特定读者进行节译。

【原文】

Cryptocurrency Market Surpasses $2 Trillion for First Time Ever

The combined market cap of all cryptocurrencies hit $2 trillion for the first time Monday, making cryptocurrency as a whole approximately as valuable as Apple, the second - largest company in the world.

Data released by CoinGecko and other cryptocurrency analysis groups revealed that the market as a whole pushed beyond $2 trillion on April 5. The milestone comes less than three months after it surpassed $1 trillion in overall value on January 7. Crypto investors and other supporters of decentralized finance factions, including Bitcoin and Ethereum, rejoiced at the news Monday morning, taking to social media to reiterate that cryptocurrencies are the future of world finance.

Institutional and retail investors have flocked to the cryptocurrency market since the start of the year, analysts said, pushing many blockchain backers to encourage others to join the massive movement into decentralized finance.

"#BTC is still just consolidating inside this range. It is this consolidation that has helped $ETH breakout to new All Time Highs. #ETH is arguably leading the market whereas $BTC is trying to catch up. Good sign so far is that orange resistance is struggling to reject #Bitcoin," wrote the pseudonymous trader known as "Rekt Capital" on Monday.

Other top investors in cryptocurrency once again touted the market's bullish ability to defy potential regulators and thrive moving forward.

"Decentralized finance (DeFi) is as significant an innovation as double entry accounting and is a great example of how Ethereum is leveraging blockchain technology," said cryptocurrency investor and entrepreneur, Correll Lashbrook, to Newsweek on Monday, adding that he's "more interested in tech than being greedy."

"Crypotcurrencies are now worth $2 trillion," Blockfolio tweeted Monday morning, prompting optimistic replies, including, "Cryptocurrencies will soon be worth $5 trillion."

Numerous factors and theories emerged to explain the rapid expansion of the market, with the strong recent performance of ETH as well as Bitcoin's approach to $60000 topping the list.

Leading New York investment manager Cathie Wood of Ark Invest told The Times of London newspaper on Monday that Bitcoin, the world's largest cryptocurrency, will "comfortably" eclipse gold's $10 trillion market capitalization.

Bitcoin's volatility has dropped to its lowest level since November 2020, CoinTelegraph reported on Monday, noting that its value has nearly doubled since January 7, when its price was around $33000. It has remained steady above $50000 fornearly one month, which has helped Ether and the altcoin market from "seeing a severe pullback."

Major changes within the cryptocurrency market were announced simultaneously on Monday. The website domain for Bitcoin. com was put up for sale at a price of $100 million, GoDaddy announced, adding that bitcoin. co. uk sold for more than $25000.

At midday, the market cap for cryptocurrencies as a whole hit $2.02 trillion. Newsweek reached out to several Bitcoin, Litecoin and Ether figures on Monday for additional remarks about the successful expansion.

After Morgan Stanley last week announced it would begin offering access to Bitcoin funds for its wealthy clients, Galaxy Digital CEO Mike Novogratz told bitcoin. com that more and more banks will increase exposure tothe crypto market in the coming months. "It could be as much as a trillion dollars comes over the next year from that giant group of wealth," he said.

原文链接：https://www.newsweek.com/cryptocurrency-market-surpasses-2-trillion-first-time-ever-1581078

【译文】

美媒：加密货币市值突破两万亿美元

参考消息网4月7日报道 美国《新闻周刊》网站4月5日发表题为《加密货币市场规模首次突破2万亿美元》的报道称，4月5日，所有加密货币的总市值首次达到2万亿美元。这使得加密货币的整体价值与世界科技巨头苹果公司不相上下。全文摘编如下：

币虎网站和其他加密货币分析组织发布的数据显示，整个加密货币市场的规模在4月5日突破2万亿美元。这一里程碑距离1月7日加密货币总市值突破1万亿美元还不到3个月。这个消息令比特币、以太币等加密货币的投资者以及其他去中心化金融资产的支持者感到欢欣鼓舞，他们在社交媒体上重申加密货币是世界金融的未来。分析人士说，自今年年初以来，机构和散户投资者纷纷涌入加密货币市场，促使许多区块链支持者鼓励其他投资者加入这场转向金融去中心化的大规模运动。

一位笔名为“Rekt Capital”的交易者当地时间周一写道：“比特币仍在这个区间内进行盘整。正是它的盘整帮助以太币突破了历史新高。以太币可以说正在引领市场，而比特币正在努力迎头赶上。”

加密货币的其他主要投资者再次吹嘘了加密货币市场无视潜在监管而继续上涨并蓬勃发展的能力。

加密货币投资者和企业家科雷尔·莱什布鲁克当地时间周一对《新闻周刊》记者说：“去中心化金融是一种与复式记账会计同样重要的创新，也是以太坊平台对区块链技术加以利用的绝佳例证。”他还说自己“更感兴趣的是技术，而不是贪婪”。

布洛克福利奥公司当地时间周一上午发布了“加密货币现在价值2万亿美元”的推文，这引发了乐观的回复，包括“加密货币的市值很快将达5万亿美元”。

人们给出了许多原因和理论来解释该市场的迅速上涨——以太币近期表现强劲和比特币价格逼近6万美元。

美国方舟投资公司的知名投资人凯茜·伍德当地时间周一对英国《泰晤士报》记者说，世界第一大加密货币比特币将“轻松”地盖过拥有10万亿美元市值的黄金。

据美国币电讯当地时间周一报道，比特币的波动性已经降至2020年11月以来的最低水平。它指出，比特币价格在1月7日还徘徊在3.3万美元上下，而自那之后已接近翻番。近一个月以来，比特币价格一直稳定在5万美元以上，帮助以太币和加密货币市场免于“大幅回落”。

译文链接：http：//m. ce. cn/gj/gd/202104/08/t20210408_36450778. shtml

▶ **点评：**

这篇报道原文是美国《新闻周刊》网站4月5日报道，译文是参考消息网的报道。整个翻译过程中，整篇采用节译的方法，基本保留了原文报道，同时又进行了部分删节，这是考虑到新闻的快、短、平等特点，将主要信息即一些代表性的评论节选翻译，同时保留原文整体信息内容，很大程度上让读者以最短的时间获取想了解的信息，符合新闻翻译的特点。

（三）挑选正面信息进行节译

有时，为了某些需求，只节译出原文中呈现的下面的信息，对读者会有帮助，也对政治、经济、社会的稳定有重要意义。

【例 13】

【原文】

Sanctions row threatens EU – China investment deal

Diplomatic escalation between Brussels and Beijing deepens uncertainty over treaty.

The EU's trade policy chief has warned that China's decision to escalate a sanctions row risks imperilling a market – access deal meant to be the cornerstone of future relations between Brussels and Beijing.

Valdis Dombrovskis, the EU's trade commissioner, said that the fate of the freshly negotiated EU – China Comprehensive Agreement on Investment—or CAI—was tied up with the diplomatic dispute, which erupted this week.

"China's retaliatory sanctions are regrettable and unacceptable," Dombrovskis said. "The prospects for the CAI's ratification will depend on how the situation evolves," he explained. "The ratification process cannot be separated from the evolving dynamics of the wider EU – China relationship."

The European Commission was already navigating choppy political waters over its decision last year to agree an investment treaty with Beijing—a move that has been attacked by human rights groups as placing the interests of business ahead of fundamental values. But the deal's fate is even more uncertain following China's decision on Monday to place sanctions on members of the European Parliament, the assembly that must decide whether the deal should ever take effect.

"The EU has been making every effort to foster a balanced, rules – based economic relationship with China, and the CAI was a major step in that direction," Dombrovskis said. "But our trade and economic agenda has European values at its core: pursuing our economic interest goes hand in hand with standing up for our values, including where necessary through sanctions."

While the politics of the CAI become ever more complicated, the economic rationale for the EU of concluding it has always been clear. It has been a long-term goal of the EU's policy towards Beijing.

The bulk of the deal, struck at the end of last year, is focused on opening up investment opportunities for EU companies operating on the Chinese market—addressing longstanding complaints about unfair treatment, and warding off the risk of EU firms operating in China at a disadvantage compared with US rivals. Specifically, it offers possibilities for European companies to increase production in promising fields such as electric cars, while eliminating requirements in some sectors to partner with local firms.

But the European Parliament's large centre-left Socialists and Democrats group has already made clear that ending the sanctions against the parliament is a "precondition" for work on ratifying the investment agreement to advance. MEPs point to the political impossibility of the parliament voting through an economic pact with a country actively attacking its members.

Even before the current row, MEPs involved in the process had emphasised that ratification would hinge in part on China providing a "road map" for implementing international conventions against the use of forced labour, and engaging with other EU human rights concerns.

Brussels secured commitments from China in these areas as part of the deal, but critics have argued that they do not go far enough.

Iuliu Winkler, lead MEP on China for the parliament's trade committee, told the Financial Times that China's decision to retaliate in the sanctions dispute amounted to "a regrettable escalation". "What I hope is that diplomacy will find a way of de-escalating," he said. "We need to build some trust, for the moment there is none between the parties."

China announced the sanctions on Monday as retaliation against travel bans and asset freezes imposed on four Chinese officials and a security organisation because of persecution and mass internments of Uyghurs in the Xinjiang region. The moves were a co – ordinated step by the EU, US, Canada and UK, prompting a furious response from the Chinese government.

China's foreign ministry announced on Tuesday that it had summoned the UK ambassador and the EU delegation representative the previous night to admonish them over the sanctions.

"When it comes to human rights, the EU has no qualification to take the mantle of a master who arrogantly lectures others," deputy foreign minister Qin Gang told EU ambassador Nicolas Chapuis, warning that the sanctions would further damage EU – China relations.

The Chinese retaliatory sanctions hit outspoken critics in the parliament of Beijing's human – rights violations, including five MEPs—among them Reinhard Bütikofer, chair of the assembly's delegation to China, and Raphaël Glucksmann, chair of a special committee on "Foreign Interference in all Democratic Processes". The measures ban them from entering China or "doing business" with it. The parliament's human rights committee was also targeted.

Winkler and other MEPs insist that there is time to salvage the situation before the real ratification process for the agreement gets under way—a step that is unlikely until late this year given the need totranslate the agreement into all of the EU's 24 official languages. But that would require China to lift sanctions and pivot to constructively addressing EU concerns.

Inma Rodríguez – Piñero, lead MEP on China trade issues for the parliament's large centre – left bloc, told the FT that "there is time enough in order to redirect the situation". "I don't believe either China or the EU wants this escalated situation," she said, adding that "now is time to wait," for diplomacy to run its course.

On paper, the benefits for China of the investment deal are largely confined to limited and reciprocal access to the EU market for renewable energy.

But EU diplomats have noted that the real attraction for Beijing was the political upside: the deal offers the potential for an improved relationship with the EU at a time when the US is seeking to put co – ordinated pressure on China, and when Brussels is readying new methods of retaliation against unfair or exploitative trading practices.

"In the short term, China's biggest consideration is to let Europe remain neutral in the US – China dispute, so the CAI is more like a carrot that China has offered. Between China and Europe, it's easier for Europe to let go of the CAI," said Bo Zhuang, chief China economist at TS Lombard in Beijing.

Despite the incentives for both sides to push the deal through, EU politicians acknowledge that its fate hangs in the balance.

"CAI is not on the table now," said Winkler of the ratification process. "There is a long road leading there—along that path China has to respond to the expectations of the European Parliament".

原文链接：https：//www. ft. com/content/6b236a71 – 512e – 4561 – a73c – b1d69b7f486b

【译文】

欧盟贸易专员东布罗夫斯基：中欧协定能否得到欧盟批准，取决于事态如何发展

欧盟配合美国炒作人权问题、制裁涉疆人员和机构，在中方强烈谴责并立刻反制后，中欧关系陷入了紧张的局面。随后，欧洲议会决定取消中欧全面投资协定审议会。这份决定中欧关系的协定未来进展究竟如何，据《金融时报》（FT）24 日报道，欧盟贸易专员瓦尔迪斯·东布罗夫斯基（Valdis Dombrovskis）认为，"中欧全面投资协定（CAI）能否得到（欧盟）批准，取决于事态如何发展"，"批准程序不可能独立于中国—欧盟关系最新动向的大背景。"

东布罗夫斯基声称，"我们的经贸议程是以欧洲价值观为核心：在追求经济利益的同时，倡导我们的价值观，包括在必要的时候，实施制裁。"他还无理指责"中国的报复性制裁是令人遗憾、无法接受的。"但矛盾的是，他同时表示不希望中国和欧盟之间的冲突进一步升级。"欧盟一直在尽一切努力与中国建立一种平衡的、基于规则的经济关系，而中欧全面投资协定是朝着这个方向迈出的重要一步。"

欧洲议会中一个较大的中左翼团体“社会主义和民主人士进步联盟”（S&D）表示，（中国）结束对议会成员的制裁是批准中欧全面投资协定的“先决条件”。几位欧洲议会议员甚至宣称，他们不可能对“一个积极攻击其成员的国家的经济协定”进行投票。

但是，还有一些议员的态度微妙，他们希望通过外交方式缓和局势。欧洲议会贸易委员会负责中国事务的议员尤留·温克勒（Iuliu Winkler）表示，中国在制裁争端中进行报复的决定相当于“令人遗憾的升级”。但他说：“我希望外交努力能找到缓和局势的方法。”

欧洲议会负责对华贸易的议员罗德里格斯—皮涅罗（Inma Rodríguez-Piero）则相信，“有足够的时间改变局势”。她补充道：“现在应该等待外交努力发挥作用。”

酝酿7年，去年12月底，中国和欧盟委员会完成了具有里程碑意义的中欧投资协定谈判，旨在推动包括德国汽车制造商在内等欧洲大型投资者的在华投资。

当时，欧盟委员会主席冯德莱恩亲自认定该协定的重要性，将其称为欧盟对华关系的“重要里程碑”（an important landmark）。

2020年12月30日晚，中欧领导人举行了视频会晤，并共同宣布如期完成中欧投资协定谈判。

但眼看协定在欧洲走到最后一步，中欧关系又因欧方的动作变得紧张。

中欧全面投资协定需要欧洲议会批准才能生效。欧洲议会原定23日就签署协定举行审议会。但上周，欧盟多国突然与美国、英国和加拿大联手，再次炒作涉疆人权议题，对负责新疆事务的官员实施制裁。很快，中方也对等宣布对欧洲10名个人和4个实体实行制裁，其中包括多名欧洲议会的议员、欧洲一些智库和学者。

值此之际，美国国务卿布林肯访问北约，再次对中欧贸易合作指指点点。据路透社3月24日报道，他在北约会议后的新闻发布会上妄称，是否对欧盟“履行承诺”、向欧洲开放经济“取决于中国”。而在另一场讲话中，布林肯又假惺惺地声称，美国不会强迫盟国“选边站”。

对于欧盟配合美国主动挑起制裁事端，15个中国驻欧盟国家使馆已在 3 月 22 日 ~24 日向驻在国提出严正交涉。

而就欧洲议会决定取消《中欧全面投资协定》的审议会议一事，中国外交部发言人华春莹在 24 日例行记者会上回应称，中欧投资协定不是一方给予另一方的“恩赐”，是互利互惠的。

译文链接：https：//baijiahao. baidu. com/s？id = 1695173566128861185&wfr = spider&for = pc

【分析】

这篇报道节译了原文的部分内容，主要将欧盟一些议员的观点节译出来，如欧盟贸易专员瓦尔迪斯·东布罗夫斯基的看法，欧洲议会贸易委员会负责中国事务的议员尤留·温克勒的看法以及一些较大团体的想法，而剩余的部分在译文报道中并没有体现。这可能是由于双方立场不同，所关注点也有所差异，因而报道的侧重点也不尽相同，但译文报道节选一些主要人员的评论可以让读者对国外态度也有所了解。

（四）从不同原文本中挑选特定信息进行节译

在面对同一新闻事件时，不同网站的报道的侧重点也是不尽相同的。在进行翻译时，有些译者也会从不同的原文报道中挑选某些特定信息进行节译。

【原文】

IMF lifts global growth forecast for 2021,

still sees ‘exceptional uncertainty’

WASHINGTON (Reuters) – The International Monetary Fund on Tuesday raised its forecast for global economic growth in 2021 and said the coronavirus – triggered downturn last year – the biggest peacetime contraction since the Great Depression – would be nearly a full percentage point less severe than expected.

The global lender said multiple vaccine approvals and the start of vaccinations in some countries had boosted hopes of an eventual end to the pandemic that has now infected nearly 100 million people and claimed the lives of more than 2. 1 million globally.

But it warned that the world economy continued to face “exceptional uncertainty” and new waves of COVID – 19 infections and variants posed risks, and global activity would remain well below pre - COVID - 19 projections made one year ago.

IMF chief economist Gita Gopinath said U. S. President Joe Biden's pledge to fund the World Health Organization's COVAX vaccine initiative marked "a very big step" to containing the pandemic and ensuring more equitable distribution of vaccines.

"Much more will be needed, because as we can see, given the mutating virus, that this is not a problem that's going away anytime soon," Gopinath told a news conference. "There is still a tremendous amount of uncertainty," she told Reuters in a separate interview. "We know that the health crisis is not over until it's over everywhere."

Gopinath said the global economy could gain $9 trillion between 2020 and 2025 if faster progress could be made in ending the health crisis, and it was clearly in the interest of advanced economies to help poorer countries recover.

"There's a complete economic sense to do this, and do it right now," she told Reuters.

The IMF estimates that close to 90 million people are likely to fall below the extreme poverty threshold during 2020 ~ 2021, with the pandemic wiping some out $22 trillion in projected output through 2025 and reversing progress made in reducing poverty over the past two decades.

Gopinath said advanced economies were recovering more quickly, and urged countries with means to continue to offer poorer nations aid, low - interest loans and debt relief. "There is still much, much to be done, but we're certainly at least in positive growth territory this year, as opposed to last year," she told the news conference.

In its latest World Economic Outlook, the IMF forecast a 2020 global *contraction of 3.5%, an improvement of 0.9 percentage points from the 4.4%* slump predicted in October, given stronger - than - expected momentum in the second half of last year.

It predicted global growth of 5.5% in 2021, 0.3 percentage points better than in October, citing expectations of a vaccine – powered uptick later in the year and added policy support in the United States, Japan and a few other large economies.

It said the U. S. economy, the largest in the world, was expected to grow by 5. 1% in 2021, an upward revision of 2 percentage points attributed to carryover from strong momentum in the second half of 2020 and the benefit accruing from about $900 billion in additional fiscal support approved in December.

The outlook would likely improve further if the U. S. Congress passes a $1. 9 trillion relief package proposed by Biden, Gopinath said, forecasting a 5% boost over three years if the package is approved by the U. S. Congress.

China's economy is expected to expand by 8. 1% in 2021 and 5. 6% in 2022, compared with the October forecasts of 8. 2% and 5. 8%, respectively, while India's economy is seen growing 11. 5% in 2021, up 2. 7 percentage points from the October forecast, after a stronger – than – expected recovery in 2020.

The Fund said countries should continue to support their economies until activity normalized to limit persistent damage from the deep recession of the past year.

Low – income countries would need continued support through grants, low – interest loans and debt relief, and some countries may require debt restructuring, the IMF said.

原文链接：https：//www. reuters. com/article/uk – imf – outlook – britain – idUSKBN29V1V9

IMF expects US and China to recover most strongly from virus economic hit

Fund predicts that Europe and emerging markets will be lagging behind in 2022

The IMF expects the US and China to be by far the most successful at steering their economies through the pandemic, leaving Europe and other emerging markets trailing in their wake.

In its updated forecasts for the global economy, the fund predicts that by 2022 recoveries in the US and China will leave their economies no more than 1. 5 percent smaller than projected before the pandemic.

Other advanced economies will still be 2. 5 percent short of their pre－pandemic path, while emerging economies excluding China will in 2022 be 8 percent smaller than expected in forecasts issued exactly a year ago.

But the reasons for the expected success in China and the US, the world's two largest economies, are sharply divergent.

China successfully implemented what the IMF called "effective containment measures" to aggressively curb the spread of COVID－19. In contrast the US has struggled to contain the virus—which continues to spread at a rampant pace—but its government spent more on economic stimulus than almost any other country, earning praise from the fund for its decisive approach.

Even before the Biden administration's proposed ＄1. 9tn additional fiscal stimulus, the IMF said the US's relative success compared with the eurozone was partly because European countries locked down their economies more tightly to contain the virus and partly because their economies were less flexible and able to adapt to lockdowns.

In general, the IMF's forecasts showed better performance in countries with greater access to vaccines and those most willing to spend more on policy stimulus, which it did not expect to be inflationary.

Gita Gopinath, the IMF's chief economist, said: "Much now depends on the outcome of this race between a mutating virus and vaccines to end the pandemic, and on the ability of policies to provide effective support until that happens."

The fund's conclusion is that globally the race is likely to be won by humans rather than the virus and reinforces the emerging new policy consensus that the best economic results will come where countries put aside worries about inflation and the possibility of excessive stimulus.

The IMF's new forecasts split the economic prospects around the world into three broad groups.

China and the US would recover almost all of the ground lost due to COVID－19. Other advanced countries were in a middling group, with a deeper economic hit and slower recoveries, which the IMF thinks could be speeded up with greater policy support.

Emerging economies with the exception of China have been hardest hit and will sustain the greatest lasting damage from the crisis, the IMF said. Containment of the virus had not been as effective as in China, while oil exporters and tourism－based economies were hit especially hard.

"Close to 90m people are likely to fall below the extreme poverty threshold during 2020－21," the IMF added.

With unemployment expected to remain at higher than normal levels across the world, there was little immediate danger of inflation and price rises were expected to average about 1.5 per cent in advanced economies, below target levels, while being below historical averages at about 4 percent in emerging economies.

For a durable and widespread recovery, the world needed to contain coronavirus, Ms Gopinath said, enabling poorer countries to have access to vaccines inaddition to the rich world.

Welcoming the US's decision to join the Covax facility to bring the necessary funding and logistics to vaccinate against COVID－19 in poorer countries, she said, "the health and economic arguments for this are overwhelming".

But she added that new variants of coronavirus were a reminder that the economic damage from the pandemic was far from over and would not disappear until the virus was controlled everywhere.

"Faster progress on ending the health crisis will raise global income cumulatively by $9tn over 2020 to 2025, with benefits for all countries, including around $4tn for advanced economies," Ms Gopinath said.

【来源】https://www.ft.com/content/341577c5-92f2-4bd3-a235-331d0db5dbbd?shareType=nongift

【译文】

IMF 上调 2021 年全球增长预测 美国和中国复苏将最为强劲

参考消息网 1 月 28 日报道 据路透社华盛顿 1 月 26 日报道，国际货币基金组织（IMF）当地时间周二上调 2021 年的全球经济增长预估，并称 2020 年新冠肺炎疫情引发的经济衰退将比预期的严重程度低近一个百分点。

IMF 称，2020 年 12 月多款疫苗被批准使用，一些国家也开始进行疫苗接种，这增加了最终结束这场新冠大流行的希望。

报道称，但 IMF 也警告，全球经济继续面临“异常高的不确定性”，新一波感染和病毒变异带来风险，全球经济活动水平仍远低于一年前在疫情暴发前所做的预测。

IMF 最新预测 2020 年全球经济萎缩 3.5%，较当年 10 月预测的萎缩 4.4% 提高 0.9 个百分点，体现出去年下半年的经济复苏动能强于预期。

报道还称，IMF 预测 2021 年全球经济增长率将为 5.5%，比 10 月时的预估高出 0.3 个百分点，理由是疫苗将推动经济在今年晚些时候加速增长，并且美国、日本和其他一些大型经济体将追加政策支持。

另据英国《金融时报》网站 1 月 26 日报道，国际货币基金组织（IMF）预计，根据目前情况，美国和中国在引领本国经济挺过新冠肺炎疫情难关方面将是最成功的两个经济体，把欧洲和其他新兴市场甩在后面。

IMF 预测，到 2022 年，美国和中国的经济规模较疫情暴发前的预测值低不到 2%。但是，中国和美国这两个世界最大经济体预期将取得成功的原因截然不同。

报道称，中国成功实施了 IMF 所称的“有效遏制措施”，以积极方式遏止了新冠疫情蔓延。相比之下，美国一直难以遏制疫情，新冠病毒仍在全美肆虐，但美国政府的经济刺激支出超过其他几乎任何国家，这种果断做法获得 IMF 的赞誉。

即使在拜登政府另外提出总额 1.9 万亿美元的财政刺激方案之前，IMF 就表示，美国比欧元区的经济表现更好，既是因为欧洲国家更加严厉地封锁经济活动以遏制疫情，也是因为欧洲经济体不够灵活、不那么善于适应防疫封锁。

报道还称，总体而言，IMF 的预测显示，新冠肺炎疫苗接种更普及以及有强烈意愿通过政策刺激增加支出的国家经济表现更好，该组织认为通过政策刺激增加支出不会造成通胀。

IMF 首席经济学家姬塔·戈皮纳特表示："现在，很多事情取决于不断变异的病毒与力求消灭疫情的疫苗之间竞赛的结果，并取决于政策能否在疫情结束之前提供有效支持。"

IMF 的结论是，在全球范围内，这场竞赛的胜利者很可能是人类而不是病毒。该组织还强化了各方开始形成的政策共识，即各国如果暂不考虑对通胀和过度刺激经济的担忧将会取得最佳的经济成果。

报道称，IMF 的最新预测将世界各地的经济前景分为三大类。

中国和美国将收复新冠危机所造成的几乎所有失地。其他发达经济体处于中间的一类，它们受到的经济冲击更深，复苏速度更慢；IMF 认为，如果得到更好的政策支持，它们的复苏速度有望加快。

IMF 表示，除中国外的新兴经济体遭受的打击最为沉重，疫情危机对这些经济体造成的持久损害也最为严重。这些经济体的抗疫措施不如中国那么有效，其中的石油出口国和依赖旅游业的经济体受到的打击尤为沉重。

报道称，IMF 表示："2020 年和 2021 年期间，有近 9000 万人将陷入极端贫困。"

由于世界各地的失业率预计将保持在偏高水平，目前几乎没有通胀风险。预计发达经济体的平均价格涨幅约为 1.5%，低于目标水平；而新兴经济体的价格涨幅约为 4%，低于历史平均水平。

戈皮纳特表示，要实现持久和大范围的复苏，世界需要遏制住新冠肺炎疫情，让较贫穷的国家也能像富国那样获得疫苗。

她补充说，新冠肺炎病毒的新变种提醒人们：这场疫情带来的经济损害仍远未结束，只有疫情在世界各地都得到控制后，经济损害才会消失。

译文链接：http://intl.ce.cn/sjjj/qy/202101/29/t20210129_36272120.shtml

【分析】

这篇中文报道选了两个外媒报道的部分进行翻译，一个是美国路透社，一个是英国的《金融时报》。可以看出，中文报道中选择了路透社的数据，而同时选取了《金融时报》的评述，并将二者巧妙地结合在一起。从节译路透社的部分可以看出，中文报道中将节选部分的信息基本完整的保留了下来，这体现了新闻报道的严谨性，也是节译的优点之一，可以较为完整的传递信息，以便读者花最少的时间读到自己最需要的信息。

第四节　摘译法

一、摘译的界定

摘译，顾名思义，便是先摘后译。摘译，即“摘取 + 翻译”，是指根据读者的特定需求选取原文核心内容或读者需要的部分内容的变译活动。摘译加快了信息的传播速度，提高了翻译效率，迎合了读者的需求。摘译的部分通常是原文的主要内容或精华部分（陈文星，2014）。财经新闻摘译也是如此，摘译内容通常是原文的主要内容或精华部分。在对财经新闻的内容进行摘译时，通常有两个选择标准：（1）按照信息重要性进行摘译，（2）按照主题信息进行摘译。下面，我们将用实例来分析译文是如何根据这两个标准来摘译的。

二、摘译的具体应用

（一）按照信息重要性进行摘译

译文只摘译重要信息，按信息的重要程度来选择摘译部分，如只摘译主题句等。只摘译主题句可以让读者瞬间把握住新闻主要信息，从而达到摄取信息的迅速性。

【例 14】

【原文】China's Long March to Geneva had taken over 15 years since its original application to become a contracting party to the GATT 1947, the multinational trade pact which served as the predecessor treaty to today's GATT 95 and related agreements, whose implementation and enforcement are now overseen by the secretariat of the global trade body called the WTO.

【译文】中国申请成为世界贸易组织的缔约方，前后用了 15 年时间。（来自公众号《译聚网》）

【分析】

摘译部分便是文章的主题句。摘译的内容涵盖了段落的核心信息，删去了原文对“the multinational trade pact”的背景解释内容。译者可能是因为考虑到读者对这些背景信息有一定了解，因此将其删除从而保证摘译版本的简洁性。并且摘译部分的翻译并非是对原文的直译，而是将原文句序做了整合，并且将原文“China's Long March to Geneva”的隐含意思翻译了出来，即“成为世界贸易组织的缔约方”。因此这一句摘译很好地实现了摘译的功能，使信息简洁明白。

【例 1】

【原文】In China, where highly restrictive measures led to an almost complete halt in activity in some sectors and regions in February, output is estimated to have contracted by 34 percent q/q, saar in the first quarter—the first contraction since 1976 (Figure 2. 1. 2). Industrial profits fell sharply by 37 percent y/y in 2020Q1, fiscal revenues of the consolidated public finance and government fund budgets declined by 14 percent y/y. Activity started to recover in early March as the domestic lockdown was relaxed. As of April, industrial production has returned to growth and vehicles sales posted the first increase since June 2018. However, companies are facing funding shortages and plummeting external demand. The recovery in services sector is lagging reflecting the lingering impacts of the outbreak.

Following a collapse in 2020Q1, China's output has bottomed out. Various indicators, including domestic flights, have rebounded, but the outlook remains uncertain amid contracting global activity. Exports contracted in 2020Q1, because of factory closures in China followed by a plunge in global demand. Bond spreads have widened but less than in other emerging market and developing economies (EMDEs). The exchange rate has remained broadly stable in contrast to that in other EMDEs. Total debt is estimated to have increased by about 17 percentage points in 2020Q1 reflecting fiscal and monetary policy support amid economic contraction.

The outbreak appears to have largely subsided in China... China and Vietnam have relaxed the national lockdowns but kept selective restrictions in place, to prevent a second wave of outbreaks.

All major regional economies have implemented large macroeconomic policy support to mitigate the economic impact of the outbreak. In China, the PBOC has provided substantial liquidity support, cut policy rates, and lowered reserve requirements to stem market sell-offs and support businesses.

Key fiscal policy measures in China included emergency health spending, tax breaks, direct transfers to vulnerable households, and deferrals and special local government bond issuances to boost investment, totaling 5.4 percent of GDP.

Outlook

Growth in China is projected to slow to 1 percent in 2020—4.9 percentage point below January forecast and the lowest rate since 1976—reflecting the significant disruptions caused by COVID-19, and then rebound above its trend pace, to 6.9 percent in 2021, as lockdowns are lifted around the world.

The pandemic will likely further slow potential growth in the region by weakening investment and the supply chains that have been an important conduit for productivity gains over the past decade (World Bank 2020a, 2020d). The negative impact is expected to be broad-based and will add to the long-term slowdown from deteriorating demographic trends and falling growth in total factor productivity (Chapter 3).

The regional outlook is predicated on major countries in the region avoiding a second wave of outbreaks. The outlook assumes that a severe contraction in 2020Q1 in China and in 2020Q2 in the rest of the region will be followed by a gradual and sustained recovery. The outlook is also predicated on the assumption that sizable fiscal and monetary policy support measures implemented by major economies are successful in averting a prolonged recession and financial crises. By the second half of 2020, these are assumed to result in a recovery in global import demand, a normalization of global financial conditions, a resumption of capital inflows to the region, and no major re – escalation in trade tensions between China and the United States.

The regional outlook is subject to significant uncertainty. The full duration and spread of the pandemic is still unknown, as is the effectiveness of the policies implemented in response. The erosion of consumer and business confidence may be longer – lasting. In addition, the spillover impacts of the outbreak through global trade, financial markets, confidence, and other second round effects continue to evolve. The containment measures in major economies may last longer than three months assumed under the baseline scenario. The recovery process in many tourism, exportoriented, remittances – and commodity – dependent EAP economies will be impeded by the slowdown in their main trading patterns, source countries, and low commodity prices. The regional outlook will also significantly deteriorate if global trade tensions re – escalate.

Risks

The balance of risks to the outlook is firmly tilted to the downside. The main risks include the possibility that the pandemic lasts longer and has more severe effects than assumed (Chapter 1). A second wave of the outbreaks in countries with subsiding active cases remains a real possibility. A sharp rise in the number of COVID – 19 patients requiring hospitalization could renew pressure on the most robust health care systems in the region (China, Malaysia, and Thailand) and overwhelm health care systems in more vulnerable countries (Lao PDR and the Pacific Islands). Moreover, it remains to be seen whether the policy accommodation being provided will be sufficient to prevent a more severe deterioration in confidence, investment, and trade.

In addition, despite prompt and massive liquidity provision, policy rate cuts to their effective lower bound, and unconventional monetary policies by central banks, global financial market stress may persist for several months and cause further capital outflows from EAP. Tighter financing conditions would weigh heavily on investment and consumption and further reduce regional growth. Eventually, this could exacerbate existing balance sheet weaknesses in highly leveraged banking, corporate, and household sectors, leading to defaults and financial crises (World Bank 2020b).

In some dimensions, major EAP economies appear to be better equipped to cope with this crisis than in the past (Kose and Ohnsorge 2019). They have a strong track record of growth, greater exchange rate flexibility, and more robust monetary, prudential, and fiscal policy frameworks. However, vulnerabilities among some EAP countries could amplify the impact of repeated sudden stops in capital flows or a rise in borrowing costs (Kose, Nagle, Ohnsorge, and Sugawara 2019). These include elevated debt (China...

A further risk is that the repeated disruptions to global trade and the supply of intermediate goods causes a retreat from global and regional value chains (Special Focus). Such a retreat could be further encouraged by tensions surrounding the Phase One agreement between China and the United States. Tensions may also arise from disagreements over the origins of, and policy responses to, the pandemic and may spill over into restrictive trade relations (World Bank 2020e).

Should these risks materialize, the regional economy could contract by 1.9 percent in 2020, and growth will remain below trend in 2021 (Chapter 1). On the upside, a gradual normalization of global trade relations remains a possibility, notwithstanding new challenges, and pandemic containment and economic policy support measures in major regional economies could be more effective than expected, leading to a sustained recovery of regional growth.

【译文】

由于中国采取了高度严格的限制措施，导致2月份某些部门及地区的活动几乎停滞，因此中国一季度的产出较去年同期估计收缩了34%（经季度调整），是自1976年以来的首次收缩。2020年一季度工业利润较去年同期急剧下降37%，综合公共财政收入和政府资金预算较去年同比下降14%。在3月上旬，随着国内疫情防控措施的放松，经济活动开始逐步恢复。因此在4月，工业生产恢复增长，汽车销售出现自2018年6月以来的首次增长。然而，企业仍面临着融资短缺和外部需求暴跌的困难。服务业的恢复仍然滞后，反映出疫情的影响仍未消除。

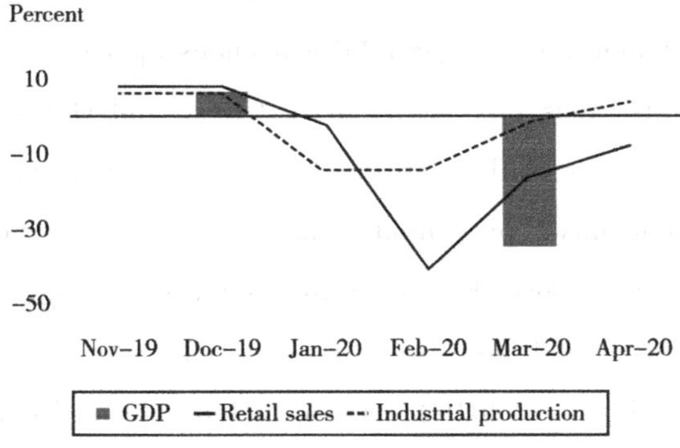

中国的产出在经历2020年一季度的暴跌之后已经从谷底反弹。众多指标，包括国内航班，都出现了反弹，但在全球活动收缩的情况下，中国经济预期仍然不确定。2020年一季度出口发生了收缩，主要因为全球需求暴跌后大量工厂停工。债券利差出现扩大，但扩大幅度小于其他新兴市场和发展中经济体。汇率总体上保持稳定，这与其他新兴市场和发展中经济体的情况相反。总债务水平在2020年一季度估计增加了大约17个百分点，反映出中国在经济紧缩中采取了财政政策和货币政策来支持经济活动。中国的新冠肺炎疫情暴发很大程度上已经平息……中国和越南已经放松了全国性的封锁，但仍选择性地保留了部分管控措施，以防止第二波新冠肺炎疫情的暴发。

该地区的主要经济体都采取了大规模的宏观经济政策来支撑经济，缓和疫情的影响。在中国，人民银行已经通过提供大量的流动性支持、调低政策利率、降低准备金要求，来阻止市场抛售和支持商业活动。中国采取的关键财政政策措施包括紧急卫生支出、减税、对弱势家庭的直接转移支付以及通过税收递延及发行地方政府特别债券来促进投资，这些措施总计达到GDP的5.4%。

展望

中国2020年的经济增速预计将下降到1%，较1月的预测值下降4.9个百分点，是自1976年以来的最低增速，反映出COVID－19对经济破坏的严重性，然后随着全世界封锁的放松，中国经济将出现反弹并超过原先预测的趋势，2021年的经济增速将能达到6.9%。

亚太地区在过去十年中主要以投资和供应链来作为生产力提升的重要中转机制，而疫情很可能会削弱该地区的投资和供应链，从而降低该地区的潜在经济增长。这种负面影响预计将非常广泛，并造成人口趋势的恶化和全要素生产率增速的下跌，从而导致长期经济增速下降。

亚太地区的经济展望预计该地区的主要国家都会避免疫情的第二波暴发。经济展望假设中国和其他亚太地区国家分别在2020年一季度和二季度出现严重的经济收缩，之后经济会逐步并持续的恢复。该展望所做的预期主要通过假设该地区主要经济体采取的大规模的财政和货币政策能成功避免长期衰退和金融危机。到2020年下半年，我们假设这些能带来全球进口需求的恢复，全球金融环境的正常化，亚太地区资本流入的恢复，以及中美贸易紧张关系不会再次升级。

亚太地区的经济预期依然有很大的不确定性。疫情的持续时间、影响范围尚未完全清楚，同样，疫情应对措施的有效性也尚未完全明晰。而消费者和商家的信心的侵蚀将会持续很长一段时间。此外，疫情通过全球贸易、金融市场、信心以及其他二次效应而造成的不利影响仍在不断进化。在基准情景的假设下，主要经济体的限制措施可能需要持续三个月以上。由于受到主要贸易模式、客源国以及商品价格下跌的拖累，亚太地区很多以旅游、出口导向、依赖汇款和大宗商品为主的经济体，它们的经济恢复将受到很大阻碍。同时，如果全球贸易紧张局势再度升级，该地区的经济预期也将会显著恶化。

风险

经济预期的风险非常明确地趋向于负面。主要的风险包括疫情持续时间、不利影响比假设更严重的可能性。疫情已经平息的国家还是存在第二波暴发的可能性。COVID－19新冠肺炎患者的急剧增加而产生的医疗需求，将会对中国、马来西亚和泰国这样医疗体系比较发达的国家产生新的压力，同时将造成老挝和其他太平洋岛国这样比较脆弱的国家的医疗体系崩溃。此外，还不能确定这些国家的政策调整是否足以避免信心、投资以及贸易的进一步恶化。

此外，尽管各国央行迅速注入了大量流动性，将利率调低至有效的利率下限，采取了非常规的货币政策，但全球金融市场的压力可能还要持续几个月，从而导致资本从亚太地区进一步流出。紧缩的金融环境将会给投资和消费带来沉重的负担，并进一步降低该地区的经济增长。最终，这将造成高杠杆银行、公司及家庭的现有资产负债表的进一步恶化，从而引发债务违约和金融危机。

在某些维度，亚太地区主要经济体展现出比以前更好的应对危机的能力。这些国家拥有强劲的经济增长记录，更具有弹性的汇率制度以及更强劲的货币、审慎考虑以及财政政策框架。然而，亚太地区国家存在的脆弱性，将放大反复出现的资本流动停止或是借款成本上升的不利影响，这些不利影响包括债务水平升高等。

目前还存在一种风险，即由于全球贸易和中间品供应的反复发生中断，导致全球和地区价值链发生退缩。而围绕在中美第一阶段贸易协议的紧张氛围更加剧了这种退缩。同时，紧张的氛围也有可能因为疫情起源地、疫情应对政策的分歧而引起，而且这种紧张氛围可能外溢，导致贸易关系收紧。

一旦这些风险实际发生，该地区的经济可能在 2020 年收缩 1.9%，而且 2021 年经济增长也将继续低于预测的趋势。从乐观角度考虑，尽管有新的挑战，全球贸易关系的逐步正常化依然存在可能，并且亚太地区主要经济体的疫情防控措施和经济支持政策可能会比预计更有效果，从而能够引导亚太地区经济增长持续恢复。

原文 & 译文链接：https：//zhuanlan. zhihu. com/p/149813267

▶ 点评：

《全球经济展望》由世界银行发布，涵盖领域广泛。译者应从读者需求出发。这篇关于《全球经济展望》的摘译，便是按信息的重要性程度来进行摘译的。由于《全球经济展望》内容较多，由于篇幅限制，这里只给出了与译文相对应的原文内容。因为中国读者是本次摘译的目标读者，因此文章中与中国相关的内容的重要性是居于第一位的。于是译者只翻译了文章中与中国有关的信息，从而方便中国读者对报告进行阅读，满足了特定读者群的阅读需求。并且对比原文和译文后可以看出，摘译部分基本忠实于原文语句，并无额外的改动与删减。这是为了保持阅读内容的客观性，较大程度上避免了译者的主观删减而造成译文信息传达错误等情况。

摘译部分可忠实于原文，也可以是对原文核心信息的重新组合。

（二）按照主题信息进行摘译

译者只摘译与主题相关的信息，此类摘译大多是在摘选译文主题信息的基础上对译文的内容顺序又做了重新调整。

【例 15】

【原文】

Mechanization rate for Xinjiang's cotton sector approaches 90 percent

A total of 2 million hectares of cotton farmland in the Xinjiang Uygur autonomous region will be harvested by machinery rather than by hand, or 106666 hectares more than last year, according to the region's Department of Agriculture and Rural Affairs.

The increase is expected to raise the mechanization rate of cotton production to 88 percent this year, as the region continues to promote mechanization in the whole process of agricultural production, the department said recently.

In Shaya county of Aksu prefecture, many tractors can be seen busily planting cotton fields, instead of lots of farmers sowing by hand, as spring temperatures rise.

Aksu, a major cotton - growing area in southern Xinjiang, saw cotton output of more than 1 million metric tons in 2020, making up about one - sixth of the country's total, according to the local government.

"A specialized agricultural machinery cooperative was founded in 2017 in Shaya to provide agricultural machinery and technology to cotton farmers," said Ma Zhanming, head of the cooperative. "The cooperative can provide mechanization service during the whole process, from spring sowing to harvest."

Farmers can pay 1650 yuan ($250) per hectare for the mechanization service, which includes plowing, planting and harvesting.

"In the past, for instance, it took at least 30 workers two months to harvest 20 hectares of cotton farmland, but now a harvesting machine can finish the harvest work on 20 hectares within one day," Ma said. "And a harvesting machine needs only two drivers."

The cooperative will manage 760 hectares of cotton farmland for 400 families this year.

"There were 132000 hectares of farmland planted with cotton in Shaya in 2020," according to Li Yang, deputy director of the county's Bureau of Agriculture and Rural Affairs. "Over 110000 hectares were harvested by machines, accounting for 85 percent of all the farmland."

"With the continuous advancement of land leveling and the construction of intensive and high - standard farmland, complete mechanization is expected to be seen in the future," he said.

In the county, there are over 54000 agricultural machines and 78 agricultural machinery cooperatives to help farmers increase efficiency and improve yields.

Farmers in other areas also benefited from advanced farming technologies and facilities.

Mijit Yimit, a cotton grower in Kuqa county, said he received income of 150000 yuan last year from his 20 hectares of cotton fields.

"I have planted cotton for 18 years," he said. "In the past, I needed to pay about 80000 yuan each season to hire workers to help harvest, but now I need only 30000 yuan."

"I have seen more application of machines for cotton planting, such as spreading fertilizers, spraying herbicides and pesticides, as well as drip irrigation, especially in recent years," he said. "The technologies and facilities also help improve the quality of cotton," he said.

Xinjiang is also striving to develop its intelligent agriculture, including promoting the Beidou satellite navigation system in driverless tractors and constructing the comprehensive data service system, local government said.

原文链接：https://www.chinadaily.com.cn/a/202104/02/WS6066514da31024ad0bab3265.html

【译文】

今年新疆棉花生产全程机械化率预计可达88%

记者走进阿克苏地区沙雅县，大片的棉花田上，是一座座大型农用机械正在有序播种，雪白的新疆棉花，从此孕育。近年来，机械化在新疆棉田得到大范围推广应用，2020年新疆棉花机采面积达2817.61万亩，今年新疆机采面积有望突破3000万亩。

"我们成立了农机专业合作社，专门为棉农提供农业机械与技术。从春耕播种到采收，全程提供机械化作业，不需要棉农操心。"新疆阿克苏地区沙雅县大欣农机专业合作社负责人马占明说。同时作为种棉农户，马占明告诉记者，农民只需要有地即可。种植棉花过程中购买社会化服务包括犁耙、播种等，总共加起来是每亩地约110元。不同合作社之间分工明确，紧密合作，提供全程机械化服务，极大地减轻棉农压力。"机械化、采棉机作业后，一台采棉机一天就可以作业300多亩地。一台采棉机两位驾驶员，十天的工作量，相当于过去300个人需要干两个月的活。"马占明说。今年大欣农机专业合作社种植的棉花面积是11400亩地，涉及农户大概400多户。

"去年，我们沙雅县种植198万亩棉花，除了个别小地块以外，85%都是机采，达到了165万亩。"阿克苏地区沙雅县农业农村局副局长李杨说，"随着土地平整的持续推进，建设集约化、高标准农田，我们棉花生产全程将完成全部机械化。"据了解，沙雅县坚持普惠共享，实施农机购置补贴政策，推进补贴范围内所有机具敞开补贴，加快创新产品购置补贴支持步伐，促进农机转型升级。目前，沙雅县农业机械总量达到54872台，动力机械16041台，农机合作社78家，农业机械化水平进一步提升。

据了解，阿克苏地区大力推广机采棉栽培模式，实现降本增效。2020年全地区推行机采棉面积551.68万亩，比2019年增加了26.38%，占棉花播种面积748万亩的73.75%；棉花机械化采收面积由2014年的6.12万亩增加至2020年的467.92万亩，棉花综合机械化水平达到89%，取得了历史性突破；采花费用由人工采摘的770元/亩降为机采的200元/亩，亩均降本增收570元/亩；棉花节水滴灌面积达到594.17万亩，比2019年增加了33.22%。

不仅是阿克苏地区沙雅县，喀什地区巴楚县棉农热合曼·热依木说："我种了三十多年棉花了，我亲眼看到我们的棉花在播种、打药、摘棉花等环节中机械化程度越来越高，还用上了滴灌技术，棉种质量也越来越好，再加上政府的各项补贴，成为我们农民致富的首选。"来自新疆库车的棉农米吉提·依米提说："我有20万平方米的农田，年收入约15万元人民币，现在都全是机械化种植与采集。"

记者从新疆维吾尔自治区农业农村机械化发展中心了解到，今年新疆将完成棉花全程机械化技术示范区建设，引导棉花生产向全程机械化转变，指导建设5个万亩以上机采棉标准化示范区，全疆新增机采棉面积160万亩以上，棉花生产全程机械化率可达88%。

在推进农业生产全程全面机械化水平进程中，今年新疆将继续坚持突出以粮棉等主要农作物为重点，为粮食、棉花等主要农产品有效供给提供技术装备支撑。抓好小麦、玉米、棉花等主要农作物和畜牧、林果、特色作物生产机械化推进工作，积极开展创建全国主要农作物全程机械化示范县工作，不断提升主要农作物生产全程机械化水平，全区主要农作物综合机械化水平达到85.2%，农林牧渔综合机械化水平达到70.4%。

此外，新疆还将推动农机农艺融合，聚焦全程全面机械化短板弱项，开展农作物品种、栽培、机械化技术融合的标准化生产试验示范，完善机械化生产技术体系。开展精准农业应用示范，推动北斗导航无人驾驶、远程监测运维功能前装应用，建设综合数据服务系统，开展智能农机装备技术演示交流活动，促进农机装备应用信息化，推动智慧农业发展。

译文链接：https：//www. 163. com/dy/article/G6ITRR9N0534AMCV. html

【分析】

从编译文本可看出，译者对原文全文内容进行了信息重组，并且只是对原文的部分内容进行摘译。译者摘译了原文中新疆阿克苏地区沙雅县大欣农机专业合作社负责人马占明的部分观点，还摘译了棉农米吉提·依米提的部分观点。同时，译者对摘译内容进行了补充，在细节方面做了部分完善。

但仔细对比原文和译文后可以发现，原文和译文的部分数据并不完全一致，如原文 Mijit Yimit 说自己种植棉花已有 18 年，而译文给的数据是三十多年。可能译者对译文数据做了审核并进行了相应修改。

【例 16】

【原文】

IMF projects China's economy will grow by 8.4% in 2021

China's economy is projected to expand by 8. 4 percent in 2021, the International Monetary Fund (IMF) said Tuesday.

The figure is 0. 3 percentage points above the IMF's January prediction, according to the latest update to its World Economic Outlook (WEO) released at the start of the IMF's and World Bank's spring meetings.

It would mark the country's strongest growth rate since 2011, because "effective containment measures, a forceful public investment response and central bank liquidity support have facilitated a strong recovery," according to IMF.

China's annual GDP growth of 2. 3 percent in 2020 indicates that the country led major economies in annual positive growth in 2020 and became the only major one to expand last year.

"Among emerging market and developing economies, China had already returned to pre – COVID GDP in 2020, whereas many others are not expected to do so until well into 2023," the IMF said, noting that its forecast for China is much higher than other major economies, including the United States, Germany and France, although behind India.

The second – largest economy has set its GDP growth rate at over 6 percent for 2021 as its economic recovery gathers steam, with Nomura analyzing that "China may not want to be perceived as 'marking to market' when setting the growth target, and it may not want to slash the growth target next year when the base effect likely subsides."

According to the IMF, China's economic growth in the next year is expected to slow to 5.6 percent. It also warned that pre – COVID – 19 risk factors continue to be relevant. For instance, "tensions between the United States and China remain elevated on numerous fronts, including international trade, intellectual property, and cybersecurity."

The IMF has also projected that the global economy will grow by 6 percent in 2021, a rate unseen since the 1970s, thanks to the unprecedented policy responses to the COVID – 19 pandemic.

原文链接：https：//news.cgtn.com/news/2021 – 04 – 06/IMF – projects – China – s – economy – to – grow – by – 8 – 4 – pct – in – 2021 – ZfckTLcci4/index.html

【译文】

财经早知道：IMF 上调今年中国经济增速预期至 8.4%

4 月 6 日，国际货币基金组织（IMF）发布《世界经济展望报告》，预计 2021 年全球经济将增长 6%，较 1 月份预测值上调 0.5 个百分点。其中，预计中国经济将增长 8.4%，较 1 月份预测值上调 0.3 个百分点。不过报告也认为，全球经济增长前景仍然具有高度不确定性，将主要取决于疫情发展及政策行动的效果等。

译文链接：https：//m.finance.caixin.com/m/2021 – 04 – 07/101686376.html

【分析】

译文按照主题需要，只摘译了相关核心内容。

对比原文和译文可知，译者只是摘译了原文的个别句子，保留了原文的核心信息，如

"China's economy is projected to expand by 8. 4 percent in 2021, the International Monetary Fund (IMF) said Tuesday" "The figure is 0. 3 percentage points above the IMF's January prediction", "The IMF has also projected that the global economy will grow by 6 percent in 2021."

译者认为，原文中的其他句子表达的信息皆为次要信息，因而全部删除不译。

同时，译者还新添了一些信息，即"较1月份预测值上调0.5个百分点"和"不过报告也认为，全球经济增长前景仍然具有高度不确定性，将主要取决于疫情发展及政策行动的效果等。"

第五节　编译法

编译是新闻翻译的重要方法，在我国媒体上，我们常常可见到由英文编译而成的财经新闻文本。一篇专业性强、大众望而生畏的英语财经新闻经编译者编译之后，就变成了普通读者喜闻乐见的汉语财经新闻编译文本。

一、编译的界定

作为一种翻译方法，编译似乎很难有具体的定义，但编译现象却是近代中国翻译史上一道奇异的风景线。研究者们也从理论译学的角度，对我国各类编译现象作了详细描述和深入探讨。黄忠廉和刘丽芬认为：编译是指对原作加工整理然后翻译的变译方法，旨在优化原作内容（黄忠廉、刘丽芬，2018：263）。方梦之在其《应用翻译研究》中提出：编译（transediting）着眼于译，是在节译的基础上译者加了编的功夫，同时适当处理中西文化和话语体系中的差异，以便更适合译入语读者的阅读习惯和阅读兴趣（方梦之，2019：328）。上述学者对"编译"的界定是从宏观的视角来描述编译的特征，是可以适用于所有文本类型的，呈现出了"编译"的普遍性。

而新闻翻译中的“编译”与上述“编译”的定义稍有不同。1989 年，卡伦·斯戴汀（Karen Stetting）首次提出了“transediting”（编译）这一概念。这里的“编译”是一个复合词，涵盖了新闻工作者对文本进行操作的两个步骤—“翻译（translating）”和“编辑（editing）”（冷冰冰，2017）。对此，刘其中持同样观点，他认为新闻编译是采用翻译和编辑的方法，按照既定的编辑方针，把用一种语文写成的新闻处理成另一种语文新闻的方法或过程（刘其中，2009：3）。显然，人们在讨论新闻翻译中的“编译”时，更强调编译的实践特征。

由此可知，财经新闻翻译中的“编译”，是译者首先在翻译过程中抓取原语财经新闻文本的主要思想，而后通过删减、补充、转换、重写、调序等手段，进而产出符合逻辑、主题鲜明、语意连贯的译语财经新闻文本的过程。

二、编译的具体方法

财经新闻的编译方法主要有删减、补充、转换、重写等。

（一）删减法（Deletion）

按照“目的论”的观点，原文只是译文的一个信息来源，“译者不可能像原文作者那样提供同样数量或同样性质的信息”（Nord 2001：33）。原文中的某些信息在译语语境中可能不再有价值，反而会占用宝贵的文本空间，损害译文的信息功能。因此，对于译者在翻译时，对译语读者可能不感兴趣的内容应该删除或简化。在一些财经新闻文本中，常常存在一些对原语读者有用，而对译语读者产出阅读不便的信息。这些信息包括语篇结构层次的信息，也包括对译语读者产出负面影响的信息。

1. 删减部分语篇结构

在英语财经新闻中，部分信息构成独特的语篇结构，发挥着独特的语篇功能，呈现出独特的语篇信息。但是编译者在编译时，会按汉语财经新闻的语篇结构来重组信息。在编译者重组的新闻语篇中，英语语篇中的一些信息可能不符合译语读者的阅读习惯，影响读者的阅读体验。编译者会将这些语篇信息删除，如英语财经新闻中的小标题，常被编译者删除。

【例 17】

【原文】

Complacency in a leaderless world

The private sector in Europe and America has been unable to create many good jobs since the beginning of the current century

Davos: The World Economic Forum's annual meeting in Davos has lost some of its pre – crisis panache. After all, before the meltdown in 2008, the captains of finance and industry could trumpet the virtues of globalisation, technology, and financial liberalisation, which supposedly heralded a new era of relentless growth. The benefits would be shared by all, if only they would do "the right thing."

Those days are gone. But Davos remains a good place to get a sense of the global zeitgeist.

It goes without saying that developing and emerging – market countries no longer look at the advanced countries as they once did. But a remark by one mining company executive from a developing country caught the spirit of change. In response to one development expert's heartfelt despair that unfair trade treaties and unfulfilled promises of aid have cost the developed countries their moral authority, he retorted: "The West never had any moral authority." Colonialism, slavery, the splintering of Africa into small countries, and a long history of resource exploitation may be matters of the distant past to the perpetrators, but not so to those who suffered as a result.

If there is a single topic that concerned the assembled leaders the most, it is economic inequality. The shift in the debate from just a yearago seems dramatic: no one even mentions the notion of trickle – down economics anymore, and few are willing to argue that there is a close congruence between social contributions and private rewards.

Land of opportunity

While the realisation that America is not the land of opportunity that it has long claimed to be is as disconcerting to others as it is to Americans, inequality of opportunity at the global scale is even greater. One cannot really claim that the world is "flat" when a typical African receives investment in his or her human capital of a few hundred dollars, while rich Americans get a gift from their parents and society in excess of a half - million dollars.

A high point of the meeting was the speech by Christine Lagarde, the International Monetary Fund's managing director, who stressed the marked change in her institution, at least at the top: deep concern about women's rights; renewed emphasis on the link between inequality and instability; and recognition that collective bargaining and minimum wages could play an important role in reducing inequality. If only the IMF programmes in Greece and elsewhere fully reflected these sentiments!

The Associated Press organised a sobering session on technology and unemployment: Can countries (particularly in the developed world) create new jobs—especially good jobs—in the face of modern technology that has replaced workers with robots and other machines in any task that can be routinised?

Overall, the private sector in Europe and America has been unable to create many good jobs since the beginning of the current century. Even in China and other parts of the world with growing manufacturing sectors, productivity improvements—often related to job - killing automated processes—account for most of the growth in output. Those suffering the most are the young, whose life prospects will be badly hurt by the extended periods of unemployment that they face today.

Dominant note

But most of those in Davos put aside these problems to celebrate the euro's survival. The dominant note was one of complacency—or even optimism. The "Draghi put" — the notion that the European Central Bank, with its deep pockets, would and could do whatever necessary to save the euro and each of the crisis countries—seemed to have worked, at least for a while. The temporary calm provided some support for those who claimed that what was required, above all, was a restoration of confidence. The hope was that Draghi's promises would be a costless way of providing that confidence, because they would never have to be fulfilled.

Critics repeatedly pointed out that the fundamental contradictions had not been resolved, and that if the euro was to survive in the long run, there would have to be a fiscal and banking union, which would require more political unification than most Europeans are willing to accept. But much of what was said in and around the meetings reflected a deep lack of solidarity. One very senior government official of a northern European country did not even put down his fork when interrupted by an earnest dinner companion who pointed out that many Spaniards now eat out of garbage cans. They should have reformed earlier, he replied, as he continued to eat his steak.

Decoupled

IMF growth forecasts released during the Davos meeting highlight the extent to which the world has become decoupled: GDP growth in the advanced industrial countries is expected to be 1.4 per cent this year, while developing countries continue to grow at a robust 5.5 per cent annual rate.

While Western leaders talked about a new emphasis on growth and employment, they offered no concrete policies backing these aspirations. In Europe, there was continued emphasis on austerity, with self-congratulations on the progress made so far, and a reaffirmation of resolve to continue along a course that has now plunged Europe as a whole into recession—and the United Kingdom into a triple-dip downturn.

Perhaps the most optimistic note came from the emerging markets: while the risk of globalisation was that it implied a new interdependence, so that flawed economic policies in the US and Europe could torpedo developing countries' economies, the more successful emerging markets have managed globalization well enough to sustain growth in the face of failures in the West.

With the US politically paralysed by the Republicans' infantile political tantrums, and Europe focused on ensuring the survival of the ill-conceived euro project, the lack of global leadership was a major complaint at Davos. In the last 25 years, we have moved from a world dominated by two superpowers to one dominated by one, and now to a leaderless, multi – polar world. While we may talk about the G7, or G8, or G20, the more apt description is G – 0. We will have to learn how to live, and thrive, in this new world. （引自海湾新闻 2013 年 2 月 10 日）

原文链接：https：//gulfnews. com/business/analysis/complacency – in – a – leaderless – world – 1. 1144438

【译文】

自鸣得意于无极世界

2008 年经济危机后，达沃斯世界经济论坛年会风光大不如前。毕竟，金融大崩溃前，金融业和工业的巨头们可以大肆鼓吹全球化、技术革新以及金融自由化的种种好处，并认为这预示着持续增长的新时代即将来临。所有人都将从中获利，但前提是巨头们做出“正确判断”。

往日一去不返。不过达沃斯仍是让人领略全球时代精神的好地方。

毋庸多言，发展中国家和新兴市场国家对待发达国家的态度已不同往昔。某发展中国家的一位矿业公司总经理一语道破其中缘故。当时，某发展研究专家感慨，由于实行不公平贸易条约且不兑现援助承诺，发达国家已然丧失道德权威，他对此表示彻底绝望。那位总经理当场反驳：“西方国家从未有过道德权威。”也许对作恶者来说，殖民、奴役分割非洲以及长期掠夺资源已是遥远的过去，但对受害者而言，却远非如此。

如果说与会领导人有什么最关心的主题，那当然是经济上的不平等。与一年前相比，年会讨论的内容发生了戏剧性的巨大转变：无人再提及涓滴经济学的概念，也没几个人认同社会贡献和个人报酬密切一致。

美国并非长期以来自我标榜的那片“机遇之地”，这一认识令包括美国人在内的世界人民都颇为不安，而在全球范围内，机会不平等的现象不断加剧。没有人能底气十足地宣称这个世界是“平”的，因为非洲人的劳动报酬一般不过区区几百美元，而富有的美国人却能从父母和社会得到超过 50 万美元的馈赠。

会议的亮点是国际货币基金组织总裁克里斯蒂娜·拉加德的发言。她着重指出了该组织至少是高层的显著变化：高度关注妇女权利，重申不平等将导致不稳定，承认集体协商与最低工资可以在减少不平等方面发挥重要作用。要是国际货币基金组织在希腊及其他地方的项目能充分反映这些观点该多好！

美联社组织了一次关于技术进步与失业的讨论，其议题发人深省：在常规化工作中，现代科技已经用机器人和机器取代了工人，那么，各国（特别是发达国家）还能够创造新的就业机会，尤其是良好的就业机会吗？

总的来说，自本世纪初以来，欧洲和美国的私营经济已无力创造大批良好的就业机会。甚至在制造业不断增长的中国和其他地区，产量增长也主要依靠生产率的提高——而生产率提高往往意味着生产自动化，从而减少了就业机会。年轻人成了最大受害者，由于当前失业时间的延长，他们的生活前景严重恶化。

可是，达沃斯的大部分与会者撇开这些问题去庆祝欧元逃过一劫。会场洋溢着自鸣得意，甚至可以说是乐观的氛围。欧洲央行行长德拉吉提出"德拉吉对策"，以其财大气粗竭尽所能拯救欧元和深陷经济危机的国家。这一对策似乎已经奏效，至少灵验了一段时间。而暂时的风平浪静为声称重拾信心高于一切的人提供了些许支持。但愿德拉吉的承诺是一剂无成本强心针，因为它们根本无需兑现。

批评者一再指出，根本矛盾并未解决，要长期拯救欧元，就必须建立财政及银行联盟，那需要更大程度上的政治统一，而大多数欧洲人并不情愿。

达沃斯会议期间国际货币基金组织公布的经济增长预期凸显了世界经济发展的脱节：今年发达工业国家的国内生产总值增长率预计为1.4%，而发展中国家预计将以5.5%的年增长率继续强势发展。

尽管西方领导人谈及要重视经济增长，促进就业却没有提出任何支持这些愿景的具体政策。欧洲国家仍继续强调紧缩政策，洋洋自得于眼前的些许进步，下定决心继续走下去，全然不顾这条路已经让整个欧洲陷入经济衰退，更让英国陷入三倍的衰退。

也许最乐观的消息来自新兴市场：全球化的风险在于，它意味着一种新的相互依存关系，美欧经济政策的缺陷可能会因此破坏发展中国家的经济，尽管如此，新兴市场日趋成熟，已能很好应对全球化，足以在西方国家经济衰败的情况下保持增长。

过去的25年间，世界已由两极格局发展为一超多强，现在则是多极化态势。尽管我们大谈G－7、G－8或者G－20，但更贴切的说法是G－0。我们必须学会如何在这个无领导的新世界里生存和茁长。（《英语世界》，2014（12），34－38）

在上述例子中，为突出部分段落的亮点内容，让读者一目了然，原英语财经新闻撰写者给出了“Land of opportunity”“Dominant note”“Decoupled”这几个小标题。而在财经新闻译文中，这种小标题可能会打断读者的思路，影响读者阅读，也不符合中文新闻的文章结构，故编译者选择删除这些小标题。

2. 删减可能产生负面影响的信息

为响应党和国家的宣传方针和相关政策，宣传积极向上的财经内容，一些与党和国家的宣传方针和相关政策不相符合，可能对大众产生负面影响的英语财经新闻中的内容也应该被删除。

【例18】

【原文】

China is Not the Source of Our Economic Problems – Corporate Greed Is

China is not an enemy. It is a nation trying to raise its living standards through education, international trade, infrastructure investment, and improved technologies. In short, it is doing what any country should do when confronted with the historical reality of being poor and far behind more powerful countries. Yet the Trump administration is now aiming to stop China's development, which could prove to be disastrous for both the United States and the entire world.

China is being made a scapegoat for rising inequality in the United States. While US trade relations with China have been mutually beneficial over the years, some US workers have been left behind, notably Midwestern factory workers facing competition due to rising productivity and comparatively low (though rising) labor costs in China. Instead of blaming China for this normal phenomenon of market competition, we should be taxing the soaring corporate profits of our own multinational corporations and using the revenues to help working – class households, rebuild crumbling infrastructure, promote new job skills and invest in cutting – edge science and technology.

We should understand that China is merely trying to make up for lost time after a very long period of geopolitical setbacks and related economic failures. Here is important historical background that is useful to understand China's economic development in the past 40 years.

In 1839, Britain attacked China because it refused to allow British traders to continue providing Chinese people with addictive opium. Britain prevailed, and the humiliation of China's defeat in the First Opium War, ending in 1842, contributed in part to a mass uprising against the Qing Dynasty called the Taiping Rebellion that ended up causing more than 20 million deaths. A Second Opium War against Britain and France ultimately led to the continued erosion of China's power and internal stability.

Toward the end of the 19th century, China lost a war to the newly industrializing Japan, and was subjected to yet more one – sided demands by Europe and the United States for trade. These humiliations led to another rebellion, followed by yet another defeat, at the hands of foreign powers.

China's Qing Dynasty fell in 1911, after which China quickly succumbed to warlords, internal strife and Japan's invasion of China beginning in 1931. The end of World War Ⅱ was followed by civil war, the creation of the People's Republic of China in 1949 and then the upheavals of Maoism, including millions of deaths from famine in the Great Leap Forward, which ended in the early 1960s, and the mass destabilization of the Cultural Revolution and its aftermath until 1977.

China's rapid development on a market basis therefore started only in 1978, *when Deng Xiaoping came to* power and launched sweeping economic reforms. While China has seen incredible growth in the past four decades, the legacy of more than a century of poverty, instability, invasion and foreign threats still looms large. Chinese leaders would like to get things right this time, and that means they are unwilling to bow to the United States or other Western powers again.

China is now the second – largest economy in the world, when GDP is measured at market prices. Yet it is a country still in the process of catching up from poverty. In 1980, according to IMF data, China's GDP per capita was a mere 2. 5% of the United States, and by 2018 had reached only 15. 3% of the US level. When GDP is measured in purchasing – power – parity terms, by using a common set of "international prices" to value GDP in all countries, China's income per capita in 2018 was a bit higher at 28. 9% of the United States.

China has roughly followed the same development strategy as Japan, Korea, Taiwan, Hong Kong and Singapore before it. From an economic standpoint, it is not doing anything particularly unusual for a country that is playing catch up. The constant US refrain that China "steals" technologies is highly simplistic.

Countries that are lagging behind upgrade their technologies in many ways, through study, imitation, purchases, mergers, foreign investments, extensive use of off – patent knowledge and, yes, copying. And with any fast – changing technologies, there are always running battles over intellectual property. That's true even among US companies today – this kind of competition is simply a part of the global economic system. Technology leaders know they shouldn't count on keeping their lead through protection, but through continued innovation.

The United States relentlessly adopted British technologies in the early 19th century. And when any country wants to close a technology gap, it recruits know – how from abroad. The US ballistic missile program, as it is well known, was built with the help of former Nazi rocket scientists recruited to the United States after World War Ⅱ.

If China were a less populous Asian country, say like South Korea, with a little more than 50 million people, it would simply be hailed by the United

States as a great development success story – which it is. But because it is so big, China refutes America's pretensions to run the world. The United States, after all, is a mere 4.2% of the world's population, less than a fourth of China's. The truth is that neither country is in a position to dominate the world today, as technologies and know – how are spreading more quickly across the globe than ever before.

Trade with China provides the United States with low – cost consumer goods and increasingly high – quality products. It also causes job losses in sectors such as manufacturing that compete directly with China. That is how trade works. To accuse China of unfairness in this is wrong – plenty of American companies have reaped the benefits of manufacturing in China or exporting goods there. And US consumers enjoy higher living standards as a result of China's low – cost goods. The US and China should continue to negotiate and develop improved rules for bilateral and multilateral trade instead of stoking a trade war with one – sided threats and over – the – top accusations.

The most basic lesson of trade theory, practice and policy is not to stop trade – which would lead to falling living standards, economic crisis and conflict. Instead, we should share the benefits of economic growth so that the winners who benefit compensate the losers.

Yet under American capitalism, which has long strayed from the cooperative spirit of the New Deal era, today's winners flat – out reject sharing their winnings. As a result of this lack of sharing, American politics are fraught with conflicts over trade. Greed comprehensively dominates Washington policies.

The real battle is not with China but with America's own giant companies, many of which are raking in fortunes while failing to pay their own workers decent wages. America's business leaders and the mega – rich push for tax cuts, more monopoly power and offshoring – anything to make a bigger profit – while rejecting any policies to make American society fairer.

Trump is lashing out against China, ostensibly believing that it will once again bow to a Western power. It is willfully trying to crush successful companies like Huawei by changing the rules of international trade abruptly and unilaterally. China has been playing by Western rules for the past 40 years, gradually catching up the way that America's Asian allies did in the past. Now the United States is trying to pull the rug out from under China by launching a new Cold War.

Unless some greater wisdom prevails, we could spin toward conflict with China, first economically, then geopolitically and militarily, with utter disaster for all. There will be no winners in such a conflict. Yet such is the profound shallowness and corruption of US politics today that we are on such a path.

A trade war with China won't solve our economic problems. Instead we need homegrown solutions: affordable health care, better schools, modernized infrastructure, higher minimum wages and a crackdown on corporate greed. In the process, we would also learn that we have far more to gain through cooperation with China rather than reckless and unfair provocation.

原文链接：https：//www. cnn. com/2019/05/26/opinions/china - is - not - the - enemy - sachs/index. html

【译文】

经济问题不在中国，而在企业的贪欲

中国不是敌人，而是一个努力通过教育、国际贸易、基础设施投资和技术改进来提高国民生活水平的国家。简而言之，面对贫穷和远远落后于强国的历史现实，中国所做的是任何国家都应做的。然而，现在特朗普政府却企图遏制中国发展，这对美国和全世界来说可能都是个灾难。

中国被当作美国不平等现象日益加剧的替罪羊。尽管多年来中美贸易关系一直是互惠互利的，但一些美国工人却被甩在了后面，尤其是中西部的工人，面临着中国生产力提高和劳动力成本相对较低（尽管不断上升）带来的竞争。美国不应将这种正常的市场竞争现象归咎于中国，而应对自己的跨国企业飞涨的利润征税，再利用这些收入帮助工薪阶层家庭，重建破败的基础设施，提升新的就业技能并投资尖端科技。

美国应该明白，中国遭遇了长期的地缘政治阻隔和与之相关的经济挫折，如今只是在努力弥补损失的时光。以下重要的历史背景有助于了解中国过去40年的经济发展。

1839年，英国入侵中国，因为中国不允许英商继续向中国输入致瘾的鸦片。1842年，第一次鸦片战争结束，英国胜利。中国蒙受战败耻辱，成为引发“太平天国运动”的一个诱因，这场大规模反清起义最终导致超2000万人死亡。抗击英法两国的第二次鸦片战争最终导致中国国力不断被削弱，内部稳定受到侵蚀。

19世纪末，中国在与刚刚走上工业化道路的日本一战中败北，同时也受到欧美更多不平等贸易影响。这些羞辱使中国国内掀起了另一场叛乱，对外则再次败于外国势力之手。

1911年清王朝分崩离析，此后中国很快被军阀掌控，接着军阀混战。1931年日本发动侵华战争。第二次世界大战结束后，内战爆发。1949年中华人民共和国成立。

1978年中国政府实施全面经济改革，中国开始以市场为基础快速发展。虽然中国在过去40年的发展中取得了令人难以置信的成就，但一个多世纪以来，贫困、动荡、外敌入侵和威胁造成的影响依然很大。

当今，以市场价格计算国内生产总值（GDP），中国则是世界第二大经济体，但其仍在努力摆脱贫困。根据国际货币基金组织的数据，1980年，中国人均GDP仅相当于美国的2.5%，到2018年，这个比例也仅是美国的15.3%。以购买力平价作为衡量GDP的标准时，即用一套通用的“国际价格”来衡量所有国家的GDP，则2018年中国的人均收入略有提高，达到了美国的28.9%。

中国大致仿效了之前日本、韩国和新加坡的发展战略。从经济角度来看，对于一个正迎头赶上的国家来说，它的所作所为并没有什么出格之处。美国总说中国“窃取”技术，这种看法过于简单化。

落后的国家通过很多方式来升级自己的技术，包括学习、模仿、购买、合并、外国投资、广泛运用非专利知识，当然，还有借鉴。而且，对于任何高速发展的技术来说，围绕知识产权的争夺总是不可避免，甚至美国公司之间至今也是如此——这种竞争只是全球经济体系的一部分。技术领域的龙头企业都知道，不应指望通过保护措施来保持自己的领先地位，而应依靠持续的创新。

19 世纪初，美国一直采用英国的技术。而且，任何国家想要缩小技术差距，都是从海外招募相关专家。众所周知，美国弹道导弹项目就是在前纳粹火箭科学家的帮助下实施的，这些科学家在第二次世界大战后被美国招募。

如果中国是一个人口较少的亚洲国家，就像韩国那样，只有5000 多万人，那么美国就会称赞中国的伟大发展是一个成功的典范——中国确实堪称成功。但中国规模巨大，驳斥了美国治理全球的妄想。毕竟，美国人口仅占世界人口的 4.2%，不到中国的四分之一。事实上，由于技术和知识在全球范围内的传播速度远超以往，因此这两个国家都无法主宰当今世界。

中美贸易为美国提供了廉价消费品和日益优质的产品，同时也会导致美国制造业等和中国直接竞争的行业工作机会的减少。这就是贸易的运作方式。在这方面指责中国不公平是错误的—许多美国公司已从在中国制造产品或对华商品出口中获益。由于中国的廉价商品，美国消费者享受了更高的生活水平。美国和中国应该继续谈判，制定完善的双边和多边贸易规则，而不是以一边倒的威胁和过分的指责挑起贸易摩擦。

贸易理论、实践和政策的最基本原则是不要停止贸易，否则将导致生活水平下降、经济危机和冲突。相反，人们应共享经济增长的好处，让受益者补偿受损者。

然而，在长期背离新政（指罗斯福新政）时代合作精神的美国资本主义制度影响下，今天的赢家断然拒绝分享他们的收益。由于缺乏共享，美国政治充满了围绕贸易的冲突。贪婪全面主导了国家政策。

美国真正的敌人不是中国，而是自己本国的大公司。其中很多大公司没有给员工支付体面的工资，反而在攫取财富。美国的商界领袖和超级富豪们都在催促减税、扩大垄断、增加离岸外包等任何能获取更大利润的事，同时拒绝任何使美国社会更加公平的政策。

特朗普正在猛烈抨击中国，从表面上看，他认为中国会再次向一个西方大国低头。美国通过突然单边地改变国际贸易规则，蓄意打压华为这样的成功企业。过去 40 年，中国一直按照西方的规则行事，逐渐像美国的亚洲盟友一样赶了上来。现在，美国试图通过发动一场新的冷战，突然给中国制造麻烦。

除非有更明智的政策，否则美国可能会陷入与中国的冲突，首先在经济上，然后在地缘政治和军事上，最终给所有人带来彻底的灾难。这样的冲突不会有赢家。然而，当下美国政治的极端浅薄和腐败使美国走上了这样一条道路。

与中国产生贸易摩擦解决不了美国的经济问题。相反，美国需要寻求国内解决方案：减轻医疗保健费用、改善办学条件、现代化改建基础设施、提高最低工资，并遏制企业的贪念。在此过程中，美国还将认识到，相较于鲁莽和不公平的挑衅，与中国合作能使我们获益更多。(《英语世界》，2020（10），58－63)

在上述译文中，新闻编译者删减了原文中以下内容：

(1) ... and then the upheavals of Maoism, including millions of deaths from famine in the Great Leap Forward, which ended in the early 1960s, and the mass destabilization of the Cultural Revolution and its aftermath until 1977.

在英语财经新闻中，作者将我国历史上的“大跃进运动”和“文化大革命”全都归因于“毛泽东主义”，这种说法刻意凸显毛泽东主席的失误，忽略了其伟大之处，是歪曲的负面新闻消息，故译者将之删除。

(2) Chinese leaders would like to get things right this time, and that means they are unwilling to bow to the United States or other Western powers again.

在英语财经新闻中，作者认为“贫困、动荡、外敌入侵和威胁造成的影响”的原因是中国国家领导人不愿向美国或西方势力低头。这种观点完全是站在西方霸权主义立场上产出的，是没有综合考虑我国的国情和国际社会立场而阐发出来的，是片面的、错误的。这种观点会对中国读者产生负面影响，不值得编译者翻译出来，也不应该在中国传播。

(3) China has roughly followed the same development strategy as Japan, Korea, Taiwan, Hong Kong and Singapore before it.

在英语财经新闻中，作者将中国台湾和中国香港这两个地区和其他国家并列，这种表述严重歪曲事实，是对我国“一国两制”政策的忽视，存在危害国家统一和领土完整等问题。编译译者意识到了这种表述的错误之处，删去了原文中的“Taiwan”和“Hong Kong”，将这句话翻译为“中国大致仿效了之前日本、韩国和新加坡的发展战略。”编译者这种删减方法符合党和国家的宣传方针和政策，维护了我国的国家主权。

(二) 补充法 (Addition)

功能翻译理论代表人物奈达指出：“跨文化交际中的一个主要难题是：在很多情况下共享信息的数量和性质存在巨大差异。”(Nida 2001：111)，在翻译过程中，译者常常需要通过注释的方法来弥补译文读者所缺乏的共享信息或预设知识，否则译文读者对某些文化专有项就无法理解（范勇，2003)。

一些涉及历史事件、人物、典故等文化专有名词的信息对英语读者来说是不言自明的常识性知识，但对大多数中国读者而言，则是陌生怪异的、难以理解的。究其原因，汉语读者的认知图式中缺乏相关的西方历史、文化、社会等方面的预设知识。对于这样的内容，就需要编译者加上适当的注释，来减少读者的阅读负担。

编译者在编译过程中加注释，也要讲究一定的技巧。由于注释多属于解释性的内容，译者首先要考虑添加多少注释量的问题，如果注释量太多，会加重读者阅读的负担，甚至误导读者过多地关注注释内容，而忽略原文原有的重要信息，干扰读者对原文信息的把握。如果注释量太少，则会使读者不能完全透彻地明白译语附带的陌生信息。其次，编译者要考虑注释部分在译文中的位置。注释可以是文后注释，也可以是文中注释。文后注释的特点是清晰、翔实，缺点是会中断读者的阅读思绪。文中注释的优点是简明、短小，不利点是不能详尽说明。对于财经新闻而言，译文的句式常常会与原文相差很大，这时，加注释时，应以注释位置符合译文的最佳通顺度为原则。

请看以下各例：

【例 19】

【原文】In the decade since the collapse of Lehman Brothers and the start of the global financial crisis, the world economy has registered stronger growth than many realize, owing in large part to China. But in the years ahead, global economic imbalances and troubling trends in the business world will continue to pose economic as well as political risks.

【译文】十年前，金融巨头雷曼兄弟破产，全球金融危机爆发，此后，世界经济增长之强劲出乎很多人意料，这很大程度上归功于中国的发展。不过，全球经济发展失衡、商业领域各种问题层出不穷仍会带来经济和政治风险。(《英语世界》，2019（5），54)

“Lehman Brothers”看似指人名，但在此处指雷曼兄弟公司。该公司是为全球公司、机构、政府和投资者提供金融服务的多元化投资银行。译者首先将其直译为“雷曼兄弟”，而后补充“金融巨头”，这说明译者已意识到中国读者可能对“Lehman Brothers”这一美国文化专有名词存在疑惑。在商务印书馆发行的《现代汉语词典》中，“巨头”多指“政治、经济界等有较大势力、能左右局势的人”。故此处可改译为“美国顶尖投行雷曼兄弟公司”，以此阐明“Lehman Brothers”的性质和在美国的地位。

【例 20】

【原文】Yet under American capitalism, which has long strayed from the cooperative spirit of the New Deal era, today's winners falt - out reject sharing their winnings. As a result of this lack of sharing, American politics are fraught with conflicts over trade. Greed comprehensively dominates Washington policies.

【译文】然而，在长期背离新政（指罗斯福新政）时代合作精神的美国资本主义制度影响下，今天的赢家断然拒绝分享他们的收益。由于缺乏共享，美国政治充满了围绕贸易的冲突。贪婪全面主导了国家政策。(《英语世界》，2020（10），62)

这一例子也是文中注释。原文中的“the New Deal”指“罗斯福新政”，是美国历史上重大事件，故原文读者对此都心知肚明。但对于中文读者来说，“新政”指革新运动，可能是中国的清末新政，也可能是美国的罗斯福新政。故译者首先将其译为“新政”，而后又用“括号”补充说明此处“新政”指罗斯福新政，即 1933 年富兰克林·罗斯福就任美国总统后实行的经济政策。译者这种补充策略能够有效规避读者产生误解的风险，有助于准确传达原文信息。

（三）转换法（Conversion）

转换法是新闻编译中广泛应用的一种手段，转换法在财经新闻编译中也屡见不鲜。英国翻译理论家约翰·卡特福德（John Catford）在其《翻译的语言学理论》（*A Linguistic Theory of Translation*）中提出了翻译转换理论。他指出：翻译转换分为两种：层次转换和范畴转换（Catford 1965：73）。范畴转换是卡特福德讨论的核心，分为结构转换、词类转换、单位转换和系统内部转换（Catford 1965：75－82）。人们在翻译财经新闻时通常会用到结构转换和词类转换。结构转换是最常见的转换方法，包括肯定与否定结构的转换、主动与被动语态的转换以及英语句子中主语突出与汉语句子中主题突出之间的转换（高梅，2015）。词类转换主要指用不同的目标语词项来替换源语词项（郑淑明、曹慧，2011），在英汉财经翻译中主要包括英语名词转换为汉语动词，英语形容词转换为汉语动词，英语介词转换为汉语动词等。

a. 财经新闻编译中的句法结构转换

在英语财经新闻中，为显示新闻的客观性，英语原文多被动语态。而在汉语中，主动语态更符合中国读者的表达习惯，故在编译过程中需要把英语原文中的被动语态在汉语中转换为主动语态。

例如：

【例 21】

【原文】The revolution in health care is being led by the innovators who are working tirelessly to improve outcomes, enhance convenience and lower costs.

【译文】领导医疗革命的那些创新者不知疲倦地改善疗效、增加便利、降低成本。(《英语世界》，2018（4），79)

在上述例子中，原文主语为“The revolution in health care”，动词为“is being led by”，为被动语态，意为“医疗革命被……领导”。译者在译文中把这一被动语态转换成了“动词（领导）＋名词（医疗革命）”组成的定语来修饰主语（那些创新者）。

【例 22】

【原文】Thus, how we manage benefits, sick leave and vocation will need to be modernized.

【译文】因此，福利、病假和休假方面的制度需要与时俱进。(《英语世界》，2018（4），79)

英语原文中的“be modernized”是被动语态，做动词“need”的不定式后置定语。译者将其处理为“与时俱进”，为主动语态。

b. 财经新闻编译中的词类转换

徐珺和自正权（2014）“基于语料库的英语财经新闻汉译本的词汇特征研究”研究结果显示：“与英语原文本相比，财经新闻的汉译文本词类使用方面的差异明显，名词和形容词明显减少，动词使用频率显著增多。”而在翻译过程中常见的词类转换有：英语名词转换为汉语动词、英语介词转换为汉语动词、英语形容词转换为汉语动词、英语形容词转换为汉语名词等。

请看以下各例：

【例 23】

【译文】That it seeks to extend the lifecycle of the products traded is fitting, considering its origins exist, in part, in the fast – fashion craze made possible by low – priced, uber – trendy chains such as Forever 21.

【原文】考虑到这一业务模式部分源自快时尚的热潮，带来这股潮流的是 Forever 21 这类超时髦的低价连锁店，所以追求延长所交易产品的生命周期倒也合情合理。(英语世界，2019（06），56)

上述财经新闻原文中的“origins”为名词（复数形式），译者为了语义的连贯将其译为了“源自”，词性由原文中的名词转换为动词。

【例 24】

【原文】In most people's minds inflation is up there with unemployment as one of the main ills you don't want an economy to come down with.

【译文】通货膨胀伴随失业，这是经济衰退的一个主要弊端。(《英语世界》，2013（4）：60 – 63)

财经新闻英语原文中的“介词 with + ……”伴随状语结构多被转换为动词。上述财经新闻中原文中的“with”意为“有；带有”，译者将其转换为动词“伴随”以简化句式，迎合汉语多短句的句式特点。

【例 25】

【原文】By way of the increased connectivity, lesser developed regions like Xinjiang are catching up with developed regions.

【译文】通过提升连通性，新疆等欠发达地区正在赶上发达地区。

（《英语世界》，2019（10），15）

英语原文中的“increased”是动词“increase”的过去分词，此处为前置定语，作形容词修饰“connectivity”，意为“增加的；增长了的”。在译文中，译者保留了原文中的方式状语结构，但意识到了在中文中介词“通过”后多加动词，故将原形容词“increased”转换为动词“提升”。

【例 26】

【原文】Meanwhile, the cities in close proximity sharing common industrial capabilities are forming economic clusters and building on their mutual expertise.

【译文】同时，彼此相邻且工业能力相当的城市正在形成经济集群，并在相同的专业基础上壮大了规模。（《英语世界》，2019（10），15）

英语原文中，名词“capabilities（能力）”的修饰语为形容词“industrial（工业的）”，名词“cluster（集群）”的修饰语为形容词“economic（经济的）”，但在翻译中，这两个形容词的词性都转换为了名词，短语“industrial capabilities”被译为了“工业能力”，“economic clusters”被译为了“经济集群”。

（四）重写法（Rewriting）

重写是新闻编译者编译新闻时最难把控的方法。重写的具体步骤为：a. 新闻编译者首先要通读原新闻全文，掌握原新闻所传递的内容，熟知原新闻中的专业知识和概念；b. 在熟知原新闻内容的情况下，编译者需灵活运用原新闻中的信息，重新组织语言，重点凸显原新闻的核心思想、主要观点。c. 编译者重写的新闻还要符合译入语新闻的风格，迎合译入语读者的阅读习惯。

下例的汉语新闻文本是整合了《华盛顿邮报》、《福布斯》、BBC 等上刊载的多篇英语新闻编译而成的。编译者根据英文新闻中的相关信息，还加上《新京报》《每日经济新闻》等刊载的汉语新闻中的信息，重新译写出了汉语新闻稿。

【例 27】（来自《福布斯》）：

Richard Thaler and the ‘Human Factor’ In Economics

Richard H. Thaler’s Nobel Prize in Economic Science underscores the importance of instilling “psychologically realistic assumptions” into analyses of economic decision - making. His work provides a more realistic understanding of human behavior in economic theory.

The Nobel committee, announcing the award in Stockholm, credited Professor Thaler with taking the behavioral field from the fringe to the academic mainstream. The committee also noted that his work drove a wide range of public policy improvements, most notably a shift toward the automatic enrollment of workers in retirement savings programs.

After getting the news of his award, Thaler, an economist at the Chicago Booth School of Business, said the basic premise of his approach to economics is that, "In order to do good economics, you have to keep in mind that people are human."

The committee said that by "exploring the consequences of limited rationality, social preferences, and lack of self - control, he has shown how these human traits systematically affect individual decisions as well as market outcomes."

The committee expanded on those three concepts:

"Limited rationality: Thaler developed the theory of mental accounting, explaining how people simplify financial decision - making by creating separate accounts in their minds, focusing on the narrow impact of each individual decision rather than its overall effect. He also showed how aversion to losses can explain why people value the same item more highly when they own it than when they don't, a phenomenon called the endowment effect. Thaler was one of the founders of the field of behavioral finance, which studies how cognitive limitations influence financial markets.

"Social preferences: Thaler's theoretical and experimental research on fairness has been influential. He showedhow consumers' fairness concerns may *stop firms from raising prices in periods of high demand, but not in times of* rising costs. Thaler and his colleagues devised the dictator game, an experimental tool that has been used in numerous studies to measure attitudes to fairness in different groups of people around the world.

"Lack of self - control: Thaler has also shed new light on the old observation that New Year's resolutions can be hard to keep. He showed how to analyze self - control problems using a planner - doer model, which is similar to the frameworks psychologists and neuroscientists now use to describe the internal tension between long - term planning and short - term doing. Succumbing to short - term temptation is an important reason why our plans to save for old age, or make healthier lifestyle choices, often fail. In his applied work, Thaler demonstrated how nudging - a term he coined - may help people exercise better self - control when saving for a pension, as well in other contexts."

A New York Times article by Thaler published on May 15, 2015, "Unless You Are Spock, Irrelevant Things Matter in Economic Behavior," offers an engaging window into his thinking. At one point he writes, "Supposedly irrelevant factors, or SIFs, matter a lot, and if we economists recognize their importance, we can do our jobs better. Behavioral economics is, to a large extent, standard economics that has been modified to incorporate SIFs."

Thaler also noted, "The field of behavioral economics has been around for more than three decades, but the application of its findings to societal problems has only recently been catching on."

Thaler is the co - author (with Cass R. Sunstein) of the best - seller Nudge (2008) in which the concepts of behavioral economics are used to tackle many of society's major problems. In 2015 he published Misbehaving: The Making of Behavioral Economics. He has also written or edited four other books: Quasi - Rational Economics, The Winner's Curse: Paradoxes and Anomalies of Economic Life, and Advances in Behavioral Finance (editor) Volumes Ⅰ and Ⅱ. He has published numerous articles in journals such as the American Economics Review, the Journal of Finance and the Journal of Political Economy.

原文链接: https://www.forbes.com/sites/katevitasek/2017/10/10/richard-thaler-and-the-human-factor-in-economics/

【例 28】(来自 BBC):

'Nudge' economist Richard Thaler wins Nobel Prize

US economist Richard Thaler, one of the founding fathers of behavioural economics, has won this year's Nobel Prize for Economics.

Prof Thaler, of Chicago Booth business school, co – wrote the global best seller Nudge, which looked at how people make bad or irrational choices.

Judges said he had demonstrated how "nudging" – a term he coined – may help people to exercise better self – control.

He will receive 9 million Swedish krona (£ 850000) from the committee. "I will try to spend it as irrationally as possible!" the 72 year – old economist said.

Nudging

Prof Thaler's work led to the UK setting up a "nudge unit" under former prime minister David Cameron. It was launched in 2010 to find innovative ways of changing public behaviour and has offices in the UK, New York, Singapore and Sydney.

One of the Nobel prize judges, Per Stroemberg, said Prof Thaler's work had explored how human psychology shaped economic decisions.

"Richard Thaler's findings have inspired many other researchers coming in his footsteps and it has paved the way for a new field in economics which we call behavioural economics," Mr Stroemberg said.

The panel said Prof Thaler's insights helped people to recognise marketing tricks and avoid bad economic decisions.

In particular, his work looked at how to "nudge" people into doing more long – term planning, such as saving for a pension.

Prof Thaler also made a cameo appearance in the Hollywood film, The Big Short, explaining the complex financial instruments that led to the financial crisis of 2007 and 2008.

Americans dominate

It is the final Nobel to be announced this year, after prizes for medicine, physics, chemistry, literature and peace were awarded last week.

The economics prize is the only Nobel not created by Alfred Nobel, and was instead launched in 1968, long after the philanthropist's death.

To date the US has dominated the prize, with American economists accounting for roughly half of laureates since it started. Between 2000 and 2013, US academics won or shared the prize every year.

Last year, UK - born Oliver Hart and Bengt Holmstrom of Finland won the award - officially called the Sveriges Riksbank Prize in Economic Sciences in Memory of Alfred Nobel - for their work on contract theory.

Prof Thaler's central insight is that we are not the rational beings beloved of more traditional economic theory.

Given two options, we are likely to pick the wrong one even if that means making ourselves less well off.

Lack of thinking time, habit and poor decision making mean that even when presented with a factual analysis (for example on healthy eating) we are still likely to pick burger and chips.

We're hungry, we're in a hurry and burger and chips is what we always buy.

Nudge theory takes account of this, based as it is on the simple premise that people will often choose what is easiest over what is wisest.

Tests have shown that putting healthier foods on a higher shelf increases sales.

The food is more likely to be in someone's eye line and therefore "nudge" that person towards the purchase - whether they had any idea about the obesity argument or not.

原文链接：https://www.bbc.com/news/business-41549753

《中国日报》整合后英语原文：

American academic who invented revolutionary theory of 'human economics' and starred alongside Selena Gomez in The Big Short wins the Nobel Prize

Peter Gardenfors, member of the committee for the Economics Prize said,

Thaler's achievements successfully integrated economics and psychology, as he made economics "more human." And his theories "help people make better economic decisions."

Thaler's work earned him a glamorous foray into the movie business when he made a cameo appearance, alongside Christian Bale, Steve Carell and Ryan Gosling, in the 2015 movie '*The Big Short*' about the credit and housing bubble collapse that led to the 2008 global financial crisis.

In his cameo, he appeared in a scene alongside pop star Selena Gomez to explain the 'hot hand fallacy,' in which people think whatever's happening now is going to continue to happen into the future.

Thaler has incorporated psychologically realistic assumptions into analyses of economic decision-making. By exploring the consequences of limited rationality, social preferences, and lack of self-control, he has shown how these human traits systematically affect individual decisions as well as market outcomes.

Limited rationality

Thaler developed the theory of mental accounting, explaining how people simplify financial decision-making by creating separate accounts in their minds, focusing on the narrow impact of each individual decision rather than its overall effect.

We may have a "vacation" budget in our heads, and a "household maintenance" budget, and we tend not to mix them. If we get an unusually good deal on our airfare to Hawaii, we won't use the savings to have the carpets cleaned; we'll spend more at the bar on our vacation, keeping the money in the appropriate bucket.

He also showed how aversion to losses can explain why people value the same item more highly when they own it than when they don't, a phenomenon called *the endowment effect*.

In the first case, you are offered the chance to bet on the toss of a coin: You can win $10 if you call the coin toss correctly, or lose $10 if you call the toss incorrectly. Most people will decline the bet.

In the second case, a bet is described differently: You are told that you are about to lose $10, but there's a 50 – 50 chance you could come out with no loss—but with the prospect of a $20 loss if the coin toss works against you. That's really the same bet as in the first example, but framed as loss avoidance rather than seeking a gain. People are much more likely to take the second bet; they will take larger risks to try to avoid a loss.

Social preferences

Thaler's theoretical and experimental research on fairness has been influential. He showed how consumers' fairness concerns may stop firms from raising prices in periods of high demand, but not in times of rising costs.

Let's say you run a building supply company located in a hurricane warning area, and everyone is coming in to buy plywood. It would be bad practice to raise prices with a sign that says: "We have raised our prices so that plywood is only bought by those who really need it."

Good practice would be to raise prices with a sign that says "Our wholesale cost of plywood has increased, and we have to pass the cost along to you. But we have not raised our profit margin."

Thaler and his colleagues devised the dictator game, an experimental tool that has been used in numerous studies to measure attitudes to fairness in different groups of people around the world.

Lack of self – control

Thaler has also shed new light on the old observation that New Year's resolutions can be hard to keep. He showed how to analyze self – control problems using a planner – doer model, which is similar to the frameworks psychologists and neuroscientists now use to describe the internal tension between long – term planning and short – term doing.

Succumbing to short – term temptation is an important reason why our plans to save for old age, or make healthier lifestyle choices, often fail. In his applied work, Thaler demonstrated how nudging – a term he coined – may help people exercise better self – control when saving for a pension, as well in other contexts.

We're hungry, we're in a hurry and burger and chips is what we always buy.

Nudge theory takes account of this, based as it is on the simple premise that people will often choose what is easiest over what is wisest.

Tests have shown that putting healthier foods on a higher shelf increases sales.

The food is more likely to be in someone's eye line and therefore "nudge" that person towards the purchase – whether they had any idea about the obesity argument or not.

【译文】

不会演戏的经济学家不是好股神，这位新晋诺奖得主有点意思

瑞典皇家科学院9日宣布，将2017年诺贝尔经济学奖授予美国经济学家理查德·H·塞勒（Richard H. Thaler），"以表彰他对行为经济学的贡献"。

诺贝尔经济学奖委员会成员皮特·加登福斯称，塞勒的研究成果成功地将经济学和心理学整合在一起，让经济学更"人性化"。他的理论"帮助人们做出更好的经济决策"。

塞勒1945年出生在美国，是行为经济学之父，现执教于芝加哥大学商学院，同时在国民经济研究局主管行为经济学的研究工作。

塞勒还是一家基金公司的创始人，专注美国小企业股。在他的行为经济学理论下，公司替摩根大通管理的一只基金表现优异，2015年基金规模激增1倍至37亿美元，目前资产总规模已达60亿美元。

不会演戏的经济学家不是好股神，如果你看过获得2016年奥斯卡最佳改编剧本奖的电影《大空头》，一定会觉得这位新晋诺贝尔奖得主有些眼熟。

塞勒曾凭借其成就得到一个进军电影业的机会，他在2015年的《大空头》中客串了一个小角色，和克里斯蒂安·贝尔、史蒂夫·卡瑞尔、瑞恩·高斯林同框出镜。这部电影讲述的是引发2008年全球金融危机的信贷与房地产泡沫崩溃。

在塞勒客串的一幕中，他出现在流行歌手赛琳娜·戈麦斯旁边，解释着“热手效应”，这个理论说的是人们认为现在发生的一切将来还会继续发生。

用塞勒徒弟、中欧国际工商学院金融学副教授余方的话来评价塞勒的学术风格，那就是有点“非主流”，“总跟别人做的研究不太一样”。

作为一位传统学术理论的挑战者，塞勒认为：人们的行为并不像传统经济学理论中认为的那样理性。

塞勒将心理学上的现实假设整合进经济决策分析中。通过探索“有限理性”“社会偏好”和“自制力缺乏”等因素的影响，揭示了这些人性特征对个体选择和市场结果产生的系统性影响。

听起来太高大上？下面我们将用尽量通俗的语言来介绍塞勒的主要理论：

有限理性

塞勒创建了“心理账户”理论，阐述了人们是如何通过在内心创建不同的账户来简化经济决策的：人们会聚焦于单个决策的狭隘影响，而不是它们的总体效果。

举例说明：

我们脑海里有一笔“度假预算”和一笔“家庭维护预算”，我们通常不会将两者混在一起。如果我们能以特别划算的价格买到飞往夏威夷的机票，我们不会把省下的钱用来清洁地毯；我们度假时会在酒吧花得更多，让这笔钱花在原本的预算上。

塞勒还向我们介绍了如何用厌恶损失来解释为什么人们拥有某件东西时，会比没有的时候更高估其价值，即“禀赋效应”。

其实“禀赋效应”在生活中有很多体现，比如下面这个经典的掷硬币打赌的例子：

在第一种情况下，你有机会玩儿掷硬币打赌：如果你猜对可以赢得10美元，如果你猜错就会输掉10美元。大多数人会放弃这个赌注。在第二种情况中，赌局的描述有所不同：你被告知将输掉10美元，但有50%的机会不输钱，不过如果猜错的话将输掉20美元。这和第一个赌局是相同的，但却被视为是在避免损失，而不是寻求利益的。人们更倾向于参加第二个赌局，冒更大的风险以尽力避免损失。

社会偏好

塞勒关于公平的理论和实验研究很有影响力。他称，消费者对公平的关注会阻止公司在需求增加的时候涨价，但却不会阻止公司在成本上升时涨价。

还是用一个通俗易懂的例子来说明：

假设你在飓风警报区开了一家建筑用品公司，所有人都来买胶合板（一种装修常用的板材）。错误的做法是将标语写成："为了将胶合板卖给真正需要的人，我们涨价了。"

要想涨价，正确的做法是将标语写成："我们的胶合板批发成本上涨了，不得不把成本转嫁给你们。但是我们的利润并没有增加。"

塞勒和他的同事还设计了"独裁者博弈"，这个实验工具被应用在大量研究中，用于衡量世界各地的不同群体对于公平的态度。

自制力缺乏

新年计划难以执行是一个世纪难题，塞勒还为解决这个问题提供了新线索。他向人们展示了如何通过"计划者—执行者模型"分析自控问题，这个模型与当前心理学家和神经科学家用来解释长期计划与短期执行间的矛盾的理论类似。

我们打算存养老金，想选择更健康的生活方式，却经常失败，一个重要的原因就是我们会向短期诱惑屈服。在塞勒的应用研究中，他展示了如何通过"助推"（他自创的术语）来帮助人们更好地控制自己存下养老金，以及完成其他事情。

"助推理论"的原理：

缺少思考时间、习惯以及失败的决策意味着即使事实分析摆在眼前，比如明知健康饮食的好处，我们仍然可能选择汉堡和薯条。

我们很饿，很着急，而汉堡薯条是我们一直购买的食物。

助推理论考虑到了这点，人们往往会做出最容易的选择，而不是最明智的选择，该理论就是建立在这个简单前提之上。

测试表明，将更健康的食品摆放在更高的货架上，销量会增加。

摆放在高层货架上的食物更容易进入消费者的视线，因此会"助推"人们购买，不论他们是否了解关于肥胖症问题。（引自 中国日报

2017 年 10 月 11 日）

原文 & 译文链接：http://language.chinadaily.com.cn/2017-10/11/content_33077941.htm

上述《中国日报》整合后的英语新闻主要是关于诺贝尔经济学奖获得者塞勒演艺事业和学术成就的报道。原文前半部分介绍了塞勒客串电影《大空头》（*The Big Short*）并与流行歌手赛琳娜·戈麦斯（Selena Gomez）一起出镜解释一个经济现象。剩余部分主要结合实例描写塞勒的经济学观点，包括“有限理性”“社会偏好”“自制力缺乏”等。

总体而言，原新闻稿用词专业、语言流畅、信息完整，对原语读者来说是一篇可读的介绍类经济新闻。但对于中文读者来说并非如此，原因在于：a. 在早已进入网络信息时代的中国，新闻更新速度极快，毫无亮点的标题难以吸引读者。b. 许多中文读者并未看过电影《大空头》，也不认识流行歌手赛琳娜·戈麦斯，因此难以掌握原新闻娱乐与专业结合的亮点。c. 中文大众读者不了解经济学术语，难以理解原新闻专业知识。

汉语编译稿在整合原新闻稿主要信息的基础上，译写了一个吸人眼球的新标题，增加了许多承上启下的过渡段落，补充了人物介绍、背景知识和术语解释。首先，编译者译写标题“不会演戏的经济学家不是好股神，这位新晋诺奖得主有点意思”，套用了“不会……不是一个好的……”这一网络用语（如郭德纲相声《我要奋斗》中的“不想当厨子的裁缝不是好司机”）吸引读者关注，且未点明诺奖得主的身份而称他“有点意思”也制造悬念，让读者对新闻主体产生兴趣。其次，编译者添加了“举例说明:”“其实‘禀赋效应’在生活中有很多体现，比如下面这个经典的掷硬币打赌的例子:”“‘助推理论’的原理:”等过渡段落使汉语编译稿衔接更加流畅。再次，编译者补充了塞勒的生平、教育背景、职业成就，他人对塞勒的评价和相关经济学理论的原理，使塞勒这一新闻主体人物更加饱满，也丰富了汉语编译稿的内容。最后，编译者一改新闻原文正式、记事的新闻文风，用词更加生活化，还增加了“非主流”“高大上”等流行词汇以缩小财经类新闻与大众读者之间的距离。

重写策略虽为最难把控的财经新闻编译策略，但对于英语和汉语这两种完全不同、来自非同族语系的语言来说，重写策略能够最大限度将原文信息融入译入语的文本和文化中。

综上所述，编译法是财经新闻翻译中行之有效的翻译和写作技巧。通过编译法，新闻编译者能站在中国读者的立场上最大限度地把外国的财经讯息和知识传入中国，这能促进我国财经新闻多元化发展，也有助于提高我国国民金融素养和理财素质。

参考文献

[1] Nida, Eugene A. Language and Calture—Contexts in Translating [M]. Shanghai: Shanghai Foreign Language Education press, 2001, 111.

[2] Nord, C. Translating as a Purposeful Activity: Functionalist Approaches Explained M]. Shanghai: Shanghai Foreign Language Education press, 2001, 33.

[3] Catford, J. C. A Linguistic Theory of Translation [M]. Oxford: Oxford University Press, 1965, 73-82.

[4] 黄忠廉，刘丽芬．外语小科研入门 [M]. 北京：商务印书馆，2018，263.

[5] 方梦之．应用翻译研究 [M]. 上海：上海外语教育出版社，2019，328.

[6] 刘其中．英汉新闻编译 [M]. 北京：清华大学出版社，2009，3.

[7] 高梅．科技英语汉译中卡特福德翻译转换理论的应用探析 [J]. 时代文学（下半月），2015 (3): 116-117.

[8] 郑淑明，曹慧．卡特福德翻译转换理论在科技英语汉译中的应用．中国科技翻译，2011，29 (4): 17-20.

[9] 徐珺，自正权．基于语料库的英语财经新闻汉译本的词汇特征研究 [J]. 中国外语，2014，11 (5): 66-74.

[10] 冷冰冰．编译策略在科普杂志翻译中的应用 [J]. 中国科技翻译，2017，30 (4): 5-8, 19.

[11] 范勇．中国高校英文网页中的种种失误 [A]. 王宏主编．翻译研究新视角 2009 年全国翻译高层研讨会论文集 [C]. 上海：上海外语教育出版社，2011，415-421.